Forms of
Practice

Forms of Practice
German-Swiss Architecture 1980–2000

Irina Davidovici

gta Verlag

Contents

7 Introduction

Backgrounds I
21 The Background of Culture
41 The Background of Theory

Forms of Practice
81 Herzog & de Meuron
Stone House, Tavole, Italy, Project 1982, Realisation 1985–88

97 Peter Zumthor
Protective Housing for Roman Archaeological Excavations
Chur, Graubünden, 1985–86

115 Gigon / Guyer
Kirchner Museum, Davos, Graubünden, 1989–92

133 Diener & Diener
Housing and Office Buildings, Warteck Brewery, Basel
Project 1991–93, Realisation 1994–96

155 Valerio Olgiati
School Extension, Paspels, Graubünden, 1996–98

171 Von Ballmoos Krucker
Stöckenacker Housing, Affoltern, Zurich
Project 1997, Realisation 2000–02

Backgrounds II
191 The Background of Practice

Thematic Interpretations
213 Towards a Swiss Model
227 Notions of Resistance
233 Degree Zero
241 The Paradox of Realism
253 A Landscape of Signs

263 Bibliography
277 Index
281 Acknowledgements

Introduction

The focus of this book is the architecture produced in the German-speaking parts of Switzerland, in the last two decades of the twentieth century. For the sake of brevity, in these pages I refer to the architectural production of this place and time simply as 'Swiss architecture'. No particular label can do justice to the heterogeneity of approaches and attitudes within this production; and yet, they also achieve some kind of *a priori* identity. There seems to be a tacit consensus of what contemporary "Swiss architecture" comprises, as a term with international validity. Nevertheless, Swiss architects are understandably reluctant to align their work with one another as if they were part of one artistic commune. They reject even more strongly the idea of national identity as common denominator.

As more practices emerge and new buildings are completed, it is ever more difficult to hold on to a sense of definition. To an extent, the time frame from 1980 to 2000 gives a clearer focus. As it becomes historically more remote, this period is associated with certain practices and a specific intellectual and professional climate. The work produced then acquired an international reputation for the integrity of its construction and the tight correlation of formal spareness, seductive materiality and contextual readings, resulting in abstract yet sensuous buildings specifically fitted to their surrounds. The first decade, the 1980s, is associated with the architecture of Jacques Herzog, Pierre de Meuron, Peter Zumthor, Roger Diener, Marcel Meili, Peter Märkli, Marianne Burkhalter and Christian Sumi. In the 1990s they were joined on the professional scene by a younger generation, among them Annette Gigon and Mike Guyer, Valerio Olgiati, Valentin Bearth and Andrea Deplazes, Gion A. Caminada, Quintus Miller and Paola Maranta. These practices contributed to the creation of a significant and multifaceted architectural discourse in which, up until the late 1990s, collective traits could be identified.

While for the Swiss themselves the term "Swiss architecture" is tainted by imprecision, for the international wider public it has a rather clear meaning, once described by Kenneth Frampton as a "basic minimalist *parti pris*".[1] For the participants themselves this understanding is simplistic, grouping various practices together as if they were significantly similar. This flattening is

---

[1] Frampton, "Minimal Moralia", 2002, p. 326.

moreover problematic when based solely on an aesthetic quality of formal restraint. The connoisseur is too aware of profound differences in the architects' approach, and indeed of their distinct artistic individualities, to feel comfortable with one umbrella term. In this book I argue differently for the validity of an idea of Swiss architecture. On no account am I attempting to equate its protagonists; the plurality implied in the book's title remains uncontested. This production is characterised by distinct forms of practice, expressing the different formation and artistic individuality of its authors. Why are they then grouped together at all? An initial answer is because of their unintended connections. Their linkage is the practice of architecture at a given historical time in a clearly defined culture. The point is not a shared "minimalist *parti pris*", but the concrete circumstances in which this aesthetic emerged and became, for better or worse, a common basis for assessment.

Before proceeding with what this book is about, I'd like first to establish what it isn't. It is not intended as a general introduction to recent Swiss architectural production, of which there have been several over the years, both more extensive and detailed. I have not compiled an exhaustive catalogue of this production, or a selection of "best" examples. Rather, this is an attempt to place a limited number of projects in a wider cultural, professional and theoretical context that goes deeper than their laconic formal appearance. The intention is to unravel the cultural dimensions, both professional and social, to which Swiss architecture is indebted.

My discussion focuses on the Eidgenössische Technische Hochschule (ETH) in Zurich to discuss the training of architects and the main interchanges between teaching and practice. Just as it does not cover all participating architects and significant buildings, likewise the argument does not extend to the courses offered at the École Polytechnique Fédérale de Lausanne (EPFL), at the Accademia di Architettura in Mendrisio, Ticino, founded in 1996, or at any of the several technical colleges.[2] While the architecture schools share ideas, students and teachers, they vary considerably in size and character. They reflect the cultural and political differences between main linguistic regions, as well as differences within the profession. Even though not all the participants trained in Zurich, ETH remains the focal point for the development and exchange of the ideas treated here.

Swiss architecture between form and decorum
The "Forms of Practice" of the title outline a tension between buildings as forms and as manifestations of the various practices, professional and otherwise, that characterise Swiss architectural production. What I would like to clarify here is what these forms of practice hold in common, and the extent to which they are connected through underlying conditions. I am addressing the idea of Swiss architecture as a cultural phenomenon.

---

2   EPFL is the French-language polytechnic counterpart of ETH and therefore it is, officially, part of the same federal institution.

This architecture seems primarily concerned with buildings as objects, as physical embodiments of a conceptual strategy. At the cost of formal intricacies, it declares a fascination with issues of physical presence and effect. This suggests on the one hand a contemplative dimension and, on the other, the unease with projecting iconographical content on concrete matter. Rather, the focus on the material thing in itself aims to avoid subjective readings and leads to the creation of architectural objects that are primarily "self-evident", simply "being".[3]

Orientation towards objects fails, however, to account fully for what the architecture communicates. This production claims an integrity that extends beyond functionality, constructional coherence and aesthetic quality. It alludes to a kind of universal intelligibility. "Our observation of the object embraces a presentiment of the world in all its wholeness because there is nothing that cannot be understood".[4] Peter Zumthor's statement illustrates this idea that the plain object embodies something more profound. Instinctively, the work transcends its aesthetic dimension through the appeal to the common ground of culture, and the common conditions for design. At this deeper level, the architecture ceases to be the heterogeneous result of individual imaginations and reaches a level of communication with the culture it emerged from in the first place. As such, the production transcends the strong minority of Swiss practices with which it is associated, and can be seen to attain a wider relevance.

The spectrum of attitudes that sustain the Swiss production is framed by the 1970s theoretical discourse imported, in the framework of ETH, from the neo-rationalism of Aldo Rossi and the neo-realism of Robert Venturi and Denise Scott Brown. The work, however, communicates to its audience more than what theoretical justifications – international in character – could account for. The oscillations between abstraction and familiarity, between a focus on the artefact and a concern with its context, point to a more complex phenomenon: a deeply communicative resonance that transcends the formal simplicity of the work and lays claim to more profound zones of understanding.

At this time, the Swiss discourse operated knowingly with the tension between formal consistency and deeper intelligibility. This interest is manifest, for example, in Marcel Meili's search for an "authenticity" that "can be retrieved from the fabric of customary activities secreted by actual modes of life in Switzerland, rather than from a typological tradition of architecture".[5] Elsewhere, Herzog & de Meuron aimed at the creation of "architecture without any distinguishable figuration, but with a hesitant non-imitating analogy […] a hint of memory, of association".[6]

Such formulations betray the concern for an elusive dimension that resists conceptualisation and which strives to articulate the self-evident and familiar. In order to understand Swiss architecture through the structure of its context, I appeal in this book to a hermeneutic method of interpretation. Rather than

---

3   Zumthor, "A Way of Looking at Things", 2006, pp. 16–17.

4   Ibid., p. 17.

5   Meili, "Ein paar Bauten, viele Pläne", 1991, p. 22. Translation from the German text.

6   Herzog and de Meuron, 2002, p. 8.

trying to arrive at conclusions about buildings, this approach emphasises their backgrounds, and their orientation towards the typical. What needs, programmatic, urban or metaphorical, does the project address? How do architectural ambition and social convention balance out in the final design? Does the new intervention recover or subvert traditional forms of urban life, and to what extent is it an alien presence?

These questions draw attention to an important quality of Swiss architecture: a sense of order that appears to bridge the customary conflict between form and decorum. Form is often considered a domain of aesthetic freedom, whereas decorum pertains to custom, tradition, all which is held in common. The notion of type and the correlative discipline of typology are at the heart of the tension between originality and convention. Recent Swiss architecture is profoundly indebted to this theoretical discourse and typology remains, implicitly or explicitly, one of its main concerns.

Typology emerged in architectural theory during the eighteenth century and was used to establish classifications of formal models, which in turn became the basis for variation in design. The tempting promise of a comprehensive range of typical forms resurfaced in the 1960s and 1970s, in reaction to the obliteration of historical types attempted by the modern movement. Through re-orientation to the historical city, type could be resurrected to provide a rationally controllable basis for architectural order.[7]

The use of typological classification in architecture is, nevertheless, limited in scope. Type is an abstract construct arising from the synthesis of precedents, and its replication allows only a partial articulation of historical reality.[8] Types embody a certain amount of design experience, and customarily address recurring situations. However, as the original inspiration for types grew out of natural science classification, already at the time of Quatremère de Quincy they formed the basis for a new mode of mimesis. His need to distinguish between type (as an abstract "image") and model (as a concrete historical precedent) pointed to a widespread confusion between the two.[9] One no longer interpreted architecture in terms of the concrete situation it addressed, but used instead the fixed template of type-forms from typological manuals. The effect was that the conditions for architecture, seen as immutable or predictable, came to be increasingly ignored. Despite the residue of building experience contained in type, typology turned buildings into concepts. Ever since, meaning has been associated less with the context in which the building stands, than with the abstract type it represents.[10]

One alternative is to view architecture as arising from its deeper situation. As Dalibor Vesely proposed, the meaning of "house" can be extracted firstly from notions and experiences of dwelling, secondly from its position in and relation to the town, and only finally from matters of appearance. The interpretation of a typical

7 See for example Argan, 1996; Rossi, 1982; Vidler, 1977.

8 Argan, 1996, p. 243.

9 Quatremère de Quincy, 1999, pp. 255–256.

10 Vesely, 1982, p. 9.

situation avoids turning the formal aspects of type into symbols of continuity. If type is understood visibly as the totality of decisions regarding form, materiality, construction, appearance, the typical can be used as a more fundamental designation of motifs of continuity, stability, and recurrence in human situations.[11]

Type operates theoretically, and is sustained by media coverage and professional expectations. However, the continuity that grants type its intelligibility remains grounded in praxis; typology is made possible by the more profound operation of common or recurring themes in culture. As a basis for interpretation in design, what is typical opens a richer domain of analogy than the formal variations of typology.

The reaction against the dry determinism of formal analysis led to Aldo Rossi's revision of typology during the mid-1970s. His *architettura analogica* was grounded in Carl Gustav Jung's model of an archaic "analogical thought" in opposition to *logos*. This model acknowledged the experiential, pre-reflective moment during which we recognise and respond to something typical.[12] However, Rossi's search for the communicative dimension of type ultimately led inwards, to personal memories and associations, highlighting the subjective sphere. In contrast, the typical is embedded in a shared praxis, pointing to something that is fundamentally held in common, and thus universally intelligible.

Swiss architecture between theory and praxis

If the ambivalence of type refers to the field of tension between form and custom, Swiss architecture can be seen to operate in this same field. Its production of forms is embedded, perhaps more than elsewhere, in exchanges between theory and practice. Practitioners are enticed to teach, and their practice-focused teaching impacts on the quality of professional training. Recent graduates are not impeded by their lack of experience and tend towards practice rather than theoretical speculation. In turn, they often work as teaching assistants, helping propagate and instil in younger students the ideas of their predecessors. Given the compactness of Swiss architectural operations, this model offers a rare opportunity to trace with some precision the relations between protagonists, the origins and developments of their intellectual positions.

For a long time, the common theoretical base has been propagated mainly through the architecture department of ETH in Zurich. Even for those trained outside it, the influence of this theory is felt in practice: it seeps in through collaborations, informal discussions with colleagues, publications of built projects or competition entries. One sees phrases from this body of theory in architects' statements about their work; these projects later become illustrations of the theory in subsequent teaching.

The body of theory has a neutral, international character, which only partially illuminates the regional specificity of the work. This suggests that the work communicates to architects and critics

[11] Ibid., p. 41.

[12] Rossi, 1996, p. 349.

something beyond what the theory can account for, that is either accidental or has its roots elsewhere in the culture. This is one question that requires clarification.

The phenomenon of Swiss architecture also raises more general questions regarding the nature of architecture, its teaching and understanding. Among its enduring ambiguities after the Enlightenment is the problem of the city. The significant political body of Switzerland is the commune, generally associated with the political sphere of villages and cities. This has inspired a group of professors at ETH to undertake a study that sees all of Switzerland as a continuous urban topography. This is seen on the one hand as an infrastructural network, accounted for statistically; on the other hand it invokes a more metaphorical understanding of the common context.[13] This enables buildings that present themselves as autonomous works of art in the landscape to share something with others which, by contrast, are so modest as to seem found in their place.

How do the claims made for these works stand up to scrutiny? How is it that a body of works apparently indebted to Modernist principles commands respect at a more profound region of understanding? Proposing answers to such questions is the vehicle for a more general theme, the way in which architecture might communicate with the depth of a culture.

Swiss architecture between ethics and aesthetics

Swiss architecture uses everyday situations as a background for formal consistency. This in turn induces a need for the work to attain a high degree of abstraction, in order that the formal consistency is not only legible, but also positively emphasised. Exacting effort goes into the construction in order to attain this visual ideal, although it is sometimes more readily represented in the graphic domain. The preference for an understated formalism has attracted, alongside the aesthetic attributes of "reductive" and "minimalist", the ethical tags of "modesty" and "appropriateness".

The aesthetic and moral dimensions of this architecture are in conflict. The former presumes absolute subjective control, the latter discretion towards and openness to the architecture's context. A resolution is attempted through a reduction of both the aesthetic and moral aspects, leading to an expression of blankness or emptiness. The architecture's laconic stance distances it from readable architectural statements; its silence is its strongest statement.

As the following chapters show, this state of affairs is embedded in architectural history, in Swiss and Western culture. However, one may note from the outset that German-Swiss architecture begins to distinguish itself around 1980 on account of its debt to the international discourse around architectural autonomy. Established in the 1960s and 1970s in reaction to sociological and scientific bases for design, the notion of autonomy was

[13] The programme *Switzerland – an Urban Portrait* ran between 1999 and 2003 at ETH Studio Basel under the direction of Roger Diener, Jacques Herzog, Pierre de Meuron, Marcel Meili and Christian Schmid. See Diener et al., 2006.

associated with the theoretical disposition of typology, and inherited its limitations.

The recourse to Francesco Milizia in Rossi's *Architettura della città* (1966) is a case in point. Inserted in an argument for the integrity of urban topography, Milizia's architecture, like Durand's, is clearest when exhibited against the blank page of didactic demonstration. Rossi's architecture advocated urban continuity through a similar reification of form. Peter Eisenman's misunderstanding of autonomy to mean a kind of geometrical emancipation is thus somewhat understandable. However, the term originally indicated the capacity of a type to support diverse, if related, activities in history. This meaning is closer to what Martin Steinmann has called "general forms".[14]

14 Steinmann, 1991.

This generality does not imply a lack of specificity, but the rejection of arbitrary or subjective formalism. Since the advent of Modernism, the withdrawal from artistic will has been debated at an ethical level. The renouncement of gesture leaves architectural form to be determined by function and material performance, usually integrated within an overall conceptual discipline. This particular claim of integrity is vulnerable to two wide misconceptions. Firstly, the veneration of materials and their detailing implies the belief that a moral order can be constituted by the very medium of architecture. Secondly, reliance on the intellectual resolution of all aspects of the architectural project places architectural order in the domain of comprehensive concepts.

Architects can hardly be blamed for this confusion. Belief in the power of concepts is a historical consequence of Enlightenment rationalism and an instrumental way of thinking, which have affected all spheres of production and exchange. Andrew Bowie explains that ever since its emergence, rationalism has been accompanied by its dialectical opposite, the philosophy of subjectivity.[15] The dissolution of stable structures of belief under the advancing power of scientific objectivity has allowed art, seen as a new receptacle of meaning, to acquire a status of aesthetic autonomy.

15 Bowie, 1990, pp. 2–12.

The dual concern in Swiss architecture, on the one hand with objectivity and on the other with art, is a manifestation of this inherently modern ambivalence. The return to material and the making of things, in the context of an increasingly rarefied theoretical climate, can be traced back to societal and economic changes that have taken place since the eighteenth century. At the same time, Swiss urban society has been deeply influenced by the Protestant work ethic, connected, in Max Weber's thinking, with the growth of capitalist culture.[16] In this respect, the attitudes that characterise its architecture illustrate issues that have simmered in Western (particularly German) philosophy throughout the modern age.

16 See Gossman, 1994, p. 67.

The only tenable position in this conundrum points to a dialectic between theory and praxis. The former implies the adherence to the field of disciplinary knowledge cultivated by universities and supported in museums and publications. The latter stands for the recovery of some form of civic society, rooted in a deep network of concrete relations operating across history, which theory in and by itself is ill equipped to understand. The resulting conflict can be summarised as one between explicit knowledge and implicit understanding, between progress and tradition, between an abstract global context and specific cultural circumstances. With regard to individual creative freedom, this translates as the tension between the open field of arbitrary, personal choice and a socio-political field of responsibilities and dependencies.

Sources

The polarities of form and context, theory and praxis, originality and convention attest to the dialectical nature of recent Swiss production. This has generated a professional literature caught between the desire for definition and the wariness of shallow generalisation. The architects' personal agendas and the variety of micro-cultures in this small territory subvert any attempts at characterisation. Indeed, most instances where strong affiliations or criticisms are declared seem to overlook one aspect or another of the production. Conversely, where impartiality is pursued, arguments tend to be either open-ended, or restricted to historical enumerations of architects and buildings. The most reliable vehicle for in-depth discussions of Swiss work remains the monograph – whether it deals with a single author, building, building type, construction material etc.

Most of the documentary material can be found in architectural journals. *Archithese* and *werk, bauen+wohnen* in the German-speaking region and *Faces* in the French have played important roles in the coverage and development of Swiss ideas.[17] Certain thematic issues act as signposts for changing theoretical developments and provide an indication of their timing. A similar role can be attributed to the catalogues attached to architecture exhibitions, which become documentary records of the Swiss discourse.[18] The more comprehensive publications on the topic gather specialised thematic essays, which tend to open the discursive range, rather than make a conclusive argument. Instead of formulating general truths, they display a heterogeneous collection of related attitudes co-existing without conflict. At a remove, they could be seen as typologies of Swiss architectures, projecting individual directions as formal variations against defined sets of criteria.[19]

In the early 1990s several attempts were made at a valid synthesis, most notably in the writings of Martin Steinmann and Marcel Meili.[20] Foremost a practitioner, Meili constructed a complex picture based on the shared theoretical background but also on the practical conditions for design. The critic Steinmann discussed the conceptual substrate of the built production, focusing on iconography and perceptual effect. His

17 Stauffer, 1998, pp. 93–94.

18 For example see Steinmann and Boga, 1975. The *Tendenzen* exhibition, shown at ETH in 1975, marked the penetration of Italian rationalist ideas into German-speaking Switzerland through the intermediary of Ticinese architecture.

19 See Gilbert and Alter, 1994; Lucan, 2001; Meseure, Tschanz, and Wang, 1998.

20 See for example Marcel Meili's essay "Ein paar Bauten, viele Pläne" and Martin Steinmann's "Neuere Architektur in der Deutschen Schweiz", both initially published in Disch, 1991.

essay "The Presence of Things" (1994) traced Swiss architecture's developments in the 1980s and early 1990s, linking projects through the elusive notion of a search for "presence".[21]

[21] Steinmann, 1994, p. 10.

In the late 1990s, under the conditions of a global building boom and increasing economic freedom, the production diversified and over-arching statements became difficult to sustain. Following Meili's article "A Few Remarks Concerning German-Swiss Architecture" (1996), the unity of discourse seems to have been silenced by the ramifications proposed in design.[22] Martin Tschanz's essay "Tendenzen und Konstruktionen" (1998) set out the common theoretical parameters of contemporary Swiss architecture in the 1970s and 1980s, but voiced the consensus that one could no longer presume a unity of direction.[23] Rather, Tschanz identified a range of parallel (or divergent) "tendencies" in the work of the main practices, spelling the end of any common ground.

[22] Meili, 1996, pp. 24–25.

[23] Tschanz, 1998, pp. 45–52.

For the present study these sources have been particularly valuable, indicating the terms of self-understanding within which the Swiss theoretical and architectural discourse propagates itself. In addition, the research benefited from informal conversations and interviews with several architects and critics, including Martin Steinmann, Stanislaus von Moos, Marcel Meili, Roger Diener, Valerio Olgiati, Peter Zumthor, Peter Märkli, Mike Guyer, Annette Gigon, Jürg Conzett and Valentin Bearth. Various sources concur on the existence of certain common conditions at the origin of the Swiss phenomenon – the ETH discourse of the 1970s and early 1980s, the advanced industrialised society, a particular federal and political structure. However, much of the written material grounds the discussion of Swiss architecture in and around the artefact. The architectural object is presented as the basis on which variation and heterogeneity are established. This approach risks overlooking the shared practical context, and anchors the discussion in the aesthetic domain.

The structure of the argument

This book explores in Swiss architecture the dialogue between two main themes: the motifs of cultural continuity arising from praxis, and the theoretical discourse reflected in the architecture's formal concerns. The first section defines the background conditions for the built production. The first chapter addresses the specific cultural themes of Swiss identity, as arising in philosophy, literature, and the architectural and urbanistic domain. The second chapter provides the theoretical background, exploring the modernist heritage of ETH in the 1960s and its developments up to the 1980s.

The next section groups together six case studies, illustrating how the theoretical discourse was applied to the built production. The buildings were deliberately chosen from among widely published projects that are familiar to most professionals and to the larger public. This familiarity is itself important. Their impact on subsequent projects (in practice) and discourse (in theory) constitutes material for the present argument. The case studies are treated chronologically and the object analysis is tied into each project's general situation. This method seeks to recover the depth of the phenomenon, rather than its material aspects. My aim has been to identify the architecture's recurrent themes, its contradictions and ambiguities, and assess the deeper promise of communication behind the artefacts' accomplished and seductive façades.

Architecture conflates the theoretical and the practical sphere; designs constantly mediate between artistic and pragmatic considerations. This dialogue with praxis is examined in the third section, which aims to establish how the commissioning and collaborative processes qualify the theoretical agendas. Here, the barrier between theory and praxis is not so clearly defined. On the one hand, the conceptual aspects of practice are passed on subliminally within the culture through a range of situations, from skilled training to casual discussions of professional positions with clients or among architects. On the other hand, the professional culture, born of a polytechnic tradition suspicious of theory, is focused on solving practical problems.

The final section comprises a series of interpretative essays, in which the common aspects of Swiss architecture are treated thematically as theoretical propositions. These essays relate back to the factual content of earlier sections. The ambiguities that result from the investigation reveal, in the reciprocity of form and practice, the tension between the claims of aesthetic freedom and the necessity to engage with fundamental motifs that otherwise resist conceptualisation.

During the late twentieth century, Swiss architecture touched upon something more fundamental than its concentration in a tiny ordered territory might suggest. The application of a certain aesthetic sensibility to concrete situations, enabled by specific cultural, economic and social conditions, lend the practice of architecture a promise of integrity. Ethical claims defined this memorable period of Swiss architecture more than any of its stylistic predilections. An understanding of the conditions that made such claims possible in the first place, and less sustainable in the long run, is necessary.

Backgrounds I

The Background
of Culture

> We rarely originate, but we are skilful at adapting; we are reluctant to push ahead and we prefer to wait; we dislike to abandon the familiar and we are sceptical of the new. The different is suspect, the exceptional is not welcome and genius ignored.[1] **Bernhard Hoesli**

[1] Hoesli quoted in Oechslin, 1998, p. 55.

Through its reductive expression, emphatic materiality, and conceptual self-sufficiency, the Swiss architectural production of the 1980s and 1990s manifests its adherence to autonomous principles that are international in character. At the same time, in a number of implicit ways, the projects reflect a shared cultural ground, determined by the architects' formative experiences and professional training. The insistence on "the significance of the idea", a characteristic dimension of this production, is shared with a more extensive modernist discourse.[2] The dominance of concepts is a trait of Western post-Enlightenment culture. Yet for the Swiss, to a greater extent than for others, it remains ingrained in local culture, interpretations of territory and ways of approaching the creative act.[3]

[2] Breitschmid, 2008.

[3] Spier, 2009.

Switzerland was not spontaneously constituted, but it is the result of centuries of considered alliances between small political and administrative units. In the absence of a single language and religion, in the context of varying boundaries, at the intersection of major commercial and artistic routes through Europe, the country has had to justify itself conceptually. Historically, its position at the junction of three major European cultures and territories – French, German and Italian – made the matter acutely sensitive in diplomatic terms. Switzerland's attempts at self-definition can be seen as deliberate, rational interpretations of European culture.

Few modern problems have absorbed Swiss thinkers more than their own cultural identity. The nation's size, its cultural and linguistic heterogeneity have generated, for most Swiss intellectuals worth their name, the need to ponder and stretch the concept of Switzerland to its limits.[4] This need for over-articulation points to a heightened sensitivity regarding issues of national and cultural character.

[4] Pender, 1979, p. 1.

The Swiss discourse around cultural identity has been returning to the same particulars that defined the country in its European context: its democratic capitalism, the mentality of tolerance and enrichment through difference, and its neutrality. Critics generally see these values as convenient idealisations, or myths, pointing to their distance from factual reality. Based on the assumption that architecture is an emanation of its cultural context, this chapter proposes an overview of Swiss perspectives on territory, culture, and Switzerland's situation in Europe.

Between idealism and materialism

> The more I reflect on your civil and political arrangements, the less can I imagine that the nature of human contrivance could produce anything better.[5] **Jean-Jacques Rousseau**

5 Rousseau, 1984, p. 61.

Swiss culture is indebted both to Protestantism and Enlightenment philosophy. Even though his thinking has largely been assimilated into French culture, Rousseau's commentaries on Swiss Protestant civic culture are relevant to the German-Swiss cultural tableau. In particular, his ambivalence towards his birthplace reflects a recurrent theme of Swiss self-understanding: the symbolic dilemma of idealism versus materialism.

In 1754, Rousseau dedicated his *Discourse on Inequality* to the citizens of Geneva. Akin to Plato's ideal Republic, their Calvinistic democracy was presented in his *Dedication* as reasonable and transparent to reason, rationally conceived, justly regulated, and free. And yet, this lyrical invocation of freedom, advocating the values of Enlightenment, represented in its historical context a hidden admonition.[6] The insistence on equality and constitutional principles was perceived by Genevan aristocracy as provocative and subversive, as indeed it was. Only ten years later, as Rousseau was forced to seek refuge from political controversy, his criticism became vehemently explicit. In *Letters from the Mountains* (1764), he concentrated on the differences between classical principles and their actual application in Geneva:

6 Rosenblatt, 1997, pp. 85–86.

> Citizens of Geneva […] you are not Romans, nor Spartans, not even Athenians. […] You are Merchants, Artisans, Burghers, always preoccupied by your own private interests, your work, your turnover and gain; people for whom freedom itself is nothing but the means to acquire without obstacles and to possess with certainty.[7]

7 Rousseau, 1964, p. 881. Translation from the French original

Rousseau presented here a society in which private economic interest overshadowed public responsibility, and cultural ambition was hindered by provincial materialism. The burghers of Geneva were characterised as "hard working men, lovers of profit, submitted by their own interests to their ministers and Laws, occupied by their trades and their crafts; all equal by rights and undistinguished by fortune".[8] These assessments exposed the distance between the utopian principles used initially in building a new society, and its historical reality. The demeaning use of higher principles as a cover for personal interests created confusion between political and administrative issues. This ambiguity had its advantages, as it assured the interested participation of all members of the community, while all civic actions remained pervaded by material considerations.

In redefining the idea of freedom as a means to financial gain, Rousseau anticipated a view that would grow in popularity with and after Karl Marx – the association of the bourgeoisie with the very opposite of liberty. The cycle of capital and investment, the certainty of possessions create a spiritual prison.[9] On the other hand, Rousseau pointed out, the impulse to amass is led by neither greed nor vanity; the people are subjugated by their own interests to their self-imposed laws; the legal and economic spheres rely on each other for support. This materialist democracy was seen to rob people of their right to be different. Its most dangerous disadvantage was the impulse to reduce all to the lowest common denominator at the expense of diversity, cultural richness and artistic achievement.

Rousseau assumed an outsider's position in relation to this state of affairs. By virtue of his disengagement, he articulated some specific and recurring motifs in the way Switzerland has been perceived, both from the outside and by its own people.

"Swiss polis": the problematic of democracy

> One thing after another will have to be sacrificed – positions, possessions, religion, civilised manners, higher learning – as long as the masses can put pressure on their *Meneurs*.[10] **Jacob Burckhardt**

The criticism levelled at Switzerland by Swiss intellectuals during the nineteenth and twentieth centuries mirrors the central theme of Rousseau's disenchantment with Geneva: the discrepancy between ideal models and their application. If Rousseau used rhetorical detachment to assess the Calvinist model, a century later Jacob Burckhardt used temporal distance to ponder the nascent Switzerland. Specifically, he used the historical study of Athens to develop an objective view of democracy and the State.[11]

Burckhardt belonged to Basel's *haute-bourgeoisie*, a distinguished social class rooted in Reformed and humanist values. Alongside great economic power, this patrician class enjoyed a prominent intellectual position in the city.[12] As a member of this elite, Burckhardt was acutely sensitive to the new political climate and the tensions between federal and cantonal powers around 1848.[13] The drama of classical democracy, a main theme in Burckhardt's *History of Greek Culture* (1898–1902), was indeed a reflection on his own times.

8 Ibid., p. 886.
9 Ibid., p. 881.
10 Jacob Burckhardt quoted in Flaig, 2003, pp. 10–11.
11 Burckhardt, 1943, p. 21.
12 See Gossman, 1994.
13 See Gossman, 2000.

Comparisons between autonomous Swiss cantons and Greek *poleis* were rife in contemporary political rhetoric. Burckhardt wanted to examine this analogy and "provide a more sober and realistic evaluation of the *polis* than those who had represented it as a model of liberty of culture".[14] Unlike Rousseau, who had unfavourably measured his contemporaries against an unattainable classical model, he meant to show the defects inherent in the model itself. The Greek *polis* ideal, which had proved especially lucrative for modern radicals, was for him "one of the greatest historical frauds ever perpetrated".[15]

Burckhardt's understanding of the *polis* echoed the writings of Alexis de Tocqueville, Benjamin Constant and Fustel de Coulanges.[16] The drama of democracy lay in the conflict between ideals and their application; the principle of political equality was inevitably tied to dreams of social and material gain. Human greed, vanity and ambition had undermined the social order of the Greek *polis*, leading to the loss of moral and cultural dimensions and, ultimately, to anarchy. In this bleak vision of democracy, the "downward spiral into the abyss of material interests saw the systematic suppression of exceptional public figures and the gradual corruption of the political process by petty interests".[17]

Burckhardt's distaste for bombastic comparisons between *polis* and canton shows the distinction he made between classical and modern histories.[18] Nevertheless, he also sought to recover "the *recurrent, constant* and *typical*" patterns underlying past and present.[19] As explained in *Reflections on History* (1868–1871), his analysis of the Athenian model provided an "Archimedean point outside events", a contemplative dimension allowing the true understanding of one's own epoch.[20] To this end Burckhardt all but erased the differences between Greek ancient and modern forms of democracy.[21]

In Burckhardt's view, democracy involved the gamble of personal interest over and against cultural values. Its fatal tendency was to ostracize those, too talented or too charismatic, who contravened the egalitarian thrust of the masses. Moreover, modern democracy faced additional challenges: the mastery of technological progress and rampant capitalism.

Despite his misgivings, the historian upheld the principles of personal freedom and humanism.[22] He remained fully aware that an alternative to democracy was unthinkable, and could "really only emerge from the depth of evil".[23] Burckhardt's anxiety regarding the masses stemmed not from aristocratic contempt, but from his revulsion towards populist demagogy. He warned against the misuse of historical ideals in order to harbour nationalism and ruthlessly promote private interests. "Intentions", he wrote, "are particularly prone to make their appearance in the guise of patriotism, so that true knowledge finds its chief rival in our preoccupation with the history of our own country".[24]

---

14 Ibid., p. 301.

15 Burckhardt quoted in ibid., p. 302.

16 Flaig, 2003, pp. 11–20. For a summary of Burckhardt's conclusions on the *polis* see Gossman, "Per me si va nella città dolente", 2003, pp. 56–59.

17 Flaig, 2003, p. 8.

18 Gossman, 2000, pp. 318–321.

19 Burckhardt, p. 17.

20 Ibid., p. 19.

21 Flaig, 2003, p. 11.

22 Gossman, "Comment", 2003, pp. 41–45.

23 Flaig, 2003, p. 8.

24 Burckhardt, 1943, p. 22.

Through the attack on the double standards of demagogy and materialism, Burckhardt brought into question the isolationist self-satisfaction of his compatriots:

> Beyond the blind praise of our own country, another and more onerous duty is incumbent upon us as citizens, namely to educate ourselves to be comprehending human beings, for whom truth and the kinship with things of the spirit is the supreme good. In the realm of thought, it is supremely just and right that all frontiers should be swept away. There is too little of high spiritual value strewn over the earth for any epoch to say: we are utterly self-sufficient; or even: we prefer our own.[25]

This critique of isolationism presented a sceptical view of nineteenth-century Switzerland. Placing "the supreme good" above and beyond matters of political frontiers undermined the political rhetoric of politicians, who presented being Swiss as a kind of moral ratification. By seeing the "masses" not as an abstract construct but as a collective, with responsibilities as well as rights, Burckhardt brought the discussion to the level of individual civic action.

The Switzerland pondered by Burckhardt and Rousseau was urban, prosperous, and intrinsically bourgeois. In this context, one may recall Max Weber's argument that rational capitalism as practiced here was shaped by the Protestant work ethic. In Protestant society, material prosperity was no justification for idleness or public display of wealth. At personal level, incessant work held the promise of salvation. Thus the economic system was supported by a religious work ethic, in which the amassing of capital was seen as a moral accomplishment, attracting even some sort of divine recognition:

> With the consciousness of standing in the fullness of God's grace and being visibly blessed by Him, the bourgeois business man, as long as he remained within the bounds of formal correctness, as long as his moral conduct was spotless and the use to which he put his wealth not objectionable, could follow his pecuniary interests as he would and feel he was fulfilling a duty in doing so.[26]

Weber's Protestant model offers a valuable indication of a deeply rooted work ethic, operating at a profound social and cultural level. This ethic has underlined, at least in part, Switzerland's successful economy in modern times. It is with this conflation of work, solvency and divine grace in mind that we move from society to the citizen, and from classical ideals to a country sustained by self-perpetuating myths.

25 Ibid.

26 Weber, 2001, p. 120.

Myth building around 1848

> At that time they had a plan. […] At that time Switzerland had an historic present.[27]
> Max Frisch

27 Frisch, 1982, p. 216.

28 Hermann Weilenmann quoted in Pender, 1979, p. 6.

29 Siegfried, 1950, p. 12.

By virtue of its multilingual harmony, democracy and neutrality, Switzerland has been described as a miniature "*Vorbild Europa*" (exemplary Europe),[28] even as "the fullest expression of our European civilisation".[29] To be sure, the attitude that Burckhardt denounced as self-satisfaction was conditioned by a deeper political insecurity. In the historical context of the early Confederation, the concept of a Swiss nation was put under considerable pressure. The new state continuously sought justification for the heterogeneity of its constituents. Switzerland was at once the fledgling of a recently recognised constitution and an archaic network of autonomous communes, the result of centuries-old pragmatic alliances. Its precarious position required reinforcement with all possible means, both ideological and pragmatic. Among these, the most durably effective was the appeal to technological progress.

Nineteenth-century Switzerland saw the development of industry and infrastructure in parallel with the programmatic development of a national identity. By enabling new connections, modernisation came to be seen as the embodiment of a metaphorical act of unification, conveniently bridging rhetoric and pragmatic interests. A typical example of the symbolism emerging from a modern materialist enterprise is the Swiss railway system. Today, this national institution still represents values of precision, efficiency, reliability and order. Programmatically, railway stations were originally conceived as expressions of progress; the mountain viaducts, as man's romantic mastery over nature. The railways established connections between previously isolated entities, which made them means towards a literal unity, an emblem of national pride. On the one hand, the remarkable skill by which an efficient railway network overlaid a natural and hostile topography validated the possibility of accomplishing spiritual ends through technological means. On the other hand, the railways were infrastructure: trains and tracks, purposeful for business interests of whatever description, a lucrative investment rather than symbol of salvation.

The railways' dual status as infrastructure and national symbol was paralleled by an educational system focused on problem solving, but equally endowed with metaphorical qualities. Since its foundation in 1855 the Zurich Polytechnikum, later to become ETH, was conceived as a first expression of federal unity, symbolising the process of modernisation. The earliest purpose of the Polytechnikum was to train engineers who would deliver infrastructural development, an essential prerequisite to economic and political unity. A positivist discipline, engineering dominated the polytechnic tradition well into the early twentieth century.

(Page 20) Mesocco, Graubünden, ca. 1855. "Vorbild Europa": the emergence of a Swiss national "mythology" based on scenic beauty

(Above) Landwasser viaduct on the Albula Railway, Filisur, Graubünden. Postcard, 1914

Modernisation, modernity and cultural identity were thus forged in Switzerland in a particular manner, idealising praxis while subjecting it to a strict process of rationalisation. Ultimately the *Neues Bauen*'s fascination with construction over and against a decorative architecture originated from the polytechnic tradition, whose effect can still be perceived.[30] Meanwhile, the investment of national ideologies in practical matters would come under sharp attack during the second half of the twentieth century.

"Spiritual defence" and post-war demystification

> Free! Free! Free! In vain I tried to make him tell me, free from what? And above all, free for what?[31] **Max Frisch**

In order to forge a Swiss cultural identity, the country's topography, politics and history were all enlisted as strands of a national mythology. The concept of Swissness has been sustained by charging the landscape, the industry, and work ethic with moral or spiritual qualities. This conceptual, even "metaphysical" virtue of everything Swiss became apparent in the phenomenon of *Geistige Landesverteidigung* (spiritual self-defence), the nationalist propaganda that grew in parallel with the Nazi threat before and during the Second World War.[32] The pillars of this ideology were the defining particularities of the Swiss political system: "federalism versus uniformity, equal rights and respect for minorities versus arrogance of race, tolerance and individual freedom versus state ideology, multi-party democracy versus one-party dictatorship".[33] The official line conflated these values with the topography, wrapping all in an exalted terminology replete with religious overtones:

> The idea of a Swiss state was born neither of race nor of the flesh, it was born of the spirit. There is something magnificent, something awesome about the fact that this tremendous idea should have led to the creation of a state whose heart is the Gotthard, the mountain that sunders and the pass that connects. It is a European, a universal idea: the idea of a spiritual community of peoples and Western civilisations! [This is] nothing other than the victory of the spirit over the flesh on the rugged terrain of the state.[34]

The sensitive link between messianic subtexts and the rise of nationalism ensured that Swiss moderate intellectuals would later vehemently denounce such pronouncements. The Second World War constituted a defining watershed for Swiss self- understanding, precisely because of its lack of visible internal repercussions.

---

30 Tschanz, 2003, p. 236.

31 Frisch, 1982, p. 289.

32 Dürrenmatt, 1982, p. 289.

33 Jud, 2005.

34 Philipp Etter, "Message of the Federal Council Concerning the Organisation and Duties of Swiss Cultural Protection and Publicity", 1938. Quoted in Bergier, 2002, p. 85.

(Above) Alpine huts seen against the Matterhorn, ca. 1907–49. The Alps as a symbol of national valour

(Right) Swiss soldier resting by a traditional house, 1942. "Spiritual defence" propaganda

The contrast with a ravaged Europe distinguished the country in a new way. Peter Bichsel's essay *Des Schweizers Schweiz* (1969) records the initial boost of nationalist values during the war:

> The war has strengthened our self-consciousness. All we needed validating is proven by the fact that we were spared: the power of our army, our probity, the strength of our state, our democracy and devoutness. […] We are convinced that it was our merit to have been spared, […] since we must have impressed God with our behaviour, our army and the beauty of our country.[35]

Bichsel's sarcasm indicates the extent to which, by the 1960s, the maintenance of neutrality had become a strain. In particular, the myth of unblemished morality ratified by honest work and devotion was brought into question by Switzerland's role in the war. This caused an attitude shift towards "*Bedürfnis nach Rechtfertigung*" (need for justification), which undermined the accepted institutions of Swiss life.[36]

Friedrich Dürrenmatt and Max Frisch held similar critical positions. Dürrenmatt's political satires concealed a deep concern with national ideological constructs, especially the misalignment of fact and idealised vision. "Switzerland's ideology consists in Switzerland's pretence of passivity", he wrote. "Switzerland is a superwolf that, by proclaiming its neutrality, declares itself a superlamb".[37] Its conceptual precariousness stemmed not from external factors, but from the pressure imposed by its own self-constructed mythology. Switzerland had to maintain its unity in distinction from its neighbours; otherwise, it might as well "go ahead and merge its economy with Southern Germany and its hotels with those in Tyrol".[38]

Like Rousseau and Burckhardt before him, Dürrenmatt believed that Switzerland's idealisation as "a metaphysical entity, a shrine" had placed unwanted expectations on the behaviour of its citizens. The typical Swiss was required to "be free, obedient, capitalistic, social-minded; a democrat, a federalist, a believer, an anti-intellectual, a man ready to defend his country".[39] This faceless person represented yet another generation of the bourgeois average, caught in a perpetual conflict with outstanding individuals.

Bichsel noted that the sense of righteousness was connected, through a peculiar ideological strand, with Switzerland's scenic beauty. The landscape itself was appropriated as a moral achievement, leading to the conceptual chain of "beautiful Switzerland – good Switzerland – progressive Switzerland – humane Switzerland".[40] Bichsel hurried to dispel the myth:

---

35 Bichsel, 1969, pp. 12–13. Translation from the German original.

36 Karl Schmid quoted in Pender, 1979, p. 4.

37 Dürrenmatt, 1982, p. 288.

38 Ibid., p. 289.

39 Ibid.

40 Bichsel, 1969, p. 13. Translation from the German original.

> We have got used to seeing Switzerland with the eyes of our tourists. […] Our notion of our country is a foreign product. We live in a legend that was built around us.[41]

This passage brings a new element into consideration: the concept of Switzerland as a formula imposed from the outside as much as from within. Bichsel raises awareness of the contemporary multi-layered understanding of Swiss territory, where the imposition of a postcard-image of Switzerland is equated with a vision of progressive and democratic prosperity. This needs to be balanced with the possibility of evading national myths, with the individual's right "not to live permanently in a state of delight".[42]

The post-war generation condemned, together with the nationalistic demagogy spurred by the war, the social passivity engendered by an older sense of self-satisfaction. The convenient use of neutrality as cover for personal interest during the war had irretrievably compromised the idyllic image of Switzerland as "a grassy province outside history".[43] Max Frisch, reprising Burckhardt's problematic of political boundaries, identified this isolationist stance as an illusion:

> The myth, which Switzerland confers upon itself, and the fact that the myth solves no problems; consequently, the hysteria of helplessness. Every problem that we ourselves have to deal with means sending the concept of Switzerland out for repair.[44]

Much of Max Frisch's writing concerns the status of national symbols in post-war Switzerland, such as the army or the idea of *Heimat*.[45] His generation faced the relativisation of those very concepts that had stood for Swiss identity. It had reached maturity in the "awareness that terms like *federalism*, *neutrality*, and *independence* represent an illusion in an age of the rule of multinational corporations".[46] Frisch's notion of Heimat was synonymous not with comfort, but with the burden of "anger and shame".[47]

This sense of indignation also permeates Frisch's fiction, through the bitter and ironic commentaries passed on 1950s Swiss society. The eponymous anti-hero of *I'm not Stiller* (1954) is a Swiss artist who, returning from the United States, refuses to reprise the identity conferred upon him by social convention and by law. The denial of his own name permits Stiller a critical detachment, not unlike Rousseau's, under whose cover he feels free to criticise. Swiss order is presented as compulsion, neatness as psychological compensation for mediocrity, and the boasts of democratic freedom as hollow formulas concealing the burden of social convention. The concept of Switzerland becomes an unnerving paradox: "so clean that one can hardly breathe for hygiene, and oppressive precisely because everything is just right".[48]

---

41 Ibid., p.15.

42 Ibid., p. 23.

43 Albin Zollinger quoted in Pender, 1979, p. 5.

44 Frisch, "Foreignization I", 1989, p. 339.

45 Frisch, "Switzerland", 1989.

46 Ibid., p. 346.

47 Ibid.

48 Frisch, 1982, pp. 12–13.

To the pervading social rigidity, Frisch opposes the myth of the artist. Motifs of redemption and sacrifice, of genuine compassion, are only accessible through the acceptance of error and fallibility. This acceptance is more readily available to the tormented artist than to the upright citizen, instigating a painful inner confrontation instead of the self-justifying procedures of a moderate and rational society. Frisch thus returns to a Romantic notion of original creativity, finding truth and freedom by turning inwards, away from the external and "oppressively adequate" manifestations of modern culture.[49]

49 Ibid., p. 13.

Reflections on architecture and urbanism

> We stroll along for nearly an hour, […] undisturbed by outstanding works of architecture, which would have interrupted our conversation.[50] **Max Frisch**

50 Ibid., p. 68.

Frisch's architectural training helped him consider the Swiss built environment, which he saw as culturally conditioned towards the average. In the novel *I'm Not Stiller* he presented the obsession with constructional quality as a compensation for moral compromise.[51] Zurich was described as a staid city, where adherence to norms was as compulsory in architecture as it was in society at large.[52] The essay "Cum Grano Salis" (1953), written at about the same time, was geared specifically towards construction and design, bringing this critique to the architectural audience. For Frisch, the tendency to endow practical actions with the gravity of moral choice was mirrored by Swiss architecture's "escape into detail, the dictatorship of the average".[53] He condemned the compromised Modernism that marked the cities and the construction of "soft" neighbourhoods designed to give the forced impression of village life. Architecture had to address the society's real needs: "The neighbourhood I need is mental-social, not a collection of dwellings".[54]

51 Ibid., pp. 213–215.

52 Ibid., p. 68.

53 Frisch, 1953, p. 329. Translation from the German original.

54 Ibid., p. 328.

Frisch called for a switch in the Swiss mind-set, from provincial pettiness to cosmopolitanism as the urban manifestation of individual freedom. The same concern motivated his participation in the polemic *achtung: die Schweiz* (1955), a manifesto co-written with Lucius Burckhardt and Markus Kutter, arguing for new solutions in urbanism.[55] The pamphlet proposed, for the 1964 national exhibition, the planning of a new city that would reflect the changes imposed by technological and social advancements, the role of the automobile, education developments etc.[56] This characteristically modernist manifesto reprised the link made by the *Neues Bauen* in the 1920s and 1930s between technological development, a rejection of tradition and the betterment of society. *Achtung: die Schweiz* was intended as a politically radical statement, and it duly attracted conservative opprobrium. In this respect, it anticipated the 1968 student movements, announcing a change in attitudes towards the middle classes, the bourgeoisie, and being Swiss.

55 Burckhardt, Frisch, and Kutter, 1955.

56 Paquot, 1998.

The debates regarding national character receded during the last decades of the twentieth century. Switzerland's cities have become more cosmopolitan than Frisch's repressed vision of Zurich in the 1950s. Nevertheless, recent polemics on Swiss character retain the sense of irony as a mask for helplessness. Werner Oechslin's "*Helvetia Docet*" (1998), an updated portrait of Swiss self-understanding, paints a less ideal picture than that of a reliably prosperous and cultivated country, actively supportive of its avant-garde architecture.[57] He presents Switzerland as still bound to its historical myths, reworking them as brands for a successful tourist industry. The culture is trivialised by the passive acceptance of, and adaptability to, external projections of a pastoral Switzerland. "The nation does not identify with the cultural achievements of its citizens, but its artists and intellectuals are expected to identify with the nation".[58]

With regard to contemporary architecture, Oechslin sees the recent production as a heterogeneous collection of attitudes, for which "Swiss" is little more than a disposable label. He does identify a perceptible Swiss character, but as a set of psychological traits, not as design features or building traditions. Swiss culture, and by implication Swiss architecture, are defined by exceptions and not by the general direction. The internationally recognised architects – Herzog & de Meuron, Peter Zumthor, Diener & Diener, Mario Botta – follow autonomous agendas, only converging through first-hand experiences of Swiss culture.

The consensus on difference conveys the idea that Swiss architecture is determined by handful of strong practices, each following its own artistic mission. Their suspicion towards the "Swiss" label indicates the careful avoidance of any dubious, national-defining cultural desiderata. This tacit understanding indicates a psychological pattern, an anxiety regarding their intrinsic Swissness. The professional circles' identification with an artistic agenda and their distaste for being read in terms of cultural stereotypes betray an aspiration towards creative independence. The architects' willingness to participate in a global discourse, away from the limitations of the national character, suggests that the drama of Stiller is not finalised after 1968, but on the contrary, it is exacerbated. Authenticity is sought away from convention, in individual acts of artistic freedom.

At the same time, the evidence on the ground suggests a more complex reading. Just as Frisch oscillated between criticising the system and acknowledging its comforts, so architecture relies on a stable professional network for the dissemination of ideas, and on a culturally established attitude towards construction for an appropriate materialisation of design. The cultural reverence manifested towards the act of building – even as a well-made thing, an investment apt for the value of the ground beneath – is incorporated in the Swiss production and reflected in the professional status of the architect. This is not a casual possession, but one that is permanently examined. It is recognised that participation in a global culture puts at risk social

---

[57] Oechslin, 1998, pp. 55–59.

[58] Ibid., p. 58. Translation from the German original.

and economic structures that, within Switzerland, can still be taken for granted. This vacillation characterises the tension between originality and the recourse to values within the culture, between objects and the praxis in which they exist.

One way out of the dilemma is through recourse to the idea of the city, a continuity in which differences can successfully co-exist. A frequently criticised Swiss trait is the "rural-romantic mentality" of a picturesque agricultural territory.[59] The discourse finds a way out of the provincial mind-set through a cosmopolitanism largely identified with urbanisation. The sense that the Swiss countryside is like false scenery, an anachronism supported by state subsidies for the sake of national pride, has led some to seek truth in the gritty, ordinary realm of cities. In this way, the Swiss polemic is tied in with the possibility of urban formulations for Switzerland as a whole.

Switzerland as urban territory

> Switzerland is essentially known.[60] **Marcel Meili**

Comparisons between Switzerland and a city are not new. In 1763 Rousseau likened its valleys, hills and mountains to the districts of a continuous town; in 1932 the architect Armin Meili referred to Switzerland as a "traditionally decentralised city".[61] The influential writings of André Corboz called in the 1980s and 1990s for an objective reappraisal of the historical distinctions between rural and urban territory, in the ever-changing context of industrialised society.[62] By metropolis he did not mean literal urban growth, or a properly defined settlement, but a conglomerate development determined by improvised market interests rather than over-arching planning strategies.[63]

Corboz sought to reconcile international theory with concrete conditions. He saw both the CIAM's *Athens Charter* of 1933, and the fierce 1960s urban conservationism it had caused, as equally problematic. The nostalgic tendency of contemporary Swiss planning to implement an idealised "village culture" was the undesirable consequence of this duality:

> The Metropolis Switzerland, which is gradually establishing itself in the collective consciousness, is again divided into microscopic pieces, offered as an accumulation of villages! After the war, the neighbourhood unit was proposed as a scientific interpretation of village, and now this regressive Utopia, representing a culture of escapism, has re-emerged.[64]

Corboz called for objectivity and concrete action against the clichés of Swiss self-understanding. He proposed that planning should deal with the improvised, unpredictable conditions dictated on the ground by economic considerations. His belief in the efficiency of planning is remarkable: it suggests a vision

59 Diener et al., 2006, p. 157.

60 Ibid., p. 136.

61 Both quoted in Corboz, 1988, p. 14.

62 See Corboz and Marot, 2001.

63 Corboz, 1988, p. 15.

64 Ibid., p. 19. Translation from the German original.

of planning law as an accurate reflection of collective, local cultural values.

Corboz's resistance against a network of private interests had a significant impact on the architectural generations at the heart of this account. Of particular interest is the publication *Switzerland – An Urban Portrait* (2006), the result of a four-year research project conducted in the framework of ETH Studio Basel by the architects Roger Diener, Jacques Herzog, Marcel Meili and Pierre de Meuron, together with the sociologist Christian Schmid.[65] The study proposed a snapshot of Switzerland at the turn of the century, equally independent from prevalent planning theories and the outdated myths of self-understanding. The information, based on actual evidence amassed from the built environment, was gathered through first-hand surveys and interviews, supplemented with statistical data.[66]

The study intended to bridge the usual schism between research and practical endeavour; its potential is political rather than conventionally theoretical. One recognises in the enterprise the leitmotif of an international theoretical hypothesis being applied to the Swiss context. The theory is grounded in Henri Lefebvre's model of societal urbanisation, a phenomenon linked to the industrialisation and urban expansion of the last two centuries.[67] This concerns not just the cities as built agglomerations, but all phenomena resulting from the urban's dominion over the rural. The hypothesis of an urban Switzerland is not meant literally in the sense of conurbation, but as the site for complex, evolving territorial exchanges and cross-border interactions. A remote village is urban inasmuch as supermarkets, Swiss Telecom phone booths and second homes are universal expressions of city life.

While Lefebvre deals with a global phenomenon, Switzerland's situation stands apart in certain respects. Its identity is grounded in conceptual thinking; its practices are permeated with a strong sense of the rational. The Swiss nation is an artificial construct, an umbrella-term covering different ethnicities, religions and languages. Its political territory comprises small overlapping territories, determined by different cultural patterns.

According to Studio Basel, Swiss territory is subject to two main ordering systems, the cultural and the administrative. Its character derives from a variety of social, linguistic and religious orientations overlaid with national, cantonal, communal divisions. On the one hand the fine network of internal borders preserves and consolidates federal unity, like tree roots preserve and consolidate the earth in which they are planted. On the other hand, it evokes a great metaphorical distance between people and things, pointing to the fragility of this condition.

The tension between autonomy and cohesion is acted out in the urban domain. "Switzerland is threatened less by a lack of solidarity between classes, social strata, or groups than by a lack of shared identity among its towns, a kind of spatial class

[65] In this context I use 'Studio Basel' to denote the collective authorship of the study on Switzerland.

[66] Herzog and Meili, 2006, pp. 136–140.

[67] Schmid, 2006, p. 165. The theoretical framework of Studio Basel was based on Lefebvre, 1991 and Lefebvre, 2003.

struggle".[68] Urban development is impeded by communal autonomy; the danger to Switzerland remains its political structure, reflecting an entrenched "system of demarcation, small-scale segmentation, small-mindedness, and egoism".[69] Studio Basel has envisaged that the country's future will be decided in a power play between communal decision-making and an inescapable urbanisation, in alignment with a global economic landscape.

The study characterises Swiss territory according to three types of criteria: networks, borders and differences. Networks of "trade, production, daily routine, communication, and migration" provide the cohesive element in the idea of a uniformly connected (democratic, federal) Switzerland.[70] Borders are a fundamental element in Swiss self-understanding, defining the political elements of federation, canton, commune but also the restrictions these imply. Finally, differences constitute the potential energy that can be released from the interaction of distinct territories. A measure of the urban is given by the way in which cultural, social, economic differences are not only recognised, but also capitalised.

Studio Basel's research stopped short of concrete proposals prone to misinterpretation. It intended to present the situation as it stood at the time of the study – a temporal cross-section through Swiss territory at the beginning of the twenty-first century. The aim was to think through its potential in isolation from the preconceptions and myths imprinted on operational policies in practice. The attempt to identify the latent potential of differences led to Studio Basel's original contribution, the formulation of a new urban typology. This was conceived not as a revisionist but as a commonsensical reading of territory, reinforcing its existing economic, social and architectural potential.[71]

The study identified five types of territorial urbanisation, each with its own socio-economic and cultural rhythm: the metropolitan regions (Geneva-Lausanne, Basel-Mulhouse-Freiburg, and Zurich), the networks of towns (in central Switzerland and around Berne), quiet zones (intra-mountainous valleys, where agricultural economy is either flourishing or still just about sustainable), Alpine resorts (characterised by seasonal variations in economic activity and inhabitant numbers) and Alpine fallow lands (those uninhabitable or steadily depopulating).

These typologies were drawn on a zoning map, which shows little correspondence with actual boundaries. Indeed, its most striking feature is the "leopard-skin pattern" of relatively autonomous patches with varying degrees of overlap. This indicates the abstract nature of the project, the withdrawal from concrete planning as such; but it also indicates the limitations of the approach. The authors themselves express scepticism with regard to the dominant cartographic representation and aerial photography. Their communicative potential is partial in comparison to a more literary (and therefore less precise)

---

[68] Herzog and Meili, 2006, p. 148.

[69] Ibid., p. 145.

[70] Schmid, 2006, p. 70.

[71] Diener et al., 2006, p. 154.

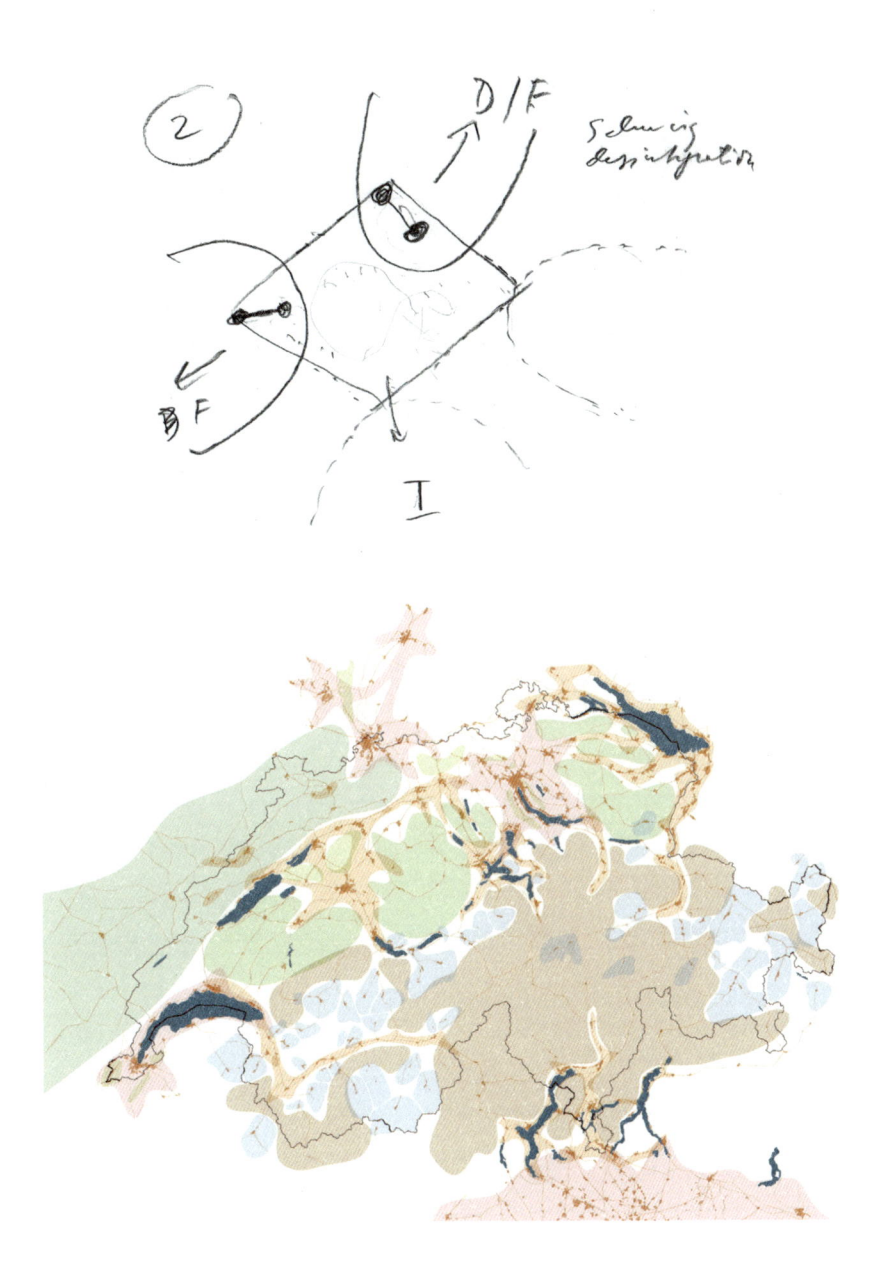

(Top) ETH Studio Basel,
Switzerland – An Urban Portrait, 2006.
Sketch showing possible future
disintegration into linguistic, cultural
and economic regions

(Bottom) ETH Studio Basel,
Switzerland – An Urban Portrait, 2006.
Urban typology of Switzerland

approach.[72] The means of representation indicate the hold of an epistemological approach on the actual thinking. One senses the influence of *Weltanschauung*, described by Heidegger as the formation of a world-picture objectifying culture and making it available as a project.[73] The authors' frustration at the limits of communication recognises the detachment from the "world", its availability only as philosophical concept or sets of statistical data.

The implicit recognition that experience extends beyond rational understanding, into a thicket of pre-reflective observations and impulses, brings us to the limitations of typological thinking. Once a type has been conceptualised through theoretical demonstration and drawn up as a spatial configuration, it loses its deeper connection to the subconscious sphere.[74] Similarly, a territorial typology cannot fully convey the reality governed on the ground by an urban order embedded in its institutional life. It is not accidental that a deeper understanding of what is typically Swiss is not drawn up in maps or diagrams, but emerges most clearly in the transcription of a conversation between authors:

> Jacques Herzog: So you believe that pragmatism basically defines the way Swiss people live and the form of their cities?
>
> Marcel Meili: Probably. The country behaves in varied, surprising, and contradictory ways, once its assets have been secured. Pragmatism means negotiation between relatively individualistic cells in order to foster collective existence.[75]

Here and in various other passages, *Switzerland – an Urban Portrait* testifies to the continuing intellectual debates around Swiss identity. It provides valuable evidence of how Switzerland is viewed by its architects, allowing some speculation on how culture and territory are re-interpreted through the built environment.

The study professes the unwillingness to subscribe to "myths" that is characteristic of post-1968 generations. The cautious ambivalence towards the established lore propagated in tourist brochures has led Studio Basel towards cartographic numerical analyses that make Switzerland into a generality. This would seem to suggest that the capitalist global city has become the paradigm, drawing on the economic procedure of statistically described trends and variations to express what is typical in culture.

One recognises in Studio Basel's mode of enquiry the theoretical discourse to which these practicing architects were exposed during their training, which also informs their built work. The focus on concrete structures and networks stands for a reification of culture, the attempt to define typical experience through typology.

[72] Herzog and Meili, 2006, pp. 137–140.
[73] Heidegger, 1977, pp. 115–154.
[74] Vesely, 1982, p. 9.
[75] Herzog and Meili, 2006, p. 156.

Studio Basel's acceptance of reality as governed by economic interest, and the reliance on objective data to understand this reality, reinforce the quantitative operative mode it otherwise criticises. The urban territory is seen as a dispersed network of types. The recourse to a typology of the territory suggests that the ethical dimensions of the need for concrete and meaningful action are translated into rational, controllable observations.

At the same time, the dichotomy of reason and feeling implied by this reification is negated in practice by the commitment to understanding and imparting knowledge demonstrated by these architects. It is significant that practitioners who could easily limit themselves to the design of autonomous projects have felt the political commitment, possibly the incentive, to engage through research with a wider social and cultural polemic. This suggests a deeper claim, manifested not in built things, but in the possibility of action.

The Background of Theory

ETH as Swiss emblem

> As a technical university in a small country, the ETH Zurich can only compete with the world's best by establishing international links [...]. The multicultural tradition of Switzerland, its cultural heritage acquired over many generations, provide in our view a strong base for this purpose.[1] **Mission Statement of ETH Zurich**

[1] ETH Executive Board, 2007.

The theory underpinning the late twentieth-century Swiss production has mainly been disseminated through the architecture department of the Swiss Federal Institute of Technology (ETH) in Zurich. A prestigious school, ETH has attracted the majority of contemporary German-Swiss practitioners mentioned in the present study. Even those who trained elsewhere were indirectly exposed, through the professional scene, to ideas discussed in ETH in the 1970s and 1980s. ETH can be seen to provide a common theoretical ground, which forms the basis of a generational self-understanding. Therefore, a closer look at its scene after 1960 will help define the formative background of the practitioners active in the 1980s and 1990s.

Before examining the content of ETH architectural theory, the school's status as a political and cultural institution demands clarification. For the Swiss, ETH is more than a higher education facility. Government funded, acting as a significant political and cultural power, ETH Zurich is a public institution in the widest sense. It relates to the city, to industrial development and to the political sphere.[2] Its mission statement emphasises the political link to the government, commitment to the local and global communities and its place in the international theoretical domain.

[2] The cultural and architectural value of the ETH is treated in Oechslin, 2005.

Within ETH, the architecture department has a high professional and representational status. It reflects the value of architecture as cultural and economic asset. The prestigious buildings of the Polytechnikum, as it was known before 1913, dominate the central cityscape of Zurich. Therefore, the re-location of the architecture school in the 1970s to the peripheral Hönggerberg campus conveyed mixed messages. Officially a glittering, expanding science campus, Hönggerberg represents at the same time a colourless exile outside the city limits.³ The artificial environment of a high-tech campus, transposed to a rural landscape, undermines the architecture school's interdependence with the urban realm.

The national significance of ETH is linked to Switzerland's history. The Polytechnikum was founded in 1855, the first institution to be created after the adoption of the Federal Constitution. Its existence therefore had a political and didactic resonance as "the expression of the federal State".⁴ ETH symbolises the political agenda of nation building through strategic modernisation. After 1848, the reinforcement of a sense of federal unity depended economically and politically on the creation of advanced, co-ordinated infrastructure. This occurred while, in the wider European context, various modernising systems were being implemented. Such measures, from centralised land administration to polytechnic education, bore witness to the wide-ranging effects of the French revolutionary ideals.

The new Switzerland needed a modern infrastructure in order to reinforce its political unity. The federal law under which the Polytechnikum originated gave priority to technical training for civil and hydraulic engineering, mechanics and chemistry, in particular to assist the connection and modernisation of remote Alpine regions. The architecture curriculum reflected this foundational ethos. Since its inception the school was shaped by the "general tendency to insist on practice rather than pure science" and the lesser role accorded to speculative theory.⁵ The school's practical and technical bias provided an innovative alternative to the established Beaux-Arts training of most Swiss architects of the time.⁶ This was propagated through the decades to form a "polytechnic culture", well integrated in the Swiss self-understanding.⁷ The present curricular structure still reflects this practical bias.

The architecture department has established a diffuse yet strong network of alliances between generations, a micro-culture that is sufficiently stable to preserve continuity and create a definite self-understanding. In comparison to other European schools, a large proportion of those teaching are involved in practice at the highest level. Federal funding allows the school, through a balance of set rules and flexibility, to accommodate established practitioners on visiting professorships and tenures. The system relies on assistants selected from among recent graduates and young practitioners. With the implacable logic of a bio-system, assistants provide the one-to-one teaching and find their own footing in business life, while allowing professors to remain engaged in practice. This creates not only a smooth transition between training and practice, but also the direct, personal contact between students and architects at several levels of the profession.

---

3   See Maurer, 2005, pp. 106–133.

4   Gubler, 1988, p. 22. Translation from the French original.

5   Ibid., p. 23.

6   This was a relatively new concept in education, following in the steps of France with its Ecole Polytechnique founded in 1794 for military engineering training, and of Germany where such new schools were provided as "technical alternatives to the liberal-arts-based academies". See Mallgrave, 1996, p. 229.

7   Gubler, 1988, p. 22. Translation from the French original.

(Above) Polytechnikum, Zurich, ca.1880

(Right) ETH Zurich, Hönggerberg.
Campus nowadays

ETH culture has a strong historical sense – partly inherited, partly re-created through theoretical re-assessments during the late 1960s and 1970s. Students have been encouraged to find culturally relevant referents in the prominent models of Swiss architectural history. Recognising the significance of culture has shifted the legitimacy of design from practical competence to typological interpretation. This kind of historical reference was intended to create and develop an objective, rather than individualist, approach to design.

This attitude is a linchpin of Swiss theory, providing a basic and widely adaptable formula throughout the 1980s and 1990s. However, it constitutes just one moment in a continuing historical development, epitomised by openness towards practice and fascination with a succession of significant figures. From Gottfried Semper, the first professor of architecture at the Polytechnikum, to Karl Moser, Otto Salvisberg and Alfred Roth, the Chairs of ETH have been selected from among architects who could mediate between practice and a theoretical or intellectual position. This series of protagonists has established a clearer architectural genealogy than in most other countries.[8]

8 See for example Allenspach, 1999; Gubler, 1975; Schmidt, 1972.

At the heart of this professional lore there is a curious ambivalence towards theory. On the one hand, one senses a slight impatience with dense texts and suspicion as to their applicability, demonstrating a view of actual building as the highest goal of architecture.[9] The appointment of studio teachers is generally assessed in the light of their accomplishments in practice. On the other hand, since the late 1960s a preference is perceptible for written discourse as supporting and often justifying the built production, clarifying the conceptual dimensions of even the most object-oriented enterprise. The reliance on form to situate meaning has led to a situation where, in order to separate style from substance, architects emphasise the work's theoretical content in order to demonstrate the ethical dimension of their architecture.

9 See Kipnis, 1997, pp. 18–19.

ETH in the 1960s: the rise of theory

(a) Bernhard Hoesli: Modernism as method

> I was convinced that Modern Architecture had become teachable… I took it for granted that the WHAT and WHY of architecture could, without saying, be assumed and that in my lessons, the main thing was to teach HOW one can design.[10] **Bernhard Hoesli**

10 Hoesli quoted in Jansen, p. 24.

The 1960s were a watershed moment for architecture teaching at ETH. Together with an increasing openness towards other disciplines, this period redefined the role of theory within the school. During the 1950s, under the leadership of Alfred Roth and the strong influence exercised by Sigfried Giedion, ETH had maintained a clear modernist direction. Nevertheless, the crisis leading to CIAM's dissolution in 1959 led to the fragmentation of teaching positions. The 1960s introduced a spectrum of attitudes, ranging from Giedion's unabated exploration of Modernist orthodoxy, to Aldo van Eyck's structuralist critique of the same.

Bernhard Hoesli (1923–1984) ran the first year course at ETH from 1959 until 1981. This *Grundkurs* became the common basis against which the polemical positions of various studios would later develop. The idea of providing a shared ground was attuned to the content of the course; rather than teaching basic skills, Hoesli sought a universally valid basis for design through the conceptualisation of "space". This non-elective introductory foundation module gave ETH pedagogy a strong systematic and conceptual direction, whose influence on Swiss education and practice endures to this day.[11]

A graduate of ETH himself, Hoesli had worked for Le Corbusier before travelling to the US in the early 1950s. Alongside Colin Rowe, he became a central figure among the so-called Texas Rangers, who taught at University of Texas in Austin. The *Grundkurs* was fundamentally a transposition of the controversial Austin pedagogy, formulated between 1951 and 1957 and later disseminated in the US through Cornell and Cooper Union. The Texas approach was a critical synthesis of academic and modernist teaching, combining the Beaux Arts reliance on tradition and the Bauhaus cultivation of innate creativity.[12] Instead of the more orthodox rupture with architectural history, Hoesli and Rowe sought to place Modernism within an architectural continuum.

This was firstly possible by defining space as the medium of architecture: "a visible and tangible thing, […] to be shaped according to the rules of formal composition".[13] The appeal to the abstract notion of space, often associated with Modernism, originated nevertheless in Beaux-Arts teaching. "Space" belongs with an intuitive understanding of architecture, based on the elimination of references to concrete historical models. This modernist topos was preceded by Durand's distillation of tradition into a series of rules with universal application. The neutral use of classical ornament in the later Beaux-Arts academy had a timeless ambition; this was not, as modernists would have it, to operate in complete freedom from historical conventions, but to freeze these into a de-historicised manner. The notion of "space", central to both attitudes, was indeed broader than in Hoesli and Rowe's use.

Secondly, the Texas group revived the need for the *idée*, previously central to Beaux-Arts method and discarded within the Bauhaus as too restrictive.[14] Hoesli and Rowe saw the necessity for concepts to structure the decision-making process and bring consistency to all aspects of the project. Finally, Austin design teaching encouraged responses to the pre-existing urban context. However, the city was understood primarily in spatial and formal terms, as a composition of sealed-off and free-flowing voids.

11 Somol, 2003, p. 11.
12 Caragonne, 1995, pp. 154–156.
13 Pearlman, 1996, p. 128.
14 Ibid., p. 127.

After returning to ETH in 1959, Hoesli continued to develop a systematic pedagogical programme for making modern architecture "teachable".[15] He sought to develop a general method that would go beyond particular circumstances:

> The method comprises: to start designing and allow the individual design steps [to] alternate with particular exercises which thereby serve to overcome typical design situations and to introduce and work on the necessary concepts and procedures.[16]

Design projects were set up as a controlled series of drawing- and model-based formal exercises, accompanied by the parallel study of avant-garde precedents. The course developed a "taxonomy of modern buildings", a kind of database that students could rely on during the process of design.[17] Several students from the 1970s recall Hoesli's lectures on modernist history, combining procedure with a thorough knowledge of precedent, as a formative experience of ETH pedagogy.

Hoesli believed "that the subject of teaching cannot be chosen according to building types […] but must be identified as problem types […]. Together with typical teaching subjects there must be, then, typical procedural matters included in the teaching content".[18] The challenge of "problem types" returns to the modernist treatment of architecture as a spatial question. The common denominator on which design could be assessed or produced was the notion of "continuous space".[19] This meant that the city could only be studied in abstract, geometric terms, or as an environmental experience of open and enclosed elements.[20]

The wider architectural context required the control of design through steps other than adherence to a formal canon. For previous generations, the works of Le Corbusier, Mies and Wright had provided a datum against which new positions could be defined. Now, due to the growing relativism of contemporary architecture, teaching had to develop the students' ability to make informed decisions.[21] In this framework design became less a matter of individual creativity, as invited by the Bauhaus, than the ability to justify decisions though the conceptualisation of common architectural tasks.

The intellectualisation of design processes and their transformation from "an empirical way of dealing with things" to "a way of thinking" became Hoesli's principle for studio teaching.[22] Intellectual activity did not schematically transform intuitive and practical design processes into an intelligible theoretical system, but had to apply this to practical considerations. In other words, Hoesli communicated to students the need to mediate between the general, neutral thrust of theory and the particulars of each situation.

---

15 Seligmann, 1989, p. 9.

16 Hoesli quoted in Jansen, 1989, p. 26.

17 Seligmann, 1989.

18 Hoesli quoted in Jansen, 1989, p. 25.

19 Hoesli, 1997, p. 92.

20 For more on Hoesli's "architectural space" see ibid., pp. 89–97.

21 Hoesli quoted in Jansen 1989, pp. 38, 40.

22 Ibid., p.40. Also see Oechslin, 1997, p. 11.

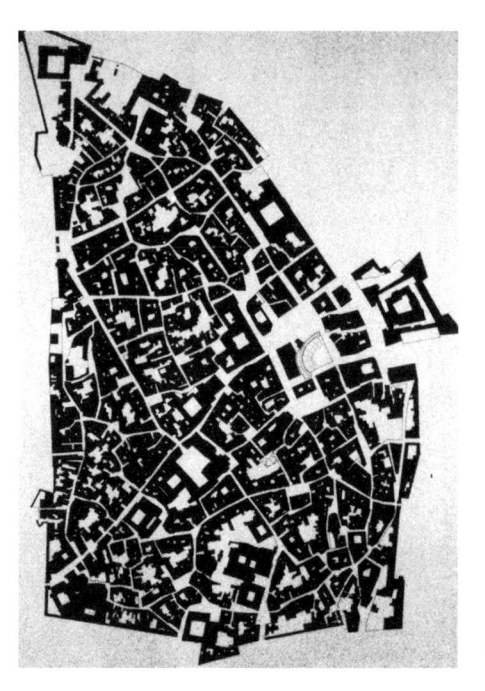

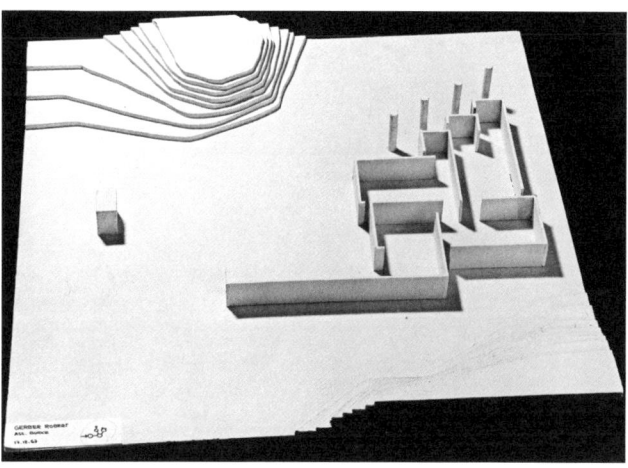

(Top left) Hoesli Studio, Urban Study
of Lecce, ca. 1978–84. The urban network
of solids and voids is seen as the
concrete manifestation of communal
and societal issues.

(Top right) *Grundkurs*. Gerbert Robert,
student work, 1967. Spatial configurations
with non-specific functions.

(Right) Bernhard Hoesli. *Untitled*,
Collage, 1977

The *Grundkurs* was the first learning experience for most German-Swiss architects active between 1980 and 2000. Its abstract methods, while confusing for many first-year students, operated retrospectively; only later would they understand the principles assimilated during this introductory course. For example, Marcel Meili identified a formal and analytical sensibility acquired from Hoesli's *Grundkurs*, which he carried on in practice:

> Hoesli was an intellectually controlled, didactically focused figure whose concerns reflected mature, conceptual modernity. At the time we were too young to comprehend the importance of what he taught us but in retrospect I can say this was a most important course, perhaps internationally, because it pursued modernity in a didactic manner. Hoesli worked with the concept of "space", which to a first year student was not understandableas such, but his course was very good at developing design strategies in an analytical way.[23]

23 Meili, 2004.

Hoesli impacted on the Swiss architectural discourse in different ways. After 1968 he came to represent a monolithic figure, associated with historical Modernism. However, his *Grundkurs* constituted an undisputed rite of passage; its design stipulations merged with the material taught in subsequent years, helping to formulate the tenets of contemporary Swiss architecture. The primacy of concept as the central generating force in design, the treatment of urban context as a mass of solids and voids, and the reliance on the abstract notion of "space" can all be traced back to Hoesli's influence.

Moreover, Hoesli's *Grundkurs* signalled the increasing significance of theory for architectural production. The need for an intellectual structure for design was a reaction against the commercially efficient Modernism dominating the international scene, the search for renewed social relevance. ETH in the 1960s saw another re-assessment of 1920s Modernism, this time in the conditions of an emerging political conscience, in the attempt to re-connect practice with the reality of social concerns.

(b) Conceptualism

> For a short while, at ETH we used to write more than draw.[24] **Martin Steinmann**

24 Steinmann, "Neuere Architektur", 2003, p. 93. Translation from the German original.

During the post-war years, while ETH offered a routine modernist education, a new school of architecture was set up in Ulm under the direction of Max Bill. The Hochschule für Gestaltung was founded in 1951 with the intention to re-establish Bauhaus principles in design teaching. The Ulm school initiated a new kind of sociological research for architecture. Bill's successor, Tomás

Bernhard Hoesli working with students,
5 February 1979

Maldonado, oriented it towards the application of social sciences in design, connecting formal production, the critical theory of the Frankfurt School, and Hannes Meyer's understanding of architecture as "environmental science".[25] The school sought methodological formulations for design, as illustrated by mathematician Horst Rittel's research into decision-making procedures. Rittel's work was a source of fascination for sociologist Lucius Burckhardt, who taught briefly in Ulm before joining ETH in 1961. Burckhardt brought process-focused impetus that would resonate in the school for over a decade.[26]

The theoretical spectrum of 1960s ETH stretches between the poles set by Hoesli and Burckhardt. Hoesli intended to overcome the "object-fixation" of Modernism by viewing form as a means to an end and not an end in itself.[27] Through set design processes he intended to systematise an aesthetic of architecture going beyond the mere issues of function. Burckhardt, influenced by the positivism of Ulm, turned architecture into a different kind of system, modelled on the social sciences. The emphasis on process and sociological investigations led to the gradual transformation of studio projects into research of multi-disciplinary processes. As a result, the ETH tendencies – much like other European schools at the time – veered from the practical towards the abstract. Marcel Meili described this scene as a "late modern climate of rampant conceptualism, in which architecture was taught as a pragmatic science".[28]

After 1968, the sociological impetus increased proportionally with the students' political involvement. The more established teachers were associated with the political establishment, causing a shift away from Hoesli's design processes and towards Burckhardt's. The lack of interest in formal resolution all but led to architecture being viewed as a branch of sociology. The studio that Burckhardt led together with architect Rolf Gutmann between 1971–73, nicknamed the "canapé", was polemical and irreverent, encouraging process-driven and open-ended projects:

> We used those methods of architectural representation that could convey that one is insufficiently informed, that one can only find this much through research, and nevertheless has to provide answers. [We tried] to remain open to solutions, to their potential, and not impose a definite, confident, perfect solution.[29]

Burckhardt's students were encouraged to compare the avant-garde's societal and formal ambitions against the actual use of modernist prototypes. They studied the manner in which *Neues Bauen* projects had been appropriated and changed over the decades – the impact of technological and social developments on the early *Siedlungen*, their adaptability to updated requirements.[30] Such comparative studies led not only to the understanding of modernist social proposals, but also their adaptability to current conditions.

25 See Frampton, "Apropos Ulm", 2002, pp 47–55; Tafuri and Dal Co, 1976, p. 42.

26 See Paquot, 1998.

27 Hoesli quoted in Jansen, 1989, p. 39.

28 Meili, 2004.

29 Paquot, 1998. Translation from the French original.

30 Burckhardt continued this research after leaving ETH in 1973. See Burckhardt, 1977, pp. 94–101.

As students at the time, Roger Diener, Pierre de Meuron and Jacques Herzog all benefited from this exposure to sociological discussions. In the first instance, instead of attending Hoesli's *Grundkurs*, Herzog and de Meuron spent their first year at EPFL in Lausanne, the French-language subsidiary of the federal ETH. Later, they joined Burckhardt's "canapé", where the study of early Modernism was conducted as an intellectual discourse.[31] In his first year, Diener studied with sociologist Hermann Zinn in a pilot unit, which placed emphasis on "interviews in the street, and not design".[32] Zinn's involvement with the Metron group from Brugg, which specialised in mass housing, provided another basis for the architectural expression of societal issues.

Symptomatic of the growing need for intellectual examination within architecture was the creation within ETH Zurich, in 1967, of the Institute for the History and Theory of Architecture (Institut für Geschichte und Theorie der Architektur, widely known as gta). The formation of gta, under the direction of architectural historian Adolf Max Vogt, re-acknowledged the relevance of historical study for contemporary design. The new department had an interdisciplinary ethos, placing theory in the service of studio teaching.[33] Vogt's inaugural speech deferred to the polytechnic spirit of ETH, stressing the need for theoretical research to fulfil itself through application.[34] However, how this was to be achieved was less clear. During the same inaugural event, Paul Hofer presented a methodology for the archaeological dating of medieval surfaces. This suggests that theory was understood at the time mainly as a corollary of historical studies. Architectural research leaned towards scientific positivism rather than the humanities.

Meanwhile, in practice, the inertia of 1960s architecture called for radical change – in design as much as in architectural criticism. Contributing the Swiss monograph to the international series *New Directions in Architecture,* Stanislaus von Moos began thus: "New directions in Swiss architecture? There are none".[35] For von Moos, contemporary production was divided into two equally dispiriting categories. The first was that of public commissions, driven by a permanent need for originality at all cost, and meaninglessly re-iterating tired modernist principles. The other was the trivial architecture of developers, inevitably resulting in comfortable bourgeois pastiche.[36]

Von Moos effectively fought with words; criticism was for him a means to bring about actual change. In 1971 he founded *archithese*, a bimonthly journal which he edited until 1976, and which he used as an opportunity to develop theoretical discourse beyond the early positivism of gta.[37] After one year the journal settled into a consistent thematic format, focusing on contemporary issues. *Archithese* invited writers from practice and various theoretical disciplines, acquiring an immediate relevance and becoming an important vehicle for the articulation of theory. Significantly, the first issues were conceived in Italy, where von Moos was exposed to the discourse of neo-rationalism.

---

31 Rüegg, 1998, p. 89.

32 Diener, 2005.

33 Vogt, 1968, pp. 13–16.

34 Vogt, 1968, p. 18.

35 Bachmann and von Moos, 1969, p. 11.

36 von Moos, 1971, p. 15.

37 Commissioned by the Union of Swiss Freelance Architects (FSAI), *archithese* came from von Moos' collaboration with FSAI president Hans Reinhard and journalist Jean-Claude Widmer. For an *archithese* historiography see Stauffer, 1998, p. 93.

The example of journals like *Casabella* and *Controspazio* opened *archithese* to the Italian debates on the historical city.

Manfredo Tafuri's reassessment of theory in *Theories and History of Architecture* (1968) affected *archithese*'s style of criticism. For Tafuri, theory meant first and foremost criticism, with the task of providing a "historical assessment of present contradictions".[38] This stance was equally detached from the tame study of pre-modern periods as it was from the capitalist system that current architecture reflected. Tafuri called for a re-examination of the foundations of Modernism, in the light of its more recent fragmentation. He advanced structuralism and semiology as models for theoretical study, fulfilling the need for an objective scientific basis for understanding the present crisis.[39]

Rooted in public debates over the future of Italian architectural heritage, Tafuri's concept of theory had a political, nominally Marxist perspective. At the same time, his theories about ancient and modern architectures constituted debates within historiography, built upon the close study of artefacts, drawings, writings and secondary literature. He was less prone to rants over how things ought to be, or even to conclusive formulations, than to identifying and characterising critical themes and their transformations in history.

This change of tone, reflected in *archithese*, soon communicated to those working at gta, including Martin Steinmann and Bruno Reichlin. Swiss theoretical discourse remains grounded in Tafuri's version of committed criticism, and shares its reliance on systematic empirical thought. This goes some way towards explaining the hold of typological thinking on the Swiss architectural imagination.

ETH in the 1970s: between typology and Realism

> Aldo [Rossi]'s profound knowledge, coupled with an artistic perspective on things, was tied into his charismatic personality. The students, spoiled by the habit of rebellion, were so surprised by Rossi's ways that they didn't notice how authoritarian his much-loved teaching was.[40] **Dolf Schnebli**

After 1968, the school's left-wing orientation resulted in the desire to expand its curriculum further towards issues of social relevance, including history and the city. At the same time, the department staff and students were advised to leave politics alone and concentrate on design once again.[41] The framework that resolved these contradictory requirements was the dialectical proposition of autonomous architecture.

---

38 Tafuri, 1980, p. 2.

39 Ibid., pp. 5–6.

40 "Viele Mythen, ein Maestro I", 1997, p. 39. Translation from the German original.

41 Paquot, 1998.

The import of autonomy in the ETH discourse has been attributed to one person in particular, the Italian architect and theorist Aldo Rossi (1931–1997). Rossi's influence has been disproportionate to the briefness of his tenure at ETH. He mesmerised the Swiss with his "humanity and extraordinary cultural knowledge, enriched by a sharp witted, active intelligence".[42] Students and teachers still testify to his personal charisma, which compensated for the somewhat cryptic content of the teaching.[43] Rossi's adoption by the school is related to his identification with the conceptual framework of autonomy. In truth, this agenda was implemented not by Rossi alone but by a group of like-minded architects from Ticino, where Italian Rationalism had already penetrated. Bruno Reichlin, Fabio Reinhart, Dolf Schnebli, Luigi Snozzi, Mario Campi, and Eraldo Consolascio were among those who facilitated Rossi's entry to ETH.[44] Crucially, they stayed there long after his departure, ensuring the propagation of autonomous ideals.

Rossi's position changed over his few years at ETH and three separate phases can be discerned in his influence. The first corresponds to Rossi's own design studio with Bruno Reichlin and Fabio Reinhart as assistants (1972–74), largely based on the theory of *Architecture and the City* (1966). The second coincides with the collaborative studio with Bernhard Hoesli and Paul Hofer (1978–79), when Rossi formulated the subjective poetics of *A Scientific Autobiography* (1981). Finally the third stage, after Rossi's departure, relates to the *Analoge Architektur* studio run by Fabio Reinhart as professor with Miroslav Šik as main assistant (1983–1991). Each of these stages has a definite character, which is reflected in the self-understanding of those studying at the time.[45]

Rossi's on-off teaching at ETH during the 1970s gradually built up into a veritable pedagogical machine, operating in several studios and further propagated through exhibitions, seminars, and thematic articles in the professional press. The subjective element he always acknowledged meant that the conceptual basis of his methods remained open to interpretation. This accounts in part for the heterogeneity of Swiss positions influenced by it. The continuity of this heritage emerges not only from Rossi's own intellectual development, but also from its assimilation and transformation in the Swiss discourse.[46]

(a) 1972—1974: Typological studio

Rossi's first teaching period at ETH was determined by his early theoretical position. His answer to the dissolution of architecture into sociological and systematic methodologies had been to seek, once again, the meaning of architecture through reference to its own values. The question of architectural autonomy was first addressed in the Rationalist discourse developed by Ernesto Nathan Rogers and the *Casabella* editorial team during the 1950s and 60s. This discourse rejected the *tabula rasa* principles of functionalist planning and proposed to bring architecture back to the historical and social context of the city. The Rationalist

---

42 Fabio Reinhart quoted in "Viele Mythen, ein Maestro II", 1998, p. 40. Translation from the German original.

43 See "Viele Mythen, ein Maestro I, II", 1997 and 1998; Moravánszky and Hopfengärtner, 2011.

44 Rossi was first invited by Dolf Schnebli to participate in an ETH seminar in February 1972. At the time, Reichlin and Reinhart wrote to the "all-powerful" Hoesli to announce Rossi's visit and propose him as candidate for a visiting professorship at ETH. They described Rossi as a "typical Italian academic in the best sense of the word, carrying out didactic, design and painterly activities sustained by historical and critical research". Moravánszky and Hopfengärtner, 2011, pp. 23–28. Translation from the Italian original.

45 Although the precise extent of Rossi's legacy is a matter of controversy, he undoubtedly contributed to the formation of a generational professional self-understanding. Several architects, while close in age, define their different positions in relation to having studied with, in parallel to, or after Rossi. A first such generation includes Jacques Herzog, Pierre de Meuron and Roger Diener, who graduated from ETH in 1975. Herzog and de Meuron were Rossi's students, Diener studied with Luigi Snozzi. The second generation, including Marcel Meili and Miroslav Šik, studied with the Rossi Hofer Hoesli urban studio of 1978–79. Rossian ideas continued to be explored in Mario Campi's studio with Eraldo Consolascio as assistant (1975–76). The early 1980s are seen as an intermediary period, with graduates (Annette Gigon, Mike Guyer among others) finding role models in practice rather than studio. In the mid- to late 1980s, Valerio Olgiati, Andrea Deplazes, Christian Kerez, Quintus Miller and Paola Maranta studied with Reinhart and Šik in the *Analoge Architektur* studio.

46 For a detailed examination of Rossi's Swiss legacy see Moravánszky and Hopfengärtner, 2011.

message was perceived as timely and consequential, at a time of unprecedented destruction and alteration of European cities.

It wasn't until 1973, when Massimo Scolari coined the term *Tendenza* on the occasion of the fifteenth Milan Triennale, that discrete Rationalist strands came together under the common rubric of an architectural programme.[47] Scolari presented architectural autonomy as a necessity: not as withdrawing from economical and social considerations, but as reclaiming architecture for itself, re-stating its specific means and sphere of action:

> For the *Tendenza*, architecture is a cognitive process that in and of itself, in the acknowledgment of its own autonomy, is today necessitating a re-founding of the discipline; that refuses interdisciplinary solutions to its own crisis; that does not pursue and immerse itself in political, economic, social, and technological events […] but rather desires to understand them so as to be able to intervene in them with lucidity.[48]

L' architettura della città, the book Rossi published in 1966, has been recognised as the clearest and most potent manifestation of this discourse.[49] Rossi put architecture in relation to the historical city, defined as a network of urban artefacts, connected by latent collective memory. He saw "individual" art and "collective" forms as equivalent manifestations of the deeper strata of commonality:

> All great manifestations of social life have in common with the work of art the fact that they are born in unconscious life. This life is collective in the former, individual in the latter; but this is only a secondary difference because […] the public provides the common denominator.[50]

Rossi believed that what is typical in culture could be identified through systematic analysis and classification. He saw in typology a method for organising the imprecise moments of transformation and difference that characterise the city at any given time. For him, the enduring street topography pointed to the reciprocity of stability and change that a city represents. He sought to uncover the constant function between the urban realm and the elements constituting it, "always considering buildings as moments and parts of the whole that is the city".[51]

Rossi defined type as "permanent and complex, a logical principle that is prior to form and that constitutes it".[52] This formulation suggests that "type" enshrined a manifestation of the collective memory condensed into form, a dimension of continuity and mediation. This understanding was indebted to Quatremère de Quincy's distinction between abstract type and concrete model, and its twentieth-century interpretation by the historian

---

47 See Hays, 1998, pp. 124–125.

48 Scolari, 1998, pp. 131–132.

49 Ibid., p. 133.

50 Rossi, 1982, p. 33.

51 Ibid., p. 35.

52 Ibid., p. 40.

Giulio Carlo Argan.[53] For Argan type was an idea, the "common root" of formal variations pertaining to a given principle. Type was not a contingent category; its meaning was stable in history, pertaining to "more profound problems which […] are thought fundamental and constant".[54] Argan's distinction between the typological and original aspects of design recalls the relation between theory and its application: a given repository with constant content that is creatively adapted to the actual conditions of design. Nevertheless, the inventive aspect of design, while "continuous and interlaced" with typological reference, constituted a critique of the precedents integrated in the type.[55]

Rossi's interpretation of type preserved the same ambiguities regarding history. Whilst it is true to say that the architectural types Rossi studied embodied years, even centuries, of refinement in practice, history itself cannot be decanted into building form. History is made up of phenomena that change at different rates. A reliance on Milizia suggests that Rossi understood types as almost-abstract configurations of specific forms, a taxonomy of buildings legitimised independently of their urban situation. His critique replaced functionalism, concerned with the schematisation of living under the defined limits of *Existenzminimum*, with typology as another instrumental system, equally removed from praxis.

In ETH, Rossi and his assistants sought to apply the discourse of autonomous architecture to studio teaching. This translated through the insistence on design's primacy over theoretical and interdisciplinary courses:

> The specific goal of any architecture school is the set up of a design strategy: its priority over all other investigations is indisputable. Design theory represents all architectures' most important and basic moment; [it] should be seen as the main axis of every architecture school.[56]

Rossi not only reinstated the supremacy of the design studio, but legitimised project-making through adherence to a set method:

> To find a basis for architecture as a science, we need the highest level of precision. We have to identify the principles, from where to start. […] We (the architects) must know how and why we design, what models to refer to, what our aims are.[57]

Rossi's design theory structured the project as the logical development of three stages: analysis, architectural idea, and design.[58] Until then, contextual studies had mostly been conducted either statistically, as part of the socio-economic approach, or morphologically, in terms of elevational physiognomies, positive and negative space etc.[59] According to Hoesli, the project entered a relationship of give-and-take with the

---

53 Quatremère de Quincy, 1999, pp.254–256.

54 Argan, 1996, p.244.

55 Ibid., pp. 245–246.

56 Rossi, 1974, p. 28. Translation from the German original.

57 Ibid., p 3. Translation from the German original.

58 Rossi, 1974, pp .1–2. Translation from the German original.

59 Max Bosshard interviewed in Maspoli and Spreyermann, 1993, p. 19.

site, accepting its morphological features after the manner of phenomenal transparency articulated by Rowe and Slutzky.[60] For Rossi, understanding a given place covered not only its morphology, but also its history. The process of historical change could provide the key to design strategies. The analysis was therefore "a critical record of the essential aspects of the existing architecture".[61] The studio emphasised the reading of urban plans, juxtaposing the contemporary city with its historical records.

The students conducted in Zurich comprehensive surveys of predominant residential types. The reading was primarily typological and morphological, with personal (subjective) experiences and impressions given less importance. The drawings focused on the repetition of "basic, permanent elements" represented in the controlled, detached manner of urban plans.[62] These studies sought to establish a rational basis for form. Once the mechanics of change were revealed, the students could import their knowledge into the design.

The second and third stages – the development of idea and design – were less deterministic. Having secured a city whose historical body resisted arbitrary form-making or economic relativism, its analysis became the basis for interpretation. The project's suitability and value could be deduced from the dialogue between original creativity and the interpretation of existing conditions.

> In reality, architecture gets its form through debate with its entire history. It grows based on its own motivations, and only through this process does it merge with the existing built world as it did in with the natural one. It is correct only if it established a dialectic relation with its originality.[63]

The "debate with history" failed however to acknowledge the differences in the rate and nature of change since the nineteenth century. Ultimately the production of form was grounded neither in function, nor in the wider conditions of capitalist industrialisation. Rather, it was based on type and its modifications under the pressure of historically determined conditions. The study of history was seen as a precondition of Realism, guaranteeing the connection between individual creativity and the surrounding culture.[64] Bruno Reichlin testifies that:

> By *architettura razionale* he [Rossi] meant the attempt to establish a system of legitimisation within the traditions of architecture, some kind of transparency between theory and praxis.[65]

[60] Hoesli, 1997.

[61] Rossi, 1974, p. 2. Translation from the German original.

[62] Maspoli and Spreyermann, 1993.

[63] Rossi, 1974, p. 24. Translation from the German original.

[64] Ibid., p. 18.

[65] Bruno Reichlin interviewed in Maspoli and Spreyermann, 1993, p. 15. Translation from the German original.

At the same time, Rossi recognised that "scientific" legitimisation was not the sole agent in the decision-making process. He increasingly considered issues of subjectivity, using his own projects in lectures to illustrate the sources and consequences of more personal choices in design.[66] This acknowledgement of autobiographical elements in architecture was the linchpin of his theory, circumscribing its rationality and later developing into the dreamlike thinking of *architettura analoga*.

Rossi's early insistence on the formal aspects of types relegated personal experience to a secondary position, emphasising an abstract version of the city. This is to be opposed to a situational understanding, in which the city becomes legible at a pre-reflective level as an expression of institutional order.[67] In spite of allegations to the contrary, the autonomous statement of architecture found it hard to escape isolation, leading to its remoteness from practical life.

(b) Swiss interpretations

> In the project for the Palazzo della Ragione in Trieste, I realised that I had simply recounted through architecture certain mornings when I read the newspaper in the great *Lichthof* of the University of Zurich. I had assimilated the light of the pyramidal, glassed covering of the Kunsthaus […]. Seeing this element repeated in many student projects which I had not personally supervised – a form derived from my work and not from the lives of these students or their education in the city – I noted how it only returned to being its own place, that is, to that place they passed every day.[68] **Aldo Rossi**

Rossi's teaching approach, described by contemporaries as "authoritarian" or "orthodox", was adopted as a formula across the ETH.[69] In a parallel studio, Luigi Snozzi maintained the orientation towards form as a reflection of pragmatic conditions, its significance relayed through recourse to history and collective memory.[70] Mario Campi's studio between 1975–76, with Eraldo Consolascio as assistant, closely followed Rossi's typological method.

A natural consequence of the general fascination with Rossi was that, alongside design method, his formal approach was likewise replicated. The geometric purism and repetitive, stark elements of Rossi's early period were adopted as a style. Student projects read like versions of Rossi's Gallaratese apartment block, Milan (1969–70), Palazzo della Ragione, Trieste (1974), or early designs for the Modena cemetery (1971). While Rossi viewed the students' tributes benignly as part of a mimetic education process, their episodic appearance in the Swiss architecture of the late 70s and early 80s was less welcome. As Meili would later note, Italian urban typologies were barely legible in the local context.[71]

---

66   Ibid., p. 13.

67   The application of situational understanding was attempted at the AA in London in the late 1970s in Dalibor Vesely's studio. See Vesely, 1982.

68   Rossi, 1979, p. 17.

69   Dolf Schnebli in "Viele Mythen, ein Maestro I", 1997, p. 39. Fabio Reinhart in "Viele Mythen, ein Maestro II", 1998, p. 41.

70   Steinmann, "Neuere Architektur", 2003, p. 94.

71   Meili, 1996, p. 24.

The tension that developed between the claims of regional cultural conditions and the expectations of a Rationalist vocabulary was first addressed in the early 1970s in the Ticino. Closer to the theoretical currents from Italy, Ticinese architecture maintained a distinctive cultural relevance to its own heritage. This creative interpretation of Italian neo-rationalism was presented at ETH in 1975 in the exhibition *Tendenzen – Neuere Architektur im Tessin*, curated by Martin Steinmann and Thomas Boga. The plural title was deliberate – Ticinese "tendencies" were not identifiable with the *Tendenza*. They reflected specific cultural circumstances, proposing a variety of interpretations of the local vernacular and modernist traditions.[72]

Steinmann's introductory essay to the catalogue, later re-published under the title "Reality as History", identified in the Ticinese work the strategy of reinterpreting the modernist tradition.[73] Starting from the dialectical proposition of architectural autonomy, Steinmann reiterated the contradiction inherent in its nature: that form is developed in relation to history and society, and yet the determining principles must be legible within the works themselves. For the Ticinese, he argued, the relation to tradition was a deliberate referential strategy:

> Tradition is more than a relationship we may or may not have to history. It is an epistemological category; it dictates that a new meaning can only be derived from a familiar one, a new norm only from the old one that it replaces.[74]

This understanding of tradition had allowed Ticinese architects to refer, in their work, both to the historical models of *Neues Bauen* and the local vernacular. The buildings were legible as translations of inherently familiar architectural motifs and forms. Ticino architecture offered the example of a widely adaptable *modus operandi*.

The idea of variations on the historical models of vernacular or indigenous Modernism had a strong impact on the developing German-Swiss discourse. Besides clarity of method, this self-referential strategy had another advantage: it came readily associated with a sense of political involvement. It brought architecture close to social concerns, constituting itself as a moral proposition. "The notion of tradition as a progressive category […] has to be saved each moment anew from becoming a tool of the ruling powers".[75] Architectural autonomy could, or had the obligation to, profess its independence from consumerist goals, and from endorsing political authority.

Beyond a certain expressive austerity, there is little continuity of appearance between 1970s Ticino architecture and what occurred in Northern Switzerland in the 1980s and 1990s. However, the idea of architecture as the interpretation of existing familiar forms and the understanding of this strategy as an act of political resistance were assimilated into the German-Swiss

[72] Steinmann, 2004.

[73] Steinmann, 1998, pp. 248–253.

[74] Ibid., p. 249.

[75] Ibid., p. 250.

Aldo Rossi, *La Casa dello studente di Chieti*, 1976

production. This can be explained at some level through cultural exchanges between Ticino and ETH, one-off events like the *Tendenzen* exhibition and day-to-day studio teaching.

While it is tempting to identify the Ticinese production with a kind of subconscious armature for subsequent Swiss architecture, it is important to recognise that autonomy was only one element of this growing structure. It was itself built on a deeper layer of modernist investigations, and was soon joined by another motif of the avant-garde re-surfacing in the contemporary discourse: the issue of Realism.

(c) 1975–80: From *Città analoga* to Las Vegas

Around 1975, in parallel to the continued interest in typology, a new focus of concern emerged: the realist research of Robert Venturi and Denise Scott Brown, disseminated through thematic *archithese* issues. To be sure, this new strand was supported by the socially conscious Realism pervading Italian culture, which resonated at the time among the students.[76] The new estates and industries in the films of Fellini and Antonioni, featuring deserted environments away from the historical city, corresponded to Venturi and Scott Brown's landscapes of the American periphery. For the Swiss students, the so-called "popular culture" encompassed an implicit and relevant commentary on bourgeois cultural values. As the question of complex realities pervaded the Rationalist discourse, Realism came into its own not as a theoretical question but, as *archithese* claimed, "in the concrete context of contemporary professional practice".[77]

At the same time, Rossi's investigations of collective memory led to a paradoxical concern with the inner triggers of artistic creativity. By the mid-1970s, the search for a more subjective approach was gaining ground over the rigid methods of typological investigation. Characteristically, Massimo Scolari renounced "the idea of treating *history*, *type*, and *monument* with the methods of historical and formal analysis" in favor of "a theory of architecture in which the theoretical principles guide the formal choices through a *genealogy of reference*".[78] For Rossi, such a genealogy was made available through analogical thought.

Rossi's "analogical architecture" expanded the Rationalist discourse to include a poetic dimension, somewhere "between inventory and memory".[79] The new argument was based on Carl Gustav Jung's distinction between logos and "analogical thought" as a deeper level of consciousness: "archaic, unexpressed, and practically inexpressible in words".[80] Fittingly, this notion eluded clear definition, operating through associations and references.

Rossi's projects in the late 1970s used the same geometric elements as his earlier buildings; what had shifted was the perception that their meaning is not fixed *a priori*, but each time reiterated according to actual conditions. This allowed him to reuse the stark repetitive elements of the Gallaratese apartment

---

76 See for example Šik's testimony in "Viele Mythen, ein Maestro I", 1997, p.44. Many other students, including Jacques Herzog, refer for example to Rossi's admiration for Fellini's films, as if they constituted part of his curriculum.

77 Von Moos, Editorial, "*Realismus in der Architektur*", *archithese* no. 19 (1976), p. 2. As a barometer of Swiss architectural debate since 1971, *archithese* devoted two issues to Realism in architecture (no.13/1975 and 19/1976) both featuring Venturi and Scott Brown contributions.

78 Scolari, 1998, p. 142.

79 See Rossi, 1996, pp. 348–352.

80 Ibid., p. 349.

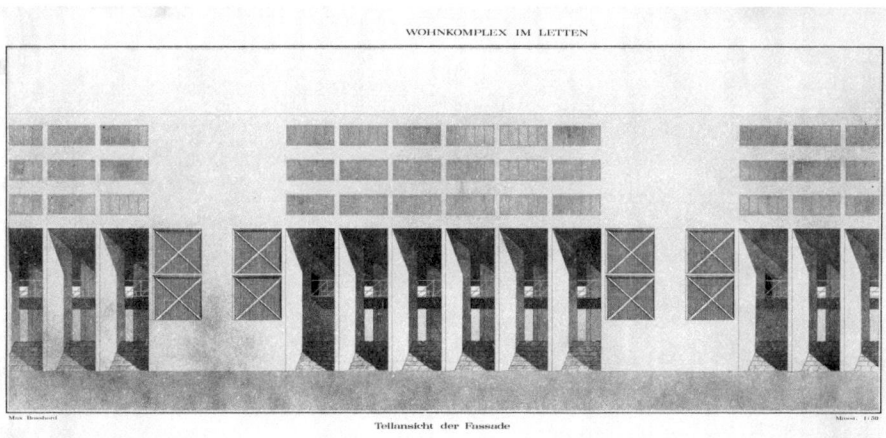

(Top) Aldo Rossi. Gallaratese housing, Milan, 1969–73. Façade

(Bottom) Residential project in Letten, Zurich. Max Bosshard, student work, 1973. Façade detail

building in the Modena cemetery to different ends – suggesting the transition from the functional attributes of types towards their use as referential images. A condition for this possibility, Rossi contended, was the focus on familiar or ordinary objects. These would place the architectonic object in a common referential sphere, linking the autobiographical moment of personal memories to a collective dimension. This subjectivity characterised Rossi's second period of ETH teaching in 1977–78, in the course of a collaborative studio with Hofer and Hoesli.[81]

At this stage, Rossi already enjoyed a quasi-mythical status, receding behind a growing mass of designs, drawings and writings. His charismatic but nebulous discourse signalled the need for followers to clarify their own position. Miroslav Šik and Marcel Meili, students of the Rossi Hoesli Hofer studio, organised in the winter of 1977–78 a seminar on the theme *Realismus*. This became a framework for discussions about Realism in the arts and literature, which were then adapted to architecture as a manner of legitimising design procedures. This seminar was conceptually structured around an article published in *archithese* in 1976 entitled "Zum Problem der innerarchitektonischen Wirklichkeit" ("On architecture's inherent reality"). Its authors, Steinmann and Reichlin, advocated an architecture that could reflect social reality while enjoying its own, sensuous and intellectual nature:

> The displacement of its own concrete reality has resulted in architecture's reduction to being a "useful item". This relates to the general tendency to separate the contemplative life from the practical, and to limit it to a compensatory, consolatory function. The practical life only admits desire, as the motor of capitalist processes, but excludes the self-sufficient pleasure [...]. The pleasure in architecture is one of these forsaken desires. In the name of Realism, we must demand the right to pleasure in architecture.[82]

By demanding *"le droit au plaisir"*, Reichlin and Steinmann legitimised a departure from the pure Rationalisms of the *Neues Bauen* and of Rossi's early scientific proclamations, in order to recognise the sensuous nature of the discipline. K. Michael Hays later saw in this proposition a practical understanding of architecture as an "experimental, transformative activity that ties an ideal of practice to concrete production" – or, rather, to concrete experience.[83]

Isolated from a hermeneutical understanding of situation, this kind of experience has echoes of subjectivity, like being aesthetically contemplative. Rossi's development since the mid-1970s, articulated in *A Scientific Autobiography* in 1981, took analogy into the subjective sphere, implying an experience of the object through perceptions and associations that were haptic rather than

[81] Hoesli intended to compare his own urban research (influenced by Rowe's *Collage City*) and didactic method with Rossi's, but the latter's interests had already shifted. Contrary to the expectations of ETH professors and students, many of whom had previously studied with Campi and Consolascio, Rossi now focused less on method and type than on cryptic, if evocative, notions like image and atmosphere. See Maspoli and Spreyermann, 1993, pp. 28–32.

[82] Reichlin and Steinmann, 1976, p. 10. Translation from the German original.

[83] Hays, 1998, p. 246.

(Left) *archithese* no. 13, *Realismus in der Architektur*, 1975. The cover shows a photograph of Venturi and Rauch's Guild House, Philadelphia, 1960–63.

(Right) *archithese* no. 19, *Realismus*, 1976. Cover

purely visual. However, this shift to subjective experience and associations transferred authority from the nominally objective typological history to that of the designer-*auteur,* an exchange that lay latent in the formalism of typology itself. This sensual understanding of architecture appears as a leitmotif in subsequent Swiss production, in particular in the work of Herzog & de Meuron and Peter Zumthor.

(d) 1983—1991 *Analoge Architektur*

The third Rossian stage in ETH coincides with the *Analoge Architektur* studio that Fabio Reinhart ran between 1983–91, with assistants Luca Ortelli, Santiago Calatrava, and Miroslav Šik, who in the end became the Analogues' driving force. As the studio's German name suggests, Reinhart and Šik effected a translation of Rossi's notion of analogous architecture. Following the impact of *Learning from Las Vegas* (1976), the studio applied it to a reading of reality imported from Venturi and Scott Brown:

> Contrary to Rossi's teaching, we located our projects in different places (the Zurich periphery) using different architectural references (the trivial forms of everyday life) and different design processes.[84]

Ultimately, the Analogue studio has come to represent Šik's position. By the time his approach was fully defined around 1987, a new generation of students (including Valerio Olgiati, Andrea Deplazes, Quintus Miller and Paola Maranta) was affected by this teaching as much as by the emerging projects and writing of the previous ETH generation. Whether embraced or contested, *Analoge Architektur* provided a new attitude towards context, which remains deeply imprinted on subsequent debates and production.

Described by Ákos Moravánszky as "an Oedipal reaction to Rossi's *città analoga*", the Analogue method rejected Rossi's typological taxonomies while adapting the poetic sensibility at work in his analogies.[85] Šik set up the studio, which soon became a school within the school, as a self-sufficient apprenticeship system, with the younger students helping their elders while learning the studio's characteristic representational techniques. Architectural ideas were conveyed through large perspectival drawings, conceived primarily in terms of images and atmospheres. Rather than idealised architectural representations like plans and sections, rendered as geometric configurations on the white space of the paper, the students were encouraged to render the project in its context. The heavy chalk lines and surfaces, depicting deep shadows and deserted interiors, were, however, more reminiscent of dream-like settings than of any concrete situation.

[84] Fabio Reinhart in "Viele Mythen, ein Maestro II", 1998, p. 41. Translation from the German original.

[85] Moravánszky, 2005, p. 27.

Three points characterised Šik's definition of *Analoge Architektur*:

i. a particular referential sphere (the so-called "classics") comprising, in opposition to Bauhaus Modernism, the alternative traditions of British and American Arts and Crafts, Viennese Secession, the "Scandinavian reformism" of Gunnar Asplund or Kay Fisker;

ii. a redefinition of "regionalism" through the focus on ordinary locations (industrial periphery, working-class residential districts) and small-scale architectures (conversions, sheds), revealing the beauty inherent in everyday environments, as opposed to monuments and landmarks;

iii. a continuity with the city, achieved through a mimetic language, resulted from the combination of distorted versions of forgotten "classics" and deference to local types and atmospheres.[86]

In opposition to Postmodernist collage techniques, this architecture operated less through the evocative power of fragments than through the melancholy, continuous erosion of "subtle allusions […] slightly obscure yet strongly emotional".[87] The Analogues proposed an elaborate, assiduous knitting of architecture in its setting, a relationship to context understood as a kind of hyperrealism.

Šik's notion of *altneu* ("oldnew") is representative of this merger. Its relation to tradition was equally opposed to pastiche conservation and to modernist innovation:

> My aim is to create a world that is neither old nor new. I want the various types of atmosphere to cancel one another out, blurring the social and temporal framework.[88]

This relationship to context is perhaps the Analogues' most provocative proposition. It brings into relief the tensions between architecture as autonomous object and typical urban order, between individual artistic expression and the universality of unmediated, concrete reality. The proposal questions the limits of architecture as a self-conscious enterprise, and tries to approximate the unconsciousness of "trivial" architecture, understood as a social, functional and economic act without artistic pretensions. However, precisely because of its conceptual nature, this claim is not realistic. The contradiction inherent in the Analogue proposition is noticeable in the tension between the limits of the architectural object and its continuation of a given setting. While part of the city to the point of indistinctness, the proposal also demands self-definition, coherence, and unity:

> Everything that originally lay on the project table, everything that has found its way into a new composition, must in the end have the effect of unity, an indivisible wholeness, as a monad.[89]

[86] See for example Šik, 2000; Šik, 1987; Šik, 2002.

[87] Šik quoted in Lucan, 2001, p. 47.

[88] Ibid., p. 49.

[89] Ibid.

This need for internal order opposes the outer urban order, as the autonomous "monad" negates the very idea of the unobtrusive project blending with its background. The artistic mimesis of typical settings is unattainable; and yet, the orientation towards the city remains a potent proposal.

ETH in the 1980s and 1990s: the content of theory

(a) Between form and culture

> Our incursions into the world of the ordinary and the everyday constitute a search for collective meanings. Following the collapse of national mythologies and territorial arrangements, this research attempts to recover the traces of an identity in the affected mobility of our contemporary culture.[90] **Marcel Meili**

90 Meili, "Ein paar Bauten", 1991, p. 22. Translation from the German original.

While all individual manifestations of German-Swiss architecture should be seen as distinct forms of practice, several elements from Rossi's theories seem to underpin their deep common ground. The typological and Analogue moments share the hope for a collective level, at which architects could make sense of a perplexing reality. The insistence on form as the concrete manifestation of universal meaning, an architecture legitimised through a conceptual framework, the tension between buildings as individual artefacts and their relationship to urban order, the recycling of primary, stark forms for contingent circumstances – all these constitute a cloud of propositions, to which architects return to define their own approach.

Implicitly or explicitly in use, such ideas form the conceptual armature of the recent Swiss production. Before its divergence became apparent in the mid-1990s, several attempts were made to formalise a common programme, based less on regionalist concerns than on the collective cultural conditions to which regionalism responded. The critics who attempted regionalist definitions found their argument straining under the marked cultural and socio-economic differences between zones like the Graubünden and the Basel–Zurich metropolitan areas. The architects, more alert to differences rather than to similarities, proved a sceptical audience. Nevertheless, some texts produced with this shared agenda had an important effect on Swiss self-understanding, galvanising these fragments in constructs of great currency. Marcel Meili's "Ein paar Bauten, viele Pläne" and Martin Steinmann's "La forme forte" (published together in 1991) are particularly significant in this context.

Meili renewed the discourse around history and Realism articulated during the previous decade. Connecting Rossi's pronouncements to the contemporary ones of *Analoge Architektur*, Meili organised the various ideas into a critique of functionalist Modernism. This was directed at the production of an intelligible architecture, resonating with social meaning:

Analoge Architektur. Project for Affoltern
Railway Station, Zurich. Rene Bosshard
student work, 1989

> We seek a kind of "authenticity of usage" [...] we are no longer interested in the optimisation of the modes of usage in buildings but in the process of sedimentation of meanings into forms, such as results through the incessant repetition of everyday use. [...] An architecture that could embody more general significations [...] could be realized through a focus of design on the problem of form, provided that our proposals would achieve a more comprehensive understanding of "use" than their scorned modernist predecessors. [...] We start with the supposition that such identity resides less in traditional building types than in the everyday activities of contemporary modes of life in Switzerland. [...] Our position is not aimed at the reconstruction of places or urban repair, but towards explaining the images and atmospheres behind a general, "typical" character.[91]

[91] Ibid. Translation from the German original.

Meili put the principles of architectural autonomy into the context of the Swiss "everyday". The argument maintained the dialectic of autonomy as if, by holding onto form, architecture was more capable of saying something about the world than by losing itself in an other-than-formal description of that world.[92] The aim was to re-establish the communicative potential of the discipline through forms, grounded neither in artistic subjectivity nor in geometric regularity, but in the residues of collective meaning left by routine activities. This attempt to understand type as the manifestation of universal meaning remained, therefore, based on form.

[92] For more on autonomy dialectic see Hays, 2001, p. 102.

Meili's implicit reliance on autonomous architecture is symptomatic both of the Swiss discourse's promise and of its limitations. The problematic of autonomy, as Alan Colquhoun has argued, is the way it displaces meaning from everyday activities related to dwelling toward matters of formal consistency:

> The "autonomy" of architecture [is] a meaningless phrase, since any principles of architecture are empty until embodied in an action, in the reality of a situation. [...] Architecture itself, considered as a culturally defined concept, is merely a "situation" at a deeper level than immediate contingency. It is therefore neither necessary nor possible to establish it as a transcendental entity outside and beyond contingency.[93]

[93] Alan Colquhoun, 1989, pp. 198–199.

The design's dependence on both architectural idea and site builds a tension between the wholeness of the perfected concept and its debts to a multifaceted and complex reality. In concrete terms, this gives rise to the tension between artefact and the situation it inhabits; its legibility as an isolated work of art in and of itself, and the urban realm in which it is positioned.

Analoge Architektur: Project for Rowing
Club, Wollishofen, Zurich. Luca Antorini
Diploma project, 1989

The promise of the Swiss project, if one may refer to such a unity, could then be found in architecture's participation in the urban order. In insisting on the relevance of form as a concretisation of practical modes of life, Meili's interpretation almost pre-empted Colquhoun's criticism. "Almost", because he still allowed form to substitute for architecture, and placed his energies in legitimising formal production. A consequence of the all-too-eager advocacy of form was, and remains, the reliance on artefacts to substitute for the activities they are supposed to shelter.

Little of Meili's legitimisation of forms as residues of usage is found in Steinmann's notion of "strong forms". With the following words, Steinmann introduced one of the most prominent paradigms of recent Swiss architecture:

> There is a trend in contemporary architecture to design buildings as simple, lucid geometric bodies – bodies whose simplicity spotlights shape, material and colour, without relating to any other building. [...] These schemes are characterised by a quest for forceful forms.[94]

94 Steinmann, "La forme forte", 2003. Translation in Lucan and Steinmann, 2001, pp. 15–16.

In this paragraph, the discussion of the projects' situation gives way to a heightened examination of their physical characteristics. "Strong" buildings are those whose armature of form and material places them in a specific relation to the site.[95] They belong there not by means of contextual quotation but by revealing, through their positioning and effect, the site's organisational structure, by making its order intelligible in confrontation with their own, independent order. This is not the mediatory construct proposed by Šik, but one that states the self-sufficiency of artefacts in relation to urban order.

95 Martin Steinmann in conversation with Jacques Lucan in Lucan and Steinmann, 2001, pp. 15–18.

In focusing on issues of presence, the "strong form" approximates the "objecthood" territory claimed by Minimalism in art during the 1960s.[96] In opposition to illusionistic representation, Minimal (literalist) art forced itself upon the observer, as a thing-in-itself protruding in the viewer's actual territory. Michael Fried ascribed transcendentalist connotations to this "theatrical" confrontation between observer and object. For him, "presentness is grace".[97] Similarly, strong forms lay claim to an architectural order miraculously established through their presence in the city.

96 Fried, 1968, pp. 116–147.

97 Ibid., p. 147.

The notion of "strong form" is as tempting as it obdurately refuses to open towards a more concrete understanding of what it entails. What does it mean, to quote for example Roger Diener, "to bring a place into order with one house"?[98] A possible answer might be offered, again, through recourse to Minimalism. Karsten Harries has argued that minimalist objects do not bring about "presentness", but merely convey it. "Presentness" is in itself an ideal, a representation of an unrealisable sense of sensual plenitude. The objects cannot be separated from meaning, and their so-called self-referentiality refers to a "secularised grace":

98 Quoted in Steinmann, 1995, p. 10.

"the presentness and plenitude that modern art pursues carry the aura of man's deepest concerns and hopes".[99] It represents the attempt to compensate, in the aesthetic field, for the loss of (cosmic) order granted traditionally.

The search for effect ultimately suggests the remoteness of "strong forms" from the praxis they should enable. The problem lies with blurring the boundary between art and architecture, which threatens precisely the architectural autonomy these projects are supposed to convey. There is little left for a discussion of how buildings are inhabited or used, modalities that are almost taken for granted during design. The notion of "strong forms" suggests that Swiss architecture has focused, instead of participation in orders of social and urban reality, on the visual and material factors of its presence.

(b) Theory within history

> If theory's real subject is history, theory must also constantly historicise itself. Theory, as much as architecture, has to be grasped in the place and time out of which it emerges.[100] **K. Michael Hays**

The content of Swiss theory can be seen as a spectrum ranging from the search for typical aspects of the culture to the formal manifestations of this search. The history of ETH suggests this oscillation emerged from a series of factors. Firstly, the "polytechnic culture" instilled a suspicion of theory without applicability, thus implying the primacy of building. Secondly, the 1920s avant-garde demonstrated the need to adhere to an ideology in order to give validity to the project. Its understanding of a "theory" behind the project was qualified by the necessity of political involvement, the possibility of social action. Thirdly, as a continuation of this, theory became a means to control decision-making processes in design, counteracting with intellectual discipline the eclecticism engendered by the market. This third notion of theory was marked by Tafuri's re-assessment of the theoretical task as an "objective and unprejudiced historical diagnosis".[101] The production covered in this book finds itself bracketed in this final understanding of theory, with echoes of the previous interpretations.

If nothing else, the material presented here shows the extent to which theory is a praxis in itself. It is not an abstract, global discourse but one permanently concretised in the theatres of its operation: in ETH studios, project reviews and lectures; in formal debates, exhibitions and gta publications; within professional journals; and finally in the translation of seminal publications by, among others, Tafuri, Rossi or Venturi. These events impact directly on what happens in design, establishing a dialogue between different areas of praxis.

Conveyed mainly through written or spoken text, the theory is seen as the contemplative part of praxis. There is a constant

---

[99] Harries, 1989, p. 31.

[100] Hays, 1998, p. 506.

[101] Tafuri, 1980, p. 3.

exchange between international theory and local discourse. And here Tafuri's location of theoretical investigations within the flow of history reveals the necessity for their constant reinterpretation. The transfer from Italy to Switzerland was made with the effort of translation, specifically in order to grasp the typical aspects of the new context.

The theoretical discourse tends to limit the vocabulary to a few key words, but this vocabulary is then overstretched to convey a variety of particular meanings. The words of theory are asked to do too much. In the Swiss discourse, watchwords like "Realism" or "Typology" became a currency that flattened the depth of issues, making them an object for design. This ambivalent terminology means that the apparent consensus regarding form conceals a variety of understandings, ranging from geometrical configuration to *Gestalt*.

This relativism is counteracted by the attempt to materialise theoretical notions in design. The result is similar to that identified by Jean-Louis Cohen regarding the adoption of Italian Rationalism in France:

> Typology is seen in many French texts from the late Seventies not as a classificatory operation allowing for the isolation of distinct types, but instead as a synonym for the notion of type. A given type identified in an urban analysis becomes une *typologie remarquable*: the analytic exercise lends its name to the empirical object.[102]

In other words, a double process occurs: under the pressure of theoretical justification, typology becomes equivalent to type, and type is concretised into form.

Swiss theory in its late manifestation (which in fact has changed least over the years) is intrinsically connected with the emphasis on form. The creative effort is oriented towards a stance outside praxis, outside the cultural claims, for which form is the appropriate object. Form *is*, and as such it becomes factual, a measure of objectivity. The fact that form conveys different meanings arises from its presumed innocence of all meanings. This explains the appeal of "strong forms", which formulate an absolute version of architecture, an architecture "beyond signs".[103]

While the perception from within the Swiss professional scene is focused on differences between practices rather than similarities, this chapter has attempted to set out the theoretical background against which these differences can be articulated. Can there be such a thing as a "Zurich school", or indeed "Swiss architecture"? While such a common denominator can only be vague, its generality permits an assessment of what is held in common. Swiss architecture's initial orientation towards the collective

102 Cohen, 1998, p. 517.

103 Steinmann, "La forme forte", 2003, p. 189.

dimensions of culture, manifest in architecture as in art, holds attention as the attempt to uncover their communicative potential. If this was a programme for most of the 1980s, in the 1990s a turn towards the increased autonomy of artefacts was already perceptible.

The ETH discourse stands for two distinct notions. Firstly its history, in parallel with the history of Modernism as a whole, shows the reflections of a changing theoretical body upon practice. To reprise a point made at the outset of this chapter: from Gottfried Semper onwards, a succession of illustrative architectural figures within ETH have initiated new directions in Swiss practice. To the names of Karl Moser, Otto Salvisberg or Alfred Roth, we can add Bernhard Hoesli and Aldo Rossi as protagonists of this history.

Secondly, with respect to the architecture produced between 1980 and 2000, ETH theory consists of the use of this history itself in order to create a common reservoir of images and references, the lexicon for a collective language. This language is linked not only to recent educational history, but also to the earlier modern architectures that gave shape to the Swiss environment, under the galvanising effect of a political agenda of modernisation.

Despite its commitment to history, the Swiss architectural discourse remains strongly indebted to scientific paradigms, and strives to be demonstrated empirically in works actually built. The emphasis on concrete constructs converts the deep claims of the situations in which architecture operates into clear judgements regarding its correctness. Theoretical descriptions are primarily concerned with creating an epistemology through which the designer exercises control over city, architecture and the lives they sustain.

Forms of
Practice

Forms of Practice

[1] Herzog and de Meuron, 1992, p. 144.

> To let reality be felt and intellectually confronted [...] we feel this to be a political necessity.[1]
> Herzog & de Meuron

[2] Tschanz, 1998.

In 1998, Martin Tschanz headed an overview of contemporary German-Swiss architecture with the plural "Tendenzen und Konstruktionen".[2] This title, adopted from the 1975 gta exhibition of Ticinese architecture, acknowledged the heterogeneity of Swiss production, its closeness to Italian neo-rationalism, as well as its own reliance on the tangibility of constructions. Tschanz argued that, while the works shared a theoretical and cultural space, they reflected the participants' individual concerns and biographical circumstances. The apparent unity of a Swiss model was not to be exclusively associated with the Zurich school, nor did it represent a deliberate decision to instigate an architectural movement. This position is representative of the Swiss architects' consensus regarding Swiss architecture.

The works' scope, however, extends beyond the authors' intentions. Firstly, regardless of their positions, the participants are reliant on common cultural and professional structures specific to Switzerland. Secondly, even if the projects of a strong minority of practices were developed in isolation, they cease to be completely autonomous from the moment of their completion. Publications, exhibitions, lectures and visits mould them into a consistent wider discourse, which then becomes a referent for subsequent architectural generations, Swiss or foreign. This chain of causality allows Swiss production to be addressed as a collection of forms of practice, illustrated by a series of case studies.

[3] See Steinmann, 1994, pp. 11–12.

[4] Meili, 1996, p. 25.

The formal production is linked both to a theoretical field and to deeper cultural structures. Swiss architecture interprets established, recognisable typologies, either by incorporating direct quotations into the design or by submitting them to various degrees of abstraction.[3] However, Marcel Meili identified a shared preoccupation with the "self-evident and precise architectural interpretation of current modes of life".[4] This suggests that Swiss production is more than a set of formal variations on common typologies.

The revisionist zeal of 1968 and the autonomy precepts learnt in the 1970s at ETH imbued the architects born around 1950 with a professional conscience extending beyond correctness of design. Their theoretical political background was grafted on a modernist building tradition, grounded in local crafts as much as in the *Werkbund* model of adapting craft to contemporary manufacturing processes.[5] Subsequent generations remained acutely perceptive to these issues, contributing a synthetic resolution of the early proposals in later projects.

One can argue that the most distinguished aspect of this production resides in its implicit claims of integrity. In design and writing, both architects and critics express the belief that architecture, beyond its programmatic role and constructional ingenuity, should manifest a deeper dimension:

> The objective is not just to make decent buildings. [...] Designing a scheme nowadays means taking a stance with respect to what we believe architecture to be. It's a commitment.[6]

> It gets boring when we're continually shown how a building is made. [...] We want more than that from architectural objects; we want them to be "objects with a spiritual purpose," to borrow from Max Bill.[7]

The earnest appeal to ambiguous notions to qualify design, ranging from the "spiritual" to art, indicate the deeper ambivalence of the Swiss phenomenon. This is apparent in oscillations between artistic individualities and collective traits, between aesthetic resolution and ethical ambitions. The aim of the following case studies is to illustrate some of the positions described by Tschanz as "Tendenzen"; to identify, beneath the heterogeneity, some recurrent themes; beneath the clarity of form, some inherent ambiguities. In order to better illustrate how the discourse developed, the case studies are treated chronologically.

---

[5] Ibid., p. 24.

[6] Lucan and Steinmann, 2001, p. 9.

[7] Ibid., p. 17.

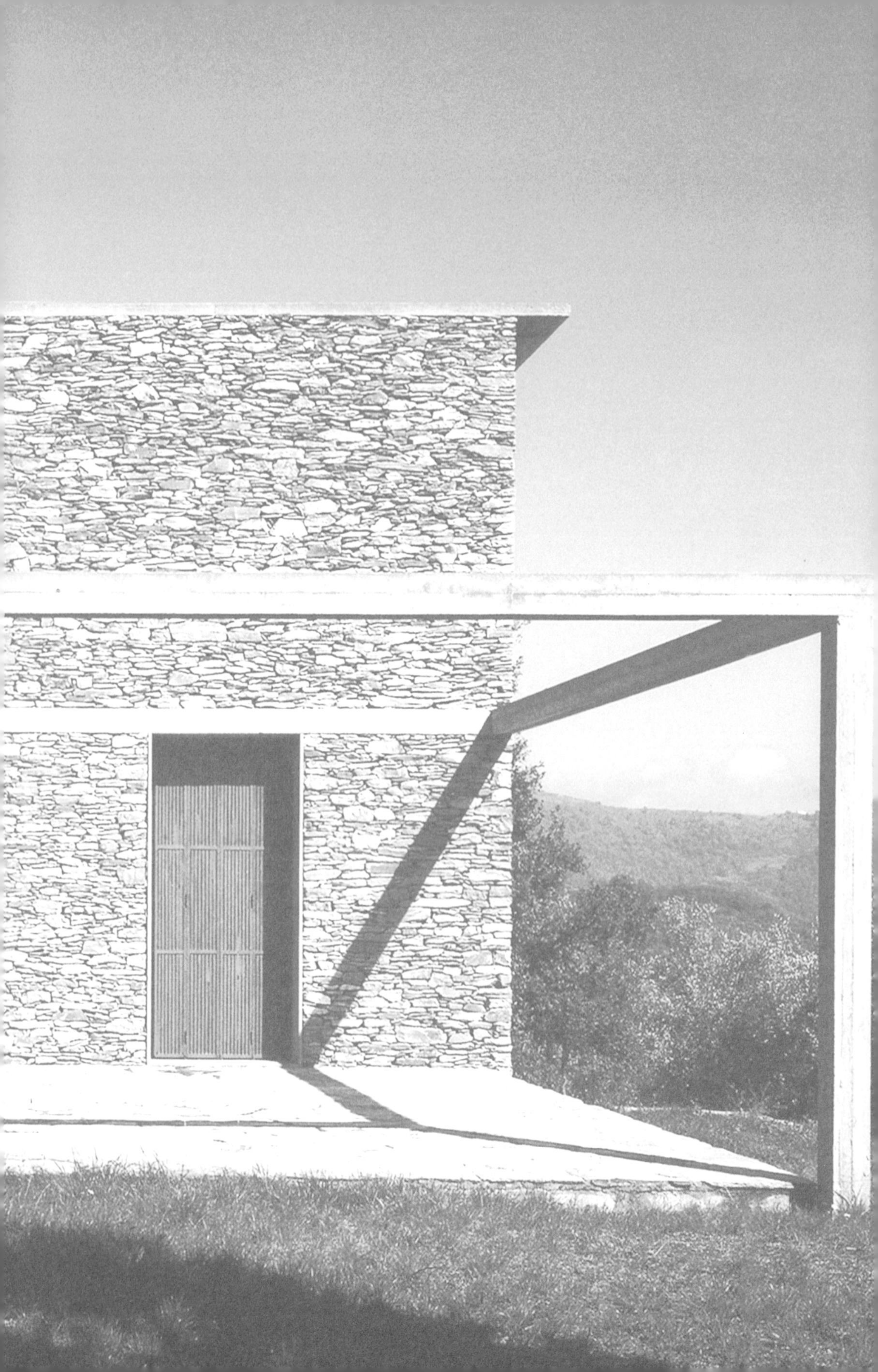

Herzog & de Meuron
Stone House, Tavole, Italy
Project 1982,
Realisation 1985–88

This case study presents some architectural motifs in Herzog & de Meuron's work that have particular relevance for the wider Swiss production. These motifs can be seen both as symptoms of an emergent architectural attitude, and as agents in its evolution.

Jacques Herzog and Pierre de Meuron's professional biography, from students of Rossi's typological studio to founding partners of a successful international practice, is well known. What is important in the present context, however, is Herzog & de Meuron's definition of their practice through differentiation. From the outset, they have disassociated themselves from the shared ETH scene, insisting on the specificity of their personal artistic and intellectual discourse. Their built work encompasses a number of major shifts, partly in order to follow personal interests and partly as a deliberate attempt to escape classification. Their 1980s and early 1990s work can be summarised as combining formal reticence with elaborately textured surfaces. In the later 1990s, as the exploration of "ornament" led to increasingly expressive forms, they rejected the connotations attached to their early output, such as "morals and perfection and […] late Protestant zeal".[1] The need to dispel moral associations and protest against narrow categorisations is forever emancipating their creativity from public and professional expectations. This is itself proof of an enduring belief in architectural integrity as a form of freedom.

Despite their declared autonomy, references to Herzog & de Meuron are embedded in the Swiss professional landscape since the 1980s. Their early reputation was built upon small-scale projects, ambitiously disseminated and conceptually justified with alert intelligence. One of these projects is the Stone House in Tavole, Italy, designed in 1982 and completed in 1998. In the meantime other projects were completed, establishing Herzog & de Meuron's profile in Switzerland and abroad: Studio Frei (1982), the Plywood House (1985), and the Laufen Ricola warehouse (1987). In spite of their modest scale, these buildings asserted themselves through formal clarity and radical use of materials.

[1] Herzog and de Meuron, 2002, p. 8.

With its longer time span, the Stone House demonstrates the existence of a coherent conceptual position beneath the formal diversity of this production. At first glance the reading it invites is object-oriented. The emphasis is on the contrast between the walls' rugged surface and the precisely edged, compact volume. The focus on concrete form as the primary means of expression implies, from the outset, a contradiction between the intellectual construct and the reality of stones. It suggests that architecture's inherent meanings should be legible in the constructed object.

In order to address the building's typical aspects, it is necessary to avoid propagating this implicit belief in its conceptual and material self-sufficiency. We should therefore consider its wider situation, encompassing village, land, and the client's desires.

"The Solitary House"

The Stone House is the Italian holiday home of a German client. This reconstructs a typical scenario of the sophisticated northerner attracted to the primitive South, seeking a twentieth-century update of the Grand Tour. The immersion in rustic aspects of Italian culture balances out the year-round demands of work in a developed Western city. We see here a reprise of the ancient tension between *otium* as leisure and *negotium* as business, developed in the Renaissance villa into the exchange between *vita contemplativa* and *vita attiva* as complementary aspects of human praxis. The presence of a studio at the top of the building attracts attention in this regard; but the client's apparent lack of participation in local culture and the relative isolation of the house seem to suggest otherwise. At design stage, the project was nicknamed "the solitary house".[2] The self-declared loneliness suggests its understanding as formal experiment, rather than a house imbedded in its local situation.

Edged between France and the Piedmont, the Ligurian Alps create a contrast between the Riviera di Ponente, with its established tourist economy, and the inland topography of bleak wooded hilltops. Here, the isolated settlements are too small and infrequent to support an urban network. The Stone House is located near the hamlet of Tavole in Prelà, a dispersed mountain commune with altitudes between 100 and 1000 metres above sea level. Prelà's population, in its hundreds, has been declining since the late nineteenth-century, a condition reflected in the large number of uninhabited properties and general decay.

The hilltop location, in an abandoned olive grove, suggests the client's desire for remoteness both from the agricultural community and the tourist mainstream. Nevertheless, their proximity enables this seclusion. The house depends upon automobile for access, on transactions with the locals for subsistence, and on the economic incentives of the holiday industry for its day to day functioning.

2   The inscription "Einsames Haus" appears on one design sketch, see Mack, 1997, p. 61, fig.E.

(Above left) Herzog & de Meuron.
Ricola Storage Building, Laufen, 1986–87

(Above right) Herzog & de Meuron.
Plywood House, Bottmingen,
Basel, 1984–85

(Right) Herzog & de Meuron.
Photographic Studio Frei, Weil am Rhein,
Germany, 1981–82

While close enough to the seaside and tourist infrastructure, the place is sufficiently remote to allow contact with a more "authentic" way of life. Paradoxically, this attitude is marked by a sense of economic and cultural privilege. The diplomatic distance from the village is a prerequisite for the fulfilment of formal ambitions, equally alien to the local vernacular and its kitsch re-interpretation in holiday bungalows.

If the house's self-sufficiency is thus relative, its design strives to suggest the opposite. The houses in the nearby village relinquish their individuality as they huddle together to form walled streets. In contrast, the Stone House stands like a watchtower in the landscape. The architects use the referential imagery of San Gimignano, suggesting the Italy of the Grand Tour. The urban element becomes part of the panoramic *tableau*, detached from its social, cultural and economic circumstances.

House as geometry

The project's attitude towards its surrounds is ambivalent. The building materially blends in with its locality, while formally declaring the intention to carve out a niche of emancipation. The design determines a "cultural space [...] clearly and intentionally cut off from the surrounding landscape".[3] This contradictory desire between fitting in and preserving autonomy is expressed in the relationship between the concrete frame and the stone infill. At a basic level the dry stone, used in a manner closest to a natural or quasi-natural condition, amounts to contextual deference; the concrete ossature asserts the project's emancipation.

The natural stone pertains to a corporeal or material dimension of existence. The walls are poised between topographical elements and man-made structures, directly referring to the surrounding agricultural stone terraces. The effort implicit in their erection has rendered the topography into a palimpsest of human toil, earth-like, equivalent to a geological process. However the house moulds the rich associations of the broken surface into a pristine geometry. The ground profiles of the terraces are rendered into the prismatic dwelling, delineated by the concrete structural system. In its non-structural cladding role, the stone offers a sophisticated rendition of rusticity.

The concrete frame forms an abstract counterpart to the stone. The geometry displays on the façade the internal division of the house into floors and rooms. The concrete and stone are two incomplete systems, relying on each other for conclusion in what Alan Colquhoun has called an "endless text".[4] Stone represents here a Romantic version of nature, a dramatic stratification of earth. The concrete frame pertains to the machine-made and to technological control, while preserving secondary primitivist connotations, in the sense of basic industrial technique. The stone/concrete pairing recalls the local constructions left unfinished for tax purposes, which display their concrete frames and rubble infill as marks of incompleteness.

[3] Ibid., p. 57.

[4] Colquhoun, "Regionalism", 2009, p. 284.

Herzog & de Meuron. Stone House, Tavole, Italy, 1982–88. The isolated location provides a vantage point for the consumption of landscape.

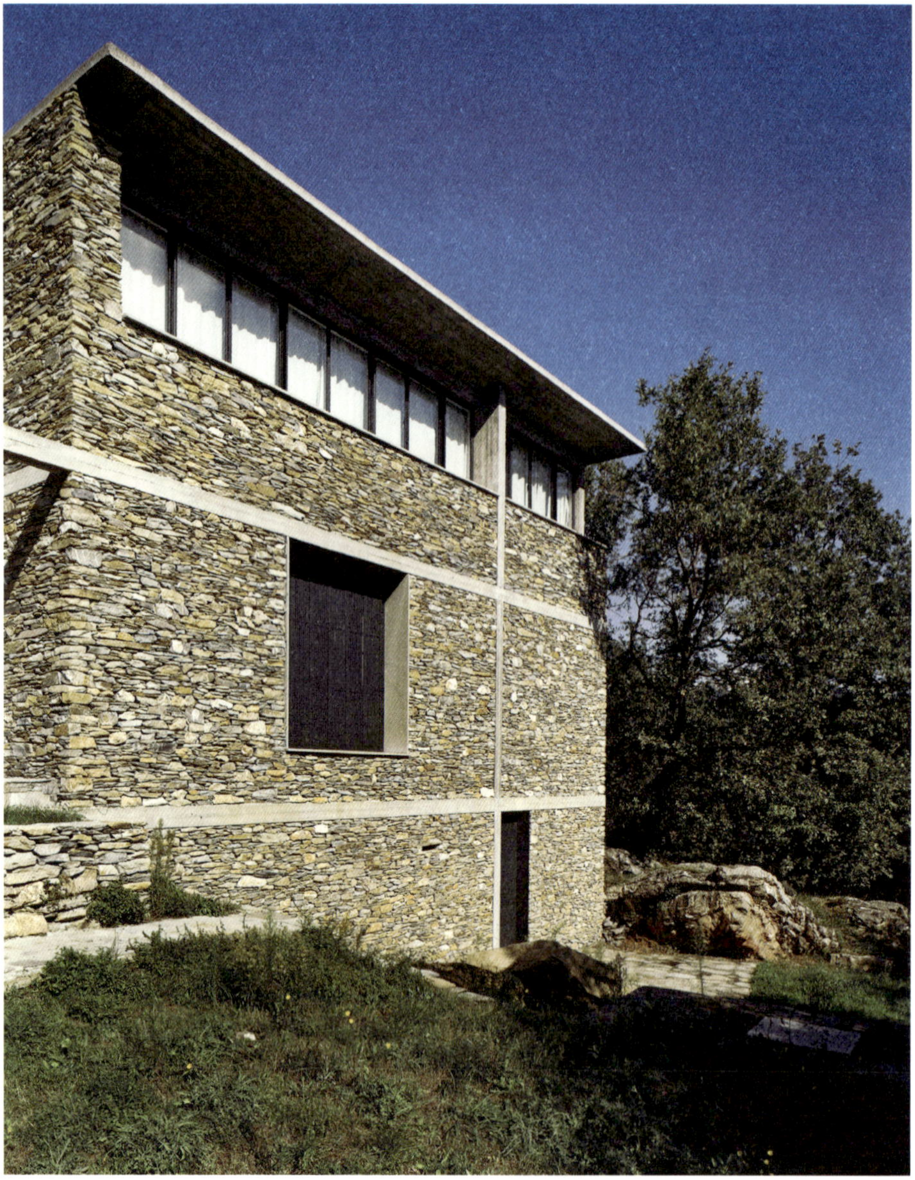

(Opposite) Herzog & de Meuron. Stone House, Tavole, Italy, 1982–88. South elevation. Modernist motifs – flat roof, strip window, prismatic volume

(Above) Herzog & de Meuron. Stone House, Tavole, Italy, 1982–88. Pergola

While straightforward in themselves, the frame construction and stone infill are set up as an altogether more mysterious combination. The artistic intention is to create a magical object held together by "an implosion of the landscape".[5] The geometric delineation of the open terrace reveals the modular structure of the overall mass and indicates its potential for extension. The pergola and terrace form an ostensibly structural system, which contrasts with the rugged rocks and contaminates them with its fragility. The device breaks down the resolute distinction between inside and outside, framing architecture and nature alike and placing them on a level of equivalence.

Simplicity / sophistication

The project's primitive appearance is achieved through the application of advanced, if not highly technological, construction means. The raised parapets conceal an inverted butterfly roof in cast concrete, and what at first seems a concrete skeleton flush with the façade is actually a slipped frame misaligned with the actual floor levels. This adjusted order doubles up as datum for the door and window lintels. Even the most contextual feature, the dry stone masonry, is elevated through geometric perfection.

The building's apparent formal and constructional simplicity aims at direct impact on the observer. The material palette intends to convey, above all, a "physical presence", a condensation of the landscape in a primal armature of form and material.[6] The object-like quality declares a return to basics. Even though later Herzog & de Meuron stated they had never tried "to simplify the world or to reduce it to so-called essentials",[7] in its isolation this project seems to suggest the retreat into a nominally "simple life".

The restorative ambitions of the Stone House recall Donald Judd's architecture in Marfa, Texas, which attains similar ends through similar means. The cleansing landscape, the modest materials, basic forms and primitive techniques are set up as a palliative to modern life. This affinity shows itself not only at a formal or technical level, but through the ethical stipulation of how life should or could be lived. The architecture enacts a return to origins, to the hidden but stable ground available to primeval culture. At the same time this need is symptomatic of the opposite being the case. It is the mark of connoisseurs and artists, whose very formation denies them an attachment to archetypes of earth and dwelling. The building represents a reification of dwelling into geometric form, whose conceptual investment distinguishes it sharply from the vernacular model.

---

[5] Mack, 1997, p. 57.

[6] Herzog & de Meuron in conversation in Steinmann et al., 1985, p. 9.

[7] Herzog and de Meuron, 2002, p. 8.

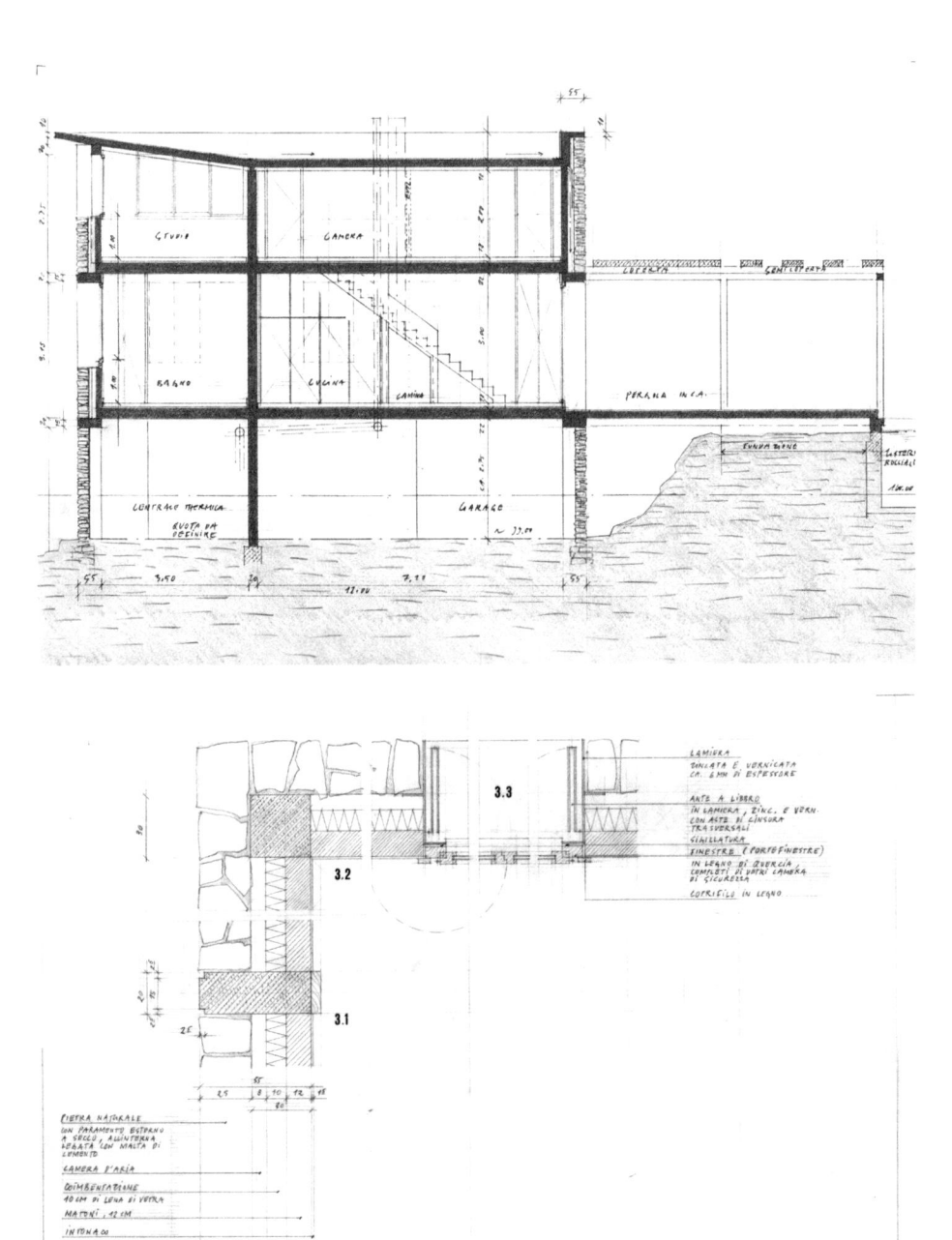

(Top) Herzog & de Meuron. Stone House, Tavole, Italy, 1982–88. Section. The terrace bridges over the irregular topography, and the inverted butterfly roof doubles up as water cistern.

(Bottom) Herzog & de Meuron. Stone House, Tavole, Italy, 1982–88. Detail of corner. The concrete contours on the façade are not actual structure, but a representation.

Objectified dwelling

All material elements of the project are connected through the articulation of a "design concept based on the fusion of plan, elevation and section".[8] This has the effect of transposing the everyday into geometric pattern. The unified, traditional order of daily life has been translated into a physical configuration of rooms and their relation to each other. How the house is occupied remains a guarded matter, much like its relationship to the settlement. Herzog and de Meuron prefer to focus on the project's conceptual resolution and issues of effect. The reluctance to address long-term dwelling suggests an interest in architecture as a timeless aesthetic experience, as opposed to its involvement in historical situations.

At the same time, the architects reject a nostalgic re-enactment of paradigmatic situations. They have seen tradition as an irretrievable value, the "distant Utopia of a complete and integrated culture".[9] The unattainable "tradition" in Herzog & de Meuron's discourse is as ambivalent as "type" is for Rossi. While impracticable, tradition nevertheless provides a charged referential ground that connects architecture with reality.

The realism of the practice is based on "pictorial analogies, their dissection and recomposition into an architectural reality".[10] With respect to dwelling, this presupposes a careful examination of existing patterns and their assimilation in conceptual terms:

> If we take a closer look at the traditional old house […] the floor plan seems simple and clear; a division following a standardised geometric pattern. If I look at it a while longer, I […] perceive this division […] as a whole assembled of autonomous parts […] as if the house in its inherited form did not arise out of division, but out of the opposite process of assemblage to create a social, functional, spatial and constructional whole, literally a unified architecture.[11]

Once identified, this sense of wholeness is interpreted formally. The integrity of the traditional house is transformed into a geometrical concern:

> If the plan form and the cross section are expressed as geometric equivalents, the spatial integration of all building parts is strengthened. The building is simultaneously an architectural expression of each single building part as well as of their unified collective form. This specific relationship between the parts and the whole is what we try to find […] in our Stone House in Tavole.[12]

8 Wang, 1992, p. 22.
9 Herzog and de Meuron, 1992, p. 143.
10 Ibid.
11 Ibid.
12 Ibid.

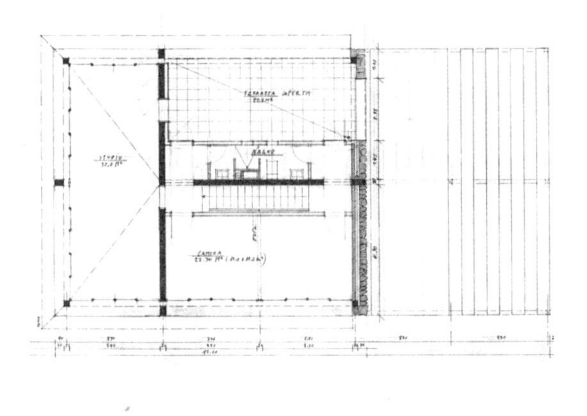

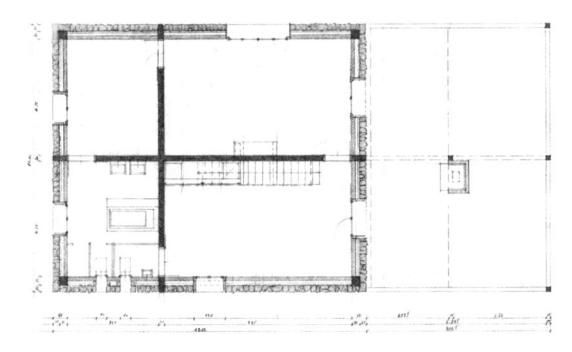

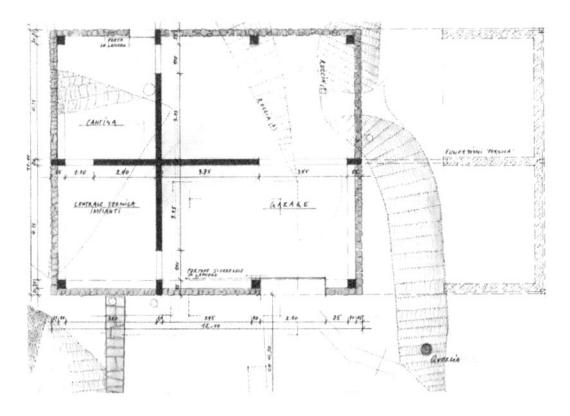

(Top) Herzog & de Meuron.
Stone House, Tavole, Italy, 1982–88.
Plan, first floor

(Middle) Herzog & de Meuron.
Stone House, Tavole, Italy, 1982–88.
Plan, ground floor

(Bottom) Herzog & de Meuron. Stone
House, Tavole, Italy, 1982–88. Plan,
basement. The cross motif is used in
plan as a visual marker for expansion
into the landscape.

These statements suggest an understanding of the traditional house as an aggregate of adjacent functions, rather than the background for dwelling. In a different context, Herzog & de Meuron later described the peasant house as an "assemblage, an architectonic entanglement of heterogeneous room types in a single, clear, externally homogeneous, self-contained structure".[13] This suggests an anxiety for formal unity, which led to the Stone House being described alternatively as an "implosion" of landscape or a "fusion" of rooms.[14]

This implosion presupposes a solid inner core, and indeed the concrete walls intersect at the centre of the plan. The concrete cross displaces the rooms into peripheral positions. Repeated in plan, section and elevation, the cruciform is conceptually justified as the attempt to guarantee a sense of overall unity.[15] However, this motif undermines the connection to earth otherwise implied by the rough masonry. Instead, a private geometrical order suspends the dry walling within the cruciform concrete frame.

The manner in which the systematic spatial division affects the house's modes of inhabitation, enabling or restricting activities, remains unexplained. The cruciform walls compress the rooms into an inflexible structure and at the same time give the impression of a dissipated interior, placing the rooms under the centrifugal force of the landscape. The staircase is incidental in relation to the wall configuration, as if the floors and rooms were conceived in isolation from each other. The implicit agenda of autonomy emerges in the specific relationships between centre and perimeter acted out at each level.

The internal configuration contributes to the strangeness of an object that presents itself, simultaneously, as both archaic and sophisticated. The primeval hut, a barely standing pile of stones, is forced into a pristine geometry through the industrial concrete frame disconnecting it from the earth. The symmetry of the west and east façades pertains to the more formal pretensions of the country house; however, the decorum of a *villa* is undermined through the rooms' detachment from one another.

Art / nature

The archaic motif juxtaposes the client's desire for a restorative refuge with the architects' ambition to create an artful approximation of nature. The architects' phrase "implosion of landscape" pertains to the intended closeness to a natural condition. At the same time, the building's formal resolution into neat planes, held together as if through an invisible will, states the artificiality of this intended primitivism, its conceptual origins. The motif of the primitive hut, the first house, automatically invokes the interpretation of nature – which, for Herzog & de Meuron, is to be undertaken through art.

The architects are keen on the correspondence between architecture and an "invading" surrounding nature.[16] In the Stone House, as in a Mannerist grotto, differences between natural and

---

13 Wang, 1992, pp. 116–119.

14 Mack, 1997, p. 57; Steinmann et al., 1985, p. 10.

15 Mack, 1997, p. 57.

16 Ibid., pp. 57–66.

artificial elements are blurred. The vegetation, topography and view are subsumed to the design, placed under the architect's remit. This approximation of the natural in the man-made is a prominent theme throughout Herzog & de Meuron's oeuvre. It demonstrates their preoccupation with the "hidden geometry of nature" as an ultimate order, invisible yet all-pervading, revealed through artistic analogy.[17]

The ambition to control nature through representation determines an orientation towards art as mimesis. "The artwork is the highest ontological state of material once it is taken out of its material context".[18] This stance originates in a Romantic notion of the artist as a demiurge, supplementing the purity of natural creation. The orientation towards art is seen as a counter-current of resistance to the meaninglessness proffered by capitalist culture. Through its capacity to replicate the "systems of relationships which exist in nature", art becomes architecture's primary claim to integrity.[19]

The magical object

Since Immanuel Kant, aesthetic contemplation has been associated with an abstracting quality. For better or worse, the art object absorbs the viewer into a timeless realm, away from everyday pressures. Karsten Harries has shown this disassociation to operate strongly into Minimalism, for which the art object must be self-referential, self-sufficient and self-justifying.[20] At the heart of minimalist concerns, the relationship between subject and object proposes a frozen moment of sensual plenitude outside history, in which things simply "are" – an idealistic proposition.

Herzog & de Meuron's concern for iconographic detachment, formal unity and conceptual coherence places their work in a similar domain. Herzog has emphasised that the manipulation of forms and materials constitutes a search for "physical presence".[21] The insistence on raw surfaces and the painterly effect of stone "pigmentation" suggests an aesthetic focus:

> The material is there to define the building but the building, to an equal degree, is there […] to make the material "visible." […] We push the material we use to an extreme to show it dismantled from any other function than "being."[22]

Nevertheless, the architecture is linked to a wide associative horizon. The Stone House oscillates between object and landscape, compactness and limitless expansion, formal villa and hut, stone pile and modular system, archaic and modern, primitive and sophisticated. This in itself shows the impossibility of "simply being".

With its focus on the direct experience of materials and form, the Stone House anticipated the thematic of Swiss developments for the next decade. The building illustrates the dialectic of

---

17 See for example "Transformation and Alienation" in Ursprung, 2002, pp. 78–141.

18 Herzog and de Meuron, 1992, p. 144.

19 Ibid., p. 145.

20 Harries, 1989, pp. 19–20.

21 Steinmann et al., 1985, pp. 8–9.

22 Zaera, 1993, p. 22.

architectural autonomy, as played out between immediate physical circumstances and a deeper understanding of context. Its unified materiality and panoramic orientation see "context" as an idealised version of nature as topography and view. The house frustrates the architects' claims of resistance against the motifs of capitalist consumerism, and reiterates the opposite as inevitable. It is a market product, a magical object inserted into a landscape understood as a dispersed collection of other such products. The concern with aesthetic contemplation undermines architecture's more participative dimensions, rendering the house truly "solitary".

The severe primitive world is juxtaposed to a sophisticated and witty *concetto*, which is as much part of Postmodernism as it is resistant to it. The Stone House takes more pride in its formal clarity and the intelligent resolution of independent requirements than its response to typical dwelling. Its assumed primitivism is attuned to a sophisticated global discourse, resonating more in the milieu that appreciates Donald Judd than that of Italian rural life. Its audience all but excludes the village yet it extends to the art world, the academic and cultural market. In these circumstances, the irony of housing foreigners in an introverted prism, subverting the conventional understanding of "house", becomes the most contextual moment of this proposal.

Peter Zumthor
Protective Housing for Roman Archaeological Excavations
Chur, Graubünden, 1985–86

Timber in theory
The Swiss interest in wood construction is not only based on its practical or environmental advantages. Rather, it has been the result of an intellectual approach seeing timber as responsive to context and capable to arouse historical associations. These associations operate at a typological and abstract level, avoiding the nostalgic imitation of vernacular forms. A predominant historical model has been the timber Modernism of the 1930s when, under harsh economic conditions, the *Neues Bauen* vocabulary of prismatic pavilions and horizontal windows was applied to wood construction. In deliberate contrast to the Heimat imagery of mountain chalets, the Modernists focused on timber prefabrication rather than on handicraft. Projects like Rudolf Gaberel's skating rink building in Davos (1934) or Emil Roth's youth hostel in Fällanden (1937) came under renewed architectural scrutiny in the 1980s and 1990s.

Nevertheless, this time the focus was on symbolic meaning rather than technical possibilities.[1] Various projects of the early 1980s used timber for its ubiquitous and ordinary qualities. Diener & Diener's St. Alban-Tal development in Basel (1985), whose concrete frame raised on pilotis was clearly modernist, was clad at the back in painted, vertical timber boarding relating to existing structures nearby. Similarly, Michael Alder clad in timber the masonry structure of the Hagmann House in Itingen, Basel (1985) as a typological reference to the suburban house. Herzog & de Meuron's Photographic Studio Frei (1981–82) and Plywood House (1984–85) used timber structurally, but emphasised the painterly and associative qualities of the plywood cladding.

Such projects anticipated an increasing intellectualisation of timber construction. Marianne Burkhalter and Christian Sumi's Forestry Depot in Turbenthal (1991–93) developed a conceptual grammar of timber elements – structural or screen-like, machine-cut planks and roughly-sawn trunks, horizontal and vertical boarding – to articulate the building's formal syntax. Marcel Meili and Markus Peter's School for Wood Technology in Biel (1990–93) used prefabricated timber elements in a didactic way. The building was conceived as a full-scale study of innovative technologies, from hollow-box units to glue-laminated girders,

[1] See Lucan, 2001, pp. 148–155; Steinmann, 1994, pp. 8, 14.

specifically in terms of structural and fire performance. The research extended implicitly to the architectural character of timber construction.

The architecture of Peter Zumthor contributed greatly to this renewed interest in timber construction. In 1985, *archithese* editor Martin Steinmann brought together the practitioners Michael Alder, Jacques Herzog, Pierre de Meuron, and Peter Zumthor to discuss the use of the material in contemporary work.[2] This forum recorded two approaches, based on differences between architectural training and crafts apprenticeship. Herzog expressed the belief that architects are shaped by their education to relate to timber construction intellectually. In contrast to this, the practical slant of the apprenticeship system teaches craftsmen to "perceive all problems from the angle of their execution".[3] As Steinmann would later note, the architect's approach engenders a sense of detachment, an insistence in design on the relationship between components rather than a sense of *Gestalt* wholeness. Conversely, for the craftsman, the material is more intimately bound with its manipulation, and construction becomes "one complete whole, made up of materials, actions and forms".[4]

The need to articulate the distinction between architect and craftsman was in part caused by the intriguing presence of Peter Zumthor. As a craftsman, his engagement with the material was of a different order. His buildings displayed their material qualities in a manner reminiscent of timeless vernacular buildings, whereas the work of his contemporaries was more indebted to the typological heritage of ETH theory.

During the *archithese* debate, Zumthor didn't entirely confirm these distinctions. On the one hand he demonstrated a sort of guild pride in his crafts formation as a joiner [*menuisier*], as opposed to carpenter, and on this basis claimed an intrinsic understanding of the material. On the other hand, he described the visual, "vibrating" quality of his façades as a deliberate aesthetic effect. The strategy of stretching a textural skin of tiny cladding elements over vast, simple volumes had the virtue of treating timber in a painterly, abstract manner. He had conceived his utilitarian buildings as finely tuned pieces of furniture. He didn't sound predominantly concerned with technique, yet he relied on it to articulate an architectural statement of wider relevance.[5]

Zumthor's attitude signalled a breach between the architects' perception of the modern craftsman and his own condition. Historically, invocations of the nominal "craftsman" have raised suspicion since the *Werkbund* industrial arts debates before the First World War. In the Swiss context, the appeal to crafts was associated with the *Landistil* and the propaganda of spiritual self-defence in the late 1930s and 1940s. Especially following the 1960s revisions of national identity, the imagery of wizened hands holding chisels remained acutely problematic. Zumthor's emergence on the Swiss professional stage re-actualised the debate in a new, non-sentimental manner.

2 Steinmann et al., 1985.
3 Ibid., p. 11.
4 Steinmann, 1994, pp. 16–17.
5 Steinmann et al., 1985, pp. 11–12.

(Top left) Emil Roth. Youth hostel, Fällanden, 1937

(Middle left) Diener & Diener. St. Alban-Tal, Basel, 1985–86

(Top right) Michael Alder. Hagmann House, Itingen, Basel, 1985

(Middle right) Burkhalter + Sumi. Forestry Station, Turbenthal, 1991–93

(Bottom right) Meili & Peter. School for Wood Technology, Biel, 1990–93

Zumthor was an outsider to the ETH scene. After a joinery apprenticeship, he trained as an architect at the Basel School of Design and the Pratt Institute in New York. His training bears the marks of a Modernism perhaps even more dogmatic than that of ETH. Nevertheless, his work philosophy is constructed around his early joinery apprenticeship and the implication of a tangible, immediate engagement with materials. This was aided by several years of work experience as a heritage architect in the Graubünden, prior to setting up in practice in 1979. Zumthor's familiarity with vernacular forms and techniques, grafted onto the joiner's tactile understanding of material, led in time to the creation of his successful image of "architect-craftsman".[6] This formation pertains less to traditional, pre-industrial craft, than to a *Werkbund* notion of craftsmanship engaged with contemporary conditions.

6   See for example Frampton, "Minimal moralia", 2002, p. 20.

The present study addresses the synthesis of technical and artistic know-how characteristic of Zumthor's earlier projects. Two of these, the Protective Housing for Roman Archaeological Excavations (Schutzbauten für Ausgrabung mit römischen Funden) in Chur and the architect's own atelier in Haldenstein, were designed and built around the same time in 1985–86. With their precise and reified use of timber, both projects combine the referential potential of naked material with the integrity of overall construction. They aim to bring an understanding of tradition in alignment to the contemporary theoretical debate, while avoiding the nostalgic replication of traditional architecture. Zumthor's work articulates a cultural ground between craft and high art, local vernacular and international Modernism.

I have focused here on the Protective Housing for Archaeological Excavations (Schutzbauten for short) because of its status as a public urban project. The building articulates a civic ambition, which subverts its intrinsic autonomy as architectural artefact.

Context

Chur, Switzerland's oldest town, was first recorded in Roman times and its history dates back to the Neolithic, Bronze and Iron Ages. It was set up strategically to control several important mountain passes; nowadays it is Graubünden's capital, a regional centre of tourism and light industry. Zumthor's Schutzbauten were set up to protect Chur's most significant Roman archaeological site. This series of interconnected buildings operates, in essence, as an annex of the Rhaetian History Museum in the historical town centre.

The site was excavated during the 1970s on the grounds of a horticultural company. Other Roman ruins identified in the area remain buried under developed land. Located at the edge of the town, on the boundary between wooded slopes and peripheral industry, the archaeological site contains the ruins of three Roman buildings, two houses and a larger inn. The excavations have revealed a series of low masonry walls, tracing two complete perimeters and a corner of the third (the rest of this third structure

(Above) Peter Zumthor. Protective
Housing for Roman Archaeological
Excavations, Chur, 1985–86

(Right) Peter Zumthor. Atelier Zumthor,
Haldenstein, 1986-86

remains buried under a garage adjacent to the site). The rooms were believed to be between 3 and 3.5 metres high, on two to three floors.

In 1985, Zumthor was commissioned to build a protective enclosure for the public display of the ruins. Rather than accommodating everything under one roof, his design approximates hypothetically each of the Roman volumes. The protective structures extrude upwards from the excavated walls, creating "a kind of abstract reconstruction" of the original perimeter.[7] The three sheds, open to air circulation, are clad in rain screens of angled timber slats, wrapped around the ruins and only interrupted at the points of access and display. Two large windows to the street, placed over the ancient doorways, and the side entry add a language of steel sheet elements that contrasts with the fine timber skin. Internally, a slender raised passageway connects the three sheds by floating above the ruins, and allows access to the low-level displays.

[7] Zumthor, 1998, p. 28.

The Schutzbauten are usually locked and unmanned, although keys are available on request at the Rhaetian Museum. However, some of the interior is put on street display for the impromptu visitor, and the provision of external light switches turns the large windows into a permanent exhibition. In its peripheral industrial neighbourhood, the project retains an *ad hoc* quality, bringing an aesthetic sensibility to the rather drab location.

The project has a double agenda; the preservation of urban memory is overlapped with an ambitious architectural statement. More than an archaeological destination, the structures are part of an architectural pilgrimage in and around Chur, an established part of its tourist circuit. In sub-Alpine suburbia, it sets up an intriguing dialectic of isolation and participation, reflected in the guarded affinity between the abstract sheds and their surroundings.

Pattern, technique, meaning

As the volumes are predetermined by the perimeter and speculated height of the ruins, the Schutzbauten's possibilities of expression are mostly focused on surface treatment. All façades are articulated by the same horizontal shadow plays. On the outside there is no indication as to the actual tectonic, which is only revealed internally.

Externally, in daylight, the enclosures appear as gravity defying, mute objects. Great effort and technical flair have been put into this impression of simplicity. The laconic forms result from a sophisticated use of laminated wood and steel in order to support the thin screens and achieve a column-less interior. The juxtaposition of joists, posts and bracings constitutes an efficient structural system, whose exertion remains invisible except at night. The cladding is presented as pure surface, freed from structural considerations and physical constraints. It is thus not a display of tectonic coherence but an idealisation of it: a *mise en*

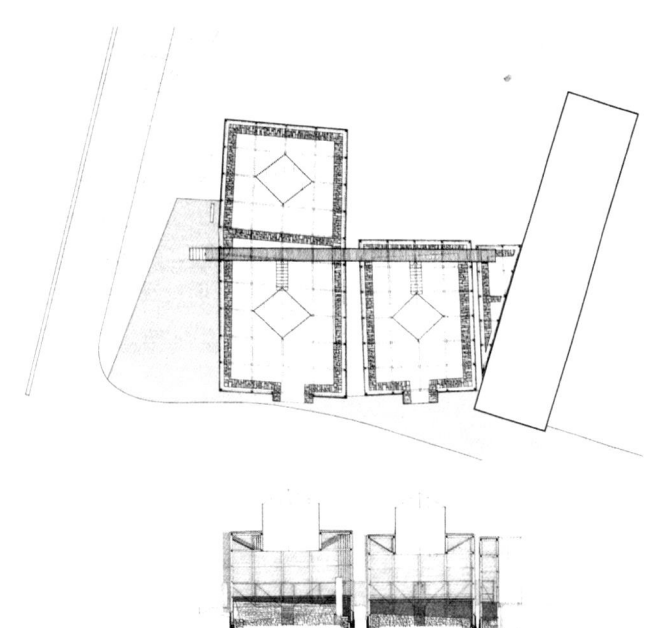

(Top) Archaeological site plan showing the excavations as part of a series of identified Roman ruins, most of them still buried

(Middle) Peter Zumthor. Protective Housing for Roman Archaeological Excavations, Chur, 1985–86. Plan showing the ruins' perimeter

(Bottom) Peter Zumthor. Protective Housing for Roman Archaeological Excavations, Chur, 1985–86. Section

scène intended to draw attention to the material and the work that went into forming it.[8]

The connections to the street and between the separate sheds establish a secondary order. The steel and leather elements – the raised steps of the side access, the window boxes and steel skylights – have a sculptural quality; they hover over the ground, suggesting only a tentative sense of connection. Thus the emphasis is placed on the contrast between the massive volumes and their delicate, screen-like skin.

The materiality of the façades stems from the local situation of a craft-oriented culture, well accustomed to wood construction.[9] Every full-height screen consists of hundreds of horizontal angled slats, each around two metres long, held in place by individual timber battens at the end and kept from twisting by additional steel rods fixed at the back. The acute precision of detail and its repetition on large expanses of surface suggests an essay on the limits of timber construction. The sheer amount of embodied energy is breathtaking. Repeated around the perimeters with the precision of a computer operation, this detail seems unrealisable almost anywhere else.

Its resonance with the local way of constructing things has provided the skills base and, by extension, a kind of economic justification. At the same time the repetitive, weathered surface has a painterly character, signalling an aesthetic sensibility different from the vernacular. The project's power thus comes from the radical, original application of local craftsmanship, whose woodworking tradition is abstracted into private formal law.

The vertical larch lamellas that clad the Haldenstein studio, designed and built at the same time, offer an additional clue to Zumthor's interpretation of tradition. There, the finesse of detail is emphasised to such a degree that the cladding recalls a piece of internal furniture rather than an architectural construction.[10] The bitumen surface of the actual wall can be glimpsed, and through it the fine strips of cladding, indicating their visual role. The use of timber is intended as an optical vibration rather than typological camouflage or actual protection.[11]

Indeed, both projects articulate differences between carpentry and joinery that are generally only apparent to experts. Through his training, Zumthor has come to regard timber primarily as a material for furniture and internal linings, rather than for structural construction or external cladding.[12] Its treatment in these projects, so extreme in external conditions, is therefore a claim to artistic individuality.

---

8 Steinmann, 1994, pp 16–17.

9 For the craft-orientation of Graubünden culture see Part III, Praxis.

10 Zumthor, 1998, p. 28.

11 Steinmann et al., 1985.

12 Ibid., pp. 7–8.

Peter Zumthor. Protective Housing
for Roman Archaeological Excavations,
Chur, 1985–86. Interior

Ambivalent traditions

This architecture displays two orders of meaning. Firstly it merges constructional logic and artistic gesture; secondly, it makes implicit reference to tradition as a repository of continuity. Subsumed under this notion of tradition there is a primitive aspect, understood not as rudimentary, but as a primordial guarantee of authenticity. In Zumthor's work, these claims of construction and tradition converge in the perfected artefact.

The Schutzbauten provide a good illustration of the primary meaning of construction in Zumthor's work. The visible relationships between elements suggest that the architecture comprises precisely what is there: the timber screens, their supports and assembly into volumes. This confirms one of Zumthor's dominant beliefs, that "the real core of all architectural work lies with the act of construction".[13]

[13] Zumthor, "A Way of Looking", 2006, p. 10.

Another issue is the concern with the buildings' presence. However carefully conceived and detailed, the extraneous elements – the leather connections, the steel stairs, protruding windows and sculptural skylights – are subsumed under the incessant vibration of fragile timber slats. The process of editing out all distracting aspects of the design, however structurally or functionally relevant, highlights the whole. The choice of materials and the form they are given provide complementary meanings. At one level, the timber construction refers to a local culture of timber craft. However, rather than propagating a vernacular convention, it is visually manipulated to veer towards abstraction. The repetition of elements borrows the seriality of Minimal structures, and exhibits the quality of an industrial pattern.

This is contrasted with the sensuality of material and its weathering. A reading of the cladding in terms of Minimalist multiples is undercut by textural variations that become apparent at close inspection. The slight tremor of the material, like lines drawn freehand, makes apparent the human labour that went into their construction. The visual tension between the large surfaces, suggestive of industrial processes, and the minute resolution that betrays the hand-made give the project a poetic richness.

This effect is specific not only of timber, but of other materials that still betray their natural unprocessed origin. Zumthor has created a similar narrative with stone in the Thermal Baths in Vals (1990–96). The contrast between geometrical planes and the hand-worked material, between the natural variations of stone and the homogeneity of concrete, implies a dialogue between technology and tradition. A close encounter with these surfaces brings to mind images of wizened faces, rugged hands, iron tools, a repository of material knowledge passed through generations. The working of materials readily available nearby in nature connects the unnamed generations to the Alpine environment. At the same time, the sharp treatment of timber edges and the industrial echo of the steel entrance and skylights signal the project's modernist origin.

(Above left) Peter Zumthor. Protective Housing for Roman Archaeological Excavations, Chur, 1985–86. Interior showing passageway

(Above right) Peter Zumthor. Protective Housing for Roman Archaeological Excavations, Chur, 1985–86. External view at night

(Right) Peter Zumthor. Protective Housing for Roman Archaeological Excavations, Chur, 1985–86. Entrance detail in steel and leather

Zumthor's understanding of tradition resembles the utopian notion of irretrievable unity that haunts Herzog & de Meuron's Stone House in Tavole. For both practices, the idea of tradition stands in for a sense of wholeness, and this wholeness is akin to natural beauty. The recourse to the authority of tradition can justify personal architectural decisions. However, the two understandings differ on the theme of architect versus craftsman, and the extent to which tradition is believed to be still attainable. In other words, to what degree can contemporary creativity rely on this authority, or emancipate itself from it for the sake of originality?

For Herzog & de Meuron tradition is a lost ideal. The best way to approximate its justifying powers is through a cerebral activity that decomposes and recomposes themes encountered in everyday reality.[14] This intellectual approach to architecture is presented as deliberate, and thus distinct from the unity of construction, form and use granted by tradition. In contrast, for Zumthor "building in the old sense of the master builders" guarantees the "self-sufficient, corporeal wholeness of an architectural object" and declares "the essential, if difficult, aim of [the] work".[15] The theory that the difference in outlook is due to their professional formation and a pre-determined relationship to material (architect from the outside, craftsman from inside) is seemingly confirmed by the meanings projected on the buildings. However, Zumthor's own distance from the nominal notion of the craftsman indicates the presence of a more complex artistic persona, which complements and promotes his production.

Despite their unquestionable differences, Zumthor's works display an anxiety towards unity similar to Herzog & de Meuron's. Certain buildings and (mostly utilitarian) objects appear to him in a state somewhat equivalent to the natural, in that they stand for a sense of wholeness. Repeatedly, in the writings of both practices, this particular category of things is referred to as "self-evident", or "just being".[16] Previously I associated this sense of self-justification with the aesthetic approach, as a secular way of achieving transcendence.

As with Herzog, Zumthor's art achieves its aim when it approximates naturalness. "If artistic processes strive for wholeness, they always attempt to give their creations a presence akin to that found in the things of nature or in the natural environment".[17] Thus both approaches find their application in artefacts. The claims of constructional and cultural integrity converge in these art-like, tradition-like, or nature-like buildings. The state of grace in which all aspects of the design are resolved in a self-evident, effortless fashion is subsumed within the complex integration of the project's various facets under what Martin Steinmann has called *"the simple whole"*.[18]

---

14 Herzog and de Meuron, 1992, p. 143.

15 Zumthor, "The Hard Core of Beauty", 2006, p. 32.

16 Zaera, 1993. Zumthor, "A Way of Looking", 2006, pp. 15–17.

17 Zumthor, "The Hard Core of Beauty", 2006, pp. 32–33.

18 Steinmann, 1994, p. 17.

(Top) Peter Zumthor,
Protective Housing for Roman
Archaeological Excavations,
Chur, 1985–86. Cladding detail

(Middle) Peter Zumthor,
Protective Housing for Roman
Archaeological Excavations,
Chur, 1985–86. Cladding as surface

(Right) Peter Zumthor,
Protective Housing for Roman
Archaeological Excavations,
Chur, 1985–86. Detail section

The crafted object

The pairing of Herzog & de Meuron and Zumthor may seem vexing for two practices preoccupied with self-definition. This parallel is, however, unavoidable considering their significant stature during the 1980s and early 1990s, both in Switzerland and abroad. While enjoying similar levels of international exposure, the practices developed along diverging lines. Responding to a global demand for original signature pieces, Herzog & de Meuron built up a prolific and heterogeneous output, sustained by an ever-increasing practice. Zumthor's beliefs crystallised in an uncompromising pursuit of excellence, which limited the scope of his operations.

The two practices have polarised professional opinion as a negative reflection of each other. In 1996 Kenneth Frampton distinguished two directions in Swiss architecture, one illustrated by Herzog & de Meuron as "artist-architects" and the other by Zumthor as "craftsman-architect". The critic advocated the latter as representing the more authentic, and thus more legitimate, manner of practice.[19] In 1998 Hans Frei reversed this reading, accusing Zumthor of precisely the kind of architecture-art practice Frampton had condemned. The ease of this reversal indicates a kind of equivalence between the two.[20] If Herzog & de Meuron and Zumthor determine a continuum between abstract thought and tangible reality, authored art versus anonymous architecture, their works represent neither extreme but an oscillation between them.

Through his circumstances, Zumthor has created a layered persona that aids in the justification of design and bestows on it a certain aura. This position is not that of a rural craftsman but of a Prospero self-exiled from the urban world yet surrounding himself with art, music and poetry. Thus an ambiguous territory opens between Zumthor's statements and his built architecture.

The focus on "self-evident" things in traditional or natural situations suggests the reliance on a primeval grounding. Buildings and things are subjected to a kind of sacred use, granted by their very plainness. The unquestionable status of the plain utilitarian object is, like the issue of crafts, a reincarnation of an earlier Modernist theme. However, Adolf Loos's advocacy of mass-produced household items, clothes and furniture and Le Corbusier's interest in *objet-type* displayed enthusiasm for new technology, whereas Zumthor's attitude implies a level of nostalgia for pre-industrial craft. The images of idealised environments that accompany Zumthor's writings suggest a version of reality controlled by an intractable artistic vision. This contradiction is embedded in his very choice of words:

19 See Frampton, "Minimal moralia", 2002. For a more detailed examination of Frampton's critique see also Davidovici, 2006.

20 Frei, 1998, p. 68.

Peter Zumthor. Atelier Zumthor,
Haldenstein, 1986-86. Elevation drawing

> Beauty always appears to me in settings, in clearly delimited pieces of reality, object-like or in the manner of a still life or like a self-contained scene, composed to perfection without the least trace of effort or artificiality. Everything is as it should be, everything is in its place. [...] The experience is unintentional. What I see is the thing itself.[21]

This "delimitation" of reality means that the irrefutable realities of casual use and conflict, dirt, expediency and kitsch are edited out. Just like in a still life, purposeful objects are severed from their purposefulness and set up for aesthetic contemplation.[22] Correspondingly, in Zumthor's buildings those elements that give stability and serviceability are subsumed under the scenography of light and shadow, material and texture, which he describes as "atmosphere".[23] Great effort and technical knowledge are directed at architecture's resolution into a complete, self-sufficient artwork. In spite of his declared fascination with utilitarian beauty, the focus in Zumthor's work remains the aesthetic experience of autonomous objects.

This object-orientation turns a blind eye to architecture's relationship to the heterogeneous urban continuum. Zumthor's trust in construction as the epitome of "factual relationships" between elements, with which the architect effects "the reduction of the contents to real things",[24] is ultimately akin to the Modernist belief in the redemptive potential of technology as the means to reach a more fundamental layer of objectivity.[25] Moreover, its significance within Swiss discourse suggests a wider belief in a reality grounded in things, in materials and the manner of their assembly, which are the precepts of architectural autonomy. The Schutzbauten's initial impression of ceremonial modesty is undercut on closer inspection by autonomy. The typological dialogue with local sheds has become an essay on visual ambiguity and accomplished technique.

The belief in the redemptive potential of construction, material and form needs to be counterbalanced by the reminder that the concrete and the tangible are not necessarily the same. There are structures of belief, determined within a society by the order of its institutions, which are not tangible and yet, as part of common and implicit cultural understandings, are sufficiently concrete to influence our way of relating to the world. Nothing, especially architecture, exists in itself, but always in connection to its context. The project, intended for the enclosure and protection of archaeological ruins, mediates between architect, town and visitors at a concrete level. Its real *topos* is not architectural presence but cultural heritage, collective memory, and the Roman origins of the European city.

---

21 Zumthor, *Thinking Architecture*, 2006, p. 76.

22 The conception of artwork as a self-evident plenitude has been a staple of the aesthetic discourse since Alexander Gottlieb Baumgarten's *Metaphysics* (1779). See Harries, 1989, pp. 21–23.

23 See Zumthor, *Atmospheres*, 2006.

24 Zumthor, "The Hard Core of Beauty", 2006, p. 33.

25 See Hannes Meyer's essay "bauen" (1928) quoted in Hays, 1992, pp. 158–159.

Peter Zumthor. Thermal Baths,
Vals, 1990–96. Interior

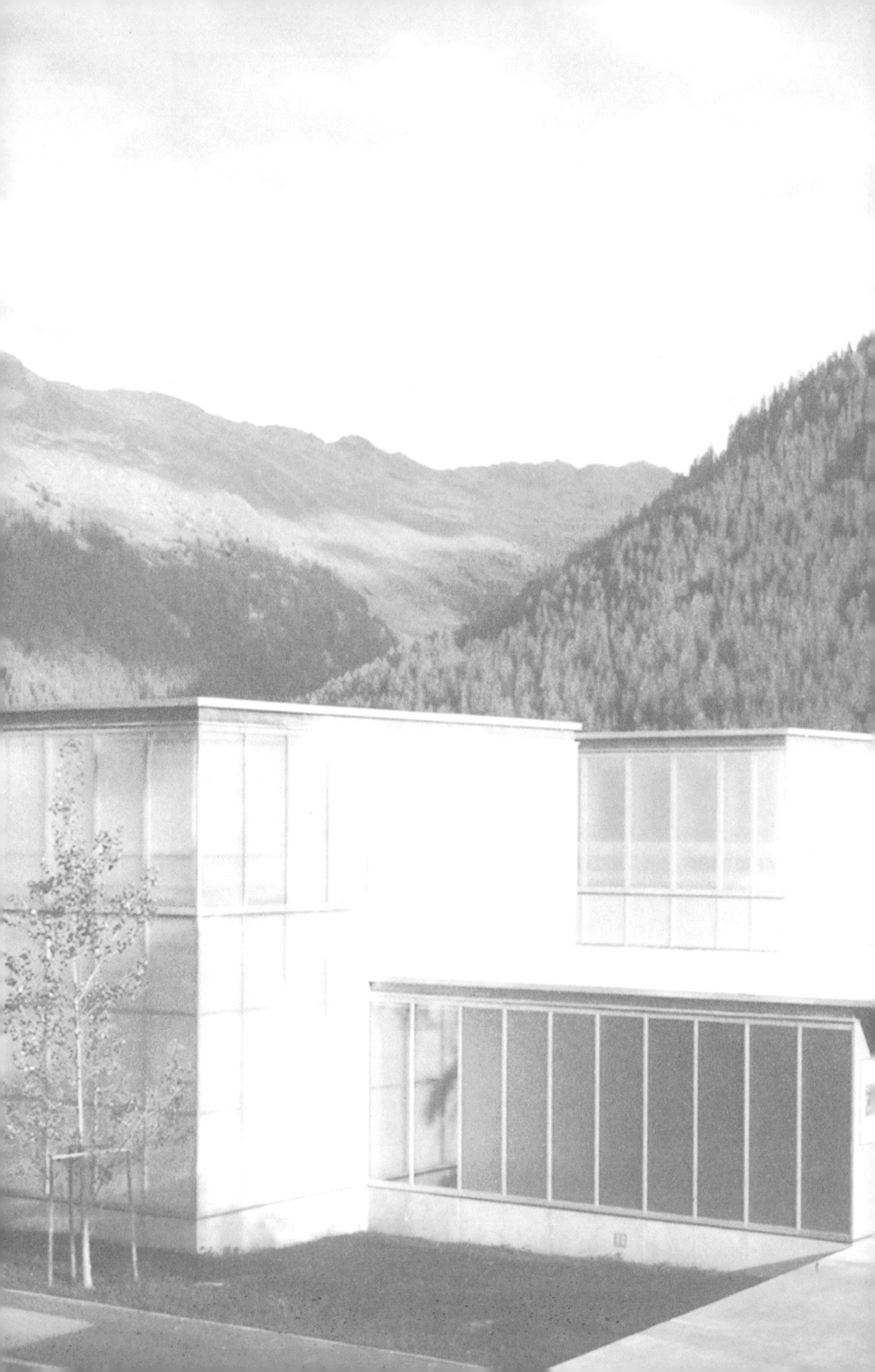

Gigon/Guyer
Kirchner Museum
Davos, Graubünden
1989–92

The Kirchner Museum, defined by conceptual focus, material presence and abstract typological references, represents a moment of synthesis for theoretical themes formulated during the 1980s. Annette Gigon and Mike Guyer's first building signals the emergence of a new generation of Swiss practitioners. Before setting up in practice in 1989, Mike Guyer worked in Rem Koolhaas's Office for Metropolitan Architecture (OMA) and Annette Gigon in Herzog & de Meuron's Basel studio. Their first collaboration reveals the generational continuities at work within Swiss practice and in relation to the international discourse.

The museum, devoted to the works of German Expressionist painter Ernst Ludwig Kirchner (1880–1938), is a prominent cultural destination in Davos.[1] An ensemble of prismatic volumes clad in translucent glass, it tends towards programmatic ambiguity, rather than the classical composition of the institutional museum type. Its luminous yet opaque skin acts, as Martin Steinmann noted, as a veil.[2] It conceals and reveals, drawing attention partly to the solids and voids beneath it, but mostly to itself. The actuality of this surface, with its emphasis on the silent and unyielding object, makes explicit the debt to the theoretical discourse of architectural autonomy. Through this emphasis, rather than simply through its materiality, the building anticipates themes soon to be explored in Herzog & de Meuron's Goetz Gallery and Peter Zumthor's Bregenz Kunsthaus.

Despite its autonomy, the project is claimed by its location and public programme as an art museum. Davos, an intrinsically modern Alpine town, and Kirchner's art deserve particular attention in the assessment of this context. An analysis of the conditions that led to the museum's realisation offers the possibility of opening up the discussion – from its assessment as architectural artefact, to its existence within an urban situation.

Kirchner and the "Magic Mountain"
One of the largest Alpine resorts in Europe, Davos grew from the fusion of two villages, Davos Platz and Davos Dorf, along the Landwasser River in Eastern Graubünden. After 1860 the settlement grew rapidly as a sanatoria town, its dry rarefied air and south-facing slopes being well suited to the cure of

1   Kirchner co-founded the Dresden *Die Brücke* avant-garde group in 1905. The name demonstrated the intention of creating, through artistic collaboration, a "bridge" to spiritual progress and individual freedom. See Scotti, 2005.

2   Steinmann, 1994, pp. 11–12.

tuberculosis. When penicillin permanently changed the nature of treatment, Davos re-branded itself into a sports and business resort. The need to rid itself of the characteristics of a place for the sick accounts, in part, for the town's extensive and eclectic developments during the second half of the twentieth century.

Two themes present themselves from the outset as particular to Davos. Firstly, its ribbon development along the valley has precluded the possibility of a clearly defined centre. The town is articulated instead by the sinuous Promenade, along which public buildings are interspersed with hotels and shops. Thus the urban order denoted by the central marketplace, church and town hall is undermined by a dispersed infrastructure associated with tourism. Secondly, the town's health services attracted a number of prominent cultural figures in the late nineteenth and early twentieth centuries.[3] This adopted community of avant-garde artists, writers and architects contributed to the town much more than the migratory business elite nowadays known as "Davos culture".

For Ernst Ludwig Kirchner, Davos and its countryside provided a clinical, political and spiritual refuge for over twenty years. At the time of his death in 1938 Kirchner left behind a vast archive of paintings, prints, sculpture and photography. Together with the works amassed by the painter's friends and patrons, this became the basis of a considerable collection. The Kirchner Foundation was founded in 1982 and a temporary museum operated in a disused post office in Davos Platz until 1992. In 1988, fifty years after the painter's death, the foundation announced a competition for a new museum building.[4] Gigon and Guyer won the commission in competition in 1989, and the building was completed in 1992.

The museum archives attest to Kirchner's respect and friendship towards the locals, but also to a sense of social and cultural isolation.[5] Throughout his stay in the Davos area, the artist oscillated between yearning for metropolitan cultural circles and the Alpine setting for bearable life. His earlier paintings of Berlin society had documented an elegant, decadent world, stimulating yet threatening. In Davos he painted the Alps as a place of recovery, the setting of a purified and renewed existence. From 1923, when his clinical treatment finished, Kirchner lived in the hamlet of Frauenkirch, above Davos. This retreat further into nature was in keeping with Die Brücke's initial anti-urban manifesto.[6] However, while his works endowed mountain existence and people with spiritual dimensions, the artist cut a detached figure, an observer with no possibility of full participation in rural life.

If the move to Frauenkirch created a perhaps necessary distance from the town's sanatorium culture, Davos offered Kirchner a respite of sophistication and a cultural horizon for intellectual friendships and patronage.[7] Kirchner's paintings of Davos, created from memory in his studio and veering towards

---

3   One of these was Thomas Mann, whose experiences in Davos during his wife's treatment were recorded in the novel *Der Zauberberg* (The Magic Mountain) first published in 1924.

4   For the Kirchner Foundation's concise history and activities see Henze, 1994, pp. 399–401.

5   Zimmermann, 2003, pp. 59–70.

6   See Grisebach, 2003.

7   Bürgi 2003, p. 143.

abstraction, suggest an ambiguous attitude towards modern urban society. These Alpine urban visions combine a sense of remoteness, civic ambition and notions of resort. In *Davos mit Kirche, Davos im Sommer* (1925) the town appears as the essence of bourgeois order, sanitised and efficient in contrast to the sublime landscape. *Rathaus Davos Platz* (1931) focuses on the juxtaposition of the medieval Church and the Town Hall, which had recently been given a modernist makeover by Rudolph Gaberel. The painting illustrates Kirchner's approval of the modern architecture as a complement to the medieval buildings and to the natural topography.[8]

8 "The new buildings give the city an altogether different appearance and make the mountains high". Kirchner quoted in Henze, 1994, p. 334.

Painted from memory in the studio, these paintings also invite less literal readings. The colour saturation exudes existential connotations. The church spire reaches to the top of the frame, dominating both compositions as an arbiter of life and death. Buildings, park, streets, light and landscape are subsumed under a situation both particular to this settlement, and paradigmatic of human existence. Kirchner envisioned the urban realm as a collective rational construct, in contrast to the unfathomable, threatening natural realm, a metaphor for individual subjective experience. The entrenched orderliness of Davos, an island of light and communality against the looming mountains, represents daily routine as a barrier against the darker forces in the artist's soul.

The world represented in these paintings is detached from the reality of the observer. The artwork size and format ensure that the sizable emotional drama remains contained within the canvas plane, sanitised by the white surface of gallery walls. This sense of aesthetic autonomy demanded an appropriate architectural response.

Modernism in the Alps

Davos is intrinsically a modernist town, more chaotic and less quaint than in Kirchner's depictions. Historically, as hotels and sanatoria replaced the medieval farmsteads, hygienic requirements for light and air circulation replaced the original settlement patterns. The order initially determined by practical, civic and religious requirements was thus superseded by rational, geometric arrangements. The characteristic building type in Davos is not the chalet but the sanatorium – itself a founding metaphor of Modernism, associated with hygiene, sunlight, rigour and renewal.

A prime argument for Davos's Modernism was its legal ratification of flat roof construction in the 1930s. The technology incorporating drainage within internal walls had been used tentatively since the 1870s, originally with a purely functional and safety role. In time the *Davoser Flachdach*, associated with modern sanatoria, became a vehicle for the wide acceptance of avant-garde architecture. The planning regulation that imposed flat-roof construction in central Davos was the result of a campaign instigated by the architect Rudolf Gaberel and historian

Erwin Poeschel. Gaberel's practice and Poeschel's articles in the professional press advocated flat roof construction as efficient, functional and hygienic.[9] Gaberel, who like Kirchner had settled permanently in Davos on health grounds, became responsible for a number of landmark *Neues Bauen* buildings, including the Zürcher Heilstätte Clinic, the Davos Platz Town Hall (painted by Kirchner) and the ice rink building, one of Davos's earliest sports facilities and a distinguished example of 1930s timber Modernism.

The flat-roof regulation displays a strong affinity with the Modern Movement, unlike other mountain towns that conceal their actual status behind a rural iconography. On the one hand, the orthogonal system of cubic terraced volumes, related to the historical health treatments, has created a consistent urban fabric. On the other, the tourist industry has undermined the traditional order of the historical villages. The 1930s Modernist landmarks are interspersed with 1960s and 1970s developments, infused with the Venturian quality of disparate billboards erected along a highway. In this mixed Modernist heritage, the predominant typologies pertain to geometry as a mode of life.

Autonomy I: white cubes

The Kirchner Museum is located in a small park near the centre of Davos Platz. The site, formerly a hotel garden off the Promenade, slopes down sharply towards a number of major sports facilities and car parks. Beneath the raised podium of the museum, the car-oriented environment raises questions about the scattered attractions of a tourist economy, undermining Davos's essential quality as a mountain town.

Gigon / Guyer's response to this dispersed location has been to reinforce the project's autonomy. The park provides a generic representation of nature, against which the building exhibits its inner logic. At a programmatic level, any museum of modern art is inherently an autonomous proposition, setting aside a space for aesthetic contemplation. In this case, autonomy is also a theoretical *topos*. The project is ordered by a self-sufficient conceptual discipline, which aims to coordinate its formal and material aspects. Each decision is precisely justified and has its place in a rational chain. The project's internal coherence renders the relation to context a secondary concern; this is the premise of its autonomy.

The overall conceptual strategy developed from two sources: curatorial requirements for the interior and local light conditions for the exterior.[10] The emphasis on Alpine "light" signals that the urban and topographical aspects of the site have been subsumed under the realm of aesthetic experience.

However, the autonomy of the project originates internally, in the typological investigation of the gallery space. The brief asked for display areas suited to a variety of media, from oil paintings, works on paper, sketchbooks, to photographs and furniture. All four galleries required white walls, a controlled environment and

[9] See for example Poeschel, 1928.

[10] Mike Guyer speaking to Matthias Bräm in Bräm, 1995, pp. 49–50.

(Top) Ernst Ludwig Kirchner.
Davos mit Kirche, Davos im Sommer,
1925, Kirchner Museum, Davos

(Middle) Ernst Ludwig Kirchner.
Rathaus Davos Platz, 1931,
Kirchner Museum, Davos

(Right) Gigon/Guyer. Kirchner Museum,
Davos, 1989–92. Situation plan

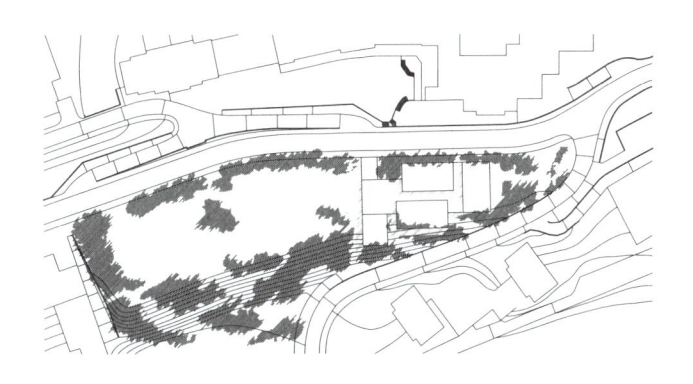

adjustable lighting. The project's conceptual rationale unfolds from the uniform, neutral character of these exhibition spaces.

The architects conceived the exhibition rooms as the abstraction of nineteenth-century art salons: "a spatial quotation of […] parquet floors, white walls and glazed roof […] simplified to prismatic spaces without cornices or baseboards".[11] Photographic records suggest that the new displays are not radically different from Kirchner's solo show at the Kunsthalle in Basel in 1923.[12] In the new museum, similarly to the neo-classical top-lit gallery, the rows of paintings of various sizes establish a horizon of distinct narratives, punctuated against the blank surface of the wall. This resemblance is not incidental; it confirms the common, or typical, dimensions of conventional displays for figurative painting.

Alan Colquhoun has connected the white cube convention with the philosophical assumption that the work of art is in itself an autonomous, self-contained object.[13] In post-war art, in particular 1960s Minimalism, illusionistic representation and the autonomous white cube as its corollary came under attack. In the case of Kirchner's work however, the artistic autonomy of both was still undisputed. The museum galleries are therefore engaged with the typological conventions of the art *salon*.

The galleries' deliberate neutrality is meant to complement the intensity of Kirchner's oeuvre. The withdrawal from expression is presented as a strategy of appropriateness. However, the design is knowingly positioned with respect to white cube conventions. The abstraction of historical precedents suggests that, beyond their stated use, the Kirchner Museum galleries are intended as object-types.

Three of the galleries are alike in size, and the fourth is shorter in length. Their overall similarity in terms of volume, materiality and light conditions avoids the creation of a hierarchy of exhibition spaces with varying characters. The consistent character reinforces the idea of multiples, as if all galleries were industrial replications of an ideal type. They present themselves as the physical embodiment of the gallery-type in its simplest form.

At the same time, the exhibition spaces depart from the typological convention of the enfilade. The visual connections allowed by the enfilade arrangement would have established a sense of continuity between individual rooms. Here, a strong sense of separation ensues, not only internally but also externally, as the volume of each gallery is distinctly defined in the overall composition.[14]

The anonymous aesthetic of the galleries, defined on the outside as distinct volumes, is rather ambiguous. At one level of association, the appearance of serial box-like volumes signals a Minimalist sensibility. At another level, the parallelepipeds provide a contextual moment, recalling the

---

11 Annette Gigon, ibid., p. 52.

12 The Basel Kunsthalle was designed by Johann Jakob Stehlin and completed in 1872.

13 See Colquhoun, "Changing Museum", 2009, pp. 335–336.

14 This late twentieth-century tendency in art museums to emphasise each room individually, partly emerging from curatorial conventions, is discussed in Colquhoun, "Changing Museum", 2009, p. 336–337.

(Above) Gigon/Guyer. Kirchner Museum, Davos, 1989–92. Gallery

(Right) Kirchner paintings shown at the June Exhibition in Kunsthalle Basel, 3–24 June 1923

hygienic requirements for "light, air and sun" typical of Davos. However, rather than the imagery of the sanatorium, the project engages that of another modernist metaphor, the factory. The repetition of object-types creates a semi-industrial appearance, while their translucent skin recalls the visionary glass architecture of Bruno Taut. If, internally, the museum acknowledges the autonomy of the artworks and demurs from open competition with them, on the outside it asserts itself as an artistic proposition drawing from a variety of historical sources.

Autonomy II: specific objects

The museum's beguiling exterior is justified pragmatically by internal requirements. In the Alpine climate, the glass ceilings to the exhibition rooms – a typological stipulation – required the provision of service spaces, glazed on all sides, to filter daylight and ensure environmental and light controls. The depth of these clerestories is significant, approximately a third of the overall external height. The expression of each room as an independent object-type was defined by this functional need for homogeneous lighting. The light source, presented on the inside as a series of magical translucent ceilings, is explained on the exterior by the addition of the technical spaces atop each opaque box. This determines the volumetric definition and the height of each gallery. The four modular prisms, towering above the interconnecting circulation area, acquire metaphorical value. The museum is presented as an industrial machine, a factory of light conditions.

The glass cladding is necessary as a light filter only at the top of each prism. However, the project uses the material all over in order to emphasise its unity. Translucent panels, framed by thin metal strips, continue from the clerestories down across the entire height of the façades. Even the flat roofs, overlooked by the nearby hotel, are covered with broken glass shards. Thus the entire ensemble, unified by the greenish-white sheen of the glass, is set apart from its surroundings through its reflection and absorption of light.

The most controversial proposition has been to enclose the opaque structural walls in the same shimmering sheath. The glass cladding is etched on the outside, preventing reflections. Grey insulation panels are visible beneath the translucent material but the eye cannot focus on them; the gaze bounces against the blurred glass surface. Martin Steinmann has memorably described this effect in terms of a veil drawn, erotically almost, across the actual façade:

> The stir caused by the Kirchner Museum [...] was not least due to its paradoxical skin: made of glass but with nothing to see except the glass itself. [...] The skin thus becomes a veil. It pretends to deny what it has to show, at the same time as pretending to show what it denies: in this way the veil itself becomes the *object of desire*.[15]

15   Steinmann, 1994, pp. 11–12.

At this level, the project aligns itself with the concerns of Minimal Art. The perceptual games with surface and depth imply the self-referential nature of the glass skin. From afar, the luminous boxes recall Donald Judd's "specific objects", with a similar equilibrium between formal neutrality, serial arrangement and sensuous materiality. The building states a tension between the industrial, repetitive look of its constituents, and the tactile treatment of its skin. However, unlike Minimalist series, this three-dimensional ensemble is carefully composed. Instead of a grid-like arrangement, the distinct volumes are held in balance, their position shifted so as to make the unity of the whole visible.

The use of glass in different states on the façades – transparent, translucent and opaque – has created a "grammar of applied substances".[16] In other words, the material has the expressive power of language, suggesting an updated *architecture parlante*. The different glass finishes express the internal contrast between two complementary spatial types: the gallery modules and the fluid circulation that connects them.

16 Bräm, 1995, p. 50.

A new typology

The Kirchner Museum's lack of enfilade arrangements has resulted in a very specific plan. The dispersed galleries and common circulation create a firm yet intuitive composition, with a looser sense of connection. The circulation space acts as a foil, clearly demarcating one pavilion from the next. Its width, determined so as to avoid overshadowing between galleries, transforms this circulation from corridor to sinuous, cave-like hall. In contrast to the white, light-filled galleries, this interstitial space appears as an unprocessed rough interior. Its walls, floor and ceiling are made of in-situ cast concrete, revealing the building's structural core. The discreetly playful gesture of aligning the floor joints with the gallery entrances reinforces the connection between rooms.

The contrast between the two types of spaces extends to their presence on the external envelope. The top-lit galleries have an internalised quality, derived from the conventional white cube. They are autonomous spaces for the contemplation of autonomous artwork. In contrast the circulation, doubling up as shop, foyer and education room, meets the façade with fully glazed openings, offering external views and the possibility of orientation.

The composition of box-like rooms and fluid circulation recalls structuralist architecture – a late modern approach pertaining to prefabrication, modules, and cellular growth. Nevertheless, if the gridded surfaces of the façades suggest the presence of a modular logic, the placement of the individual galleries creates a looser internal circuit. On the one hand this *promenade architecturale* underlines the internal self-sufficiency of the ensemble; on the other, it engenders a pattern similar to that of Davos houses. In what is perhaps the project's most contextual aspect, the galleries' separation into discrete entities evokes the

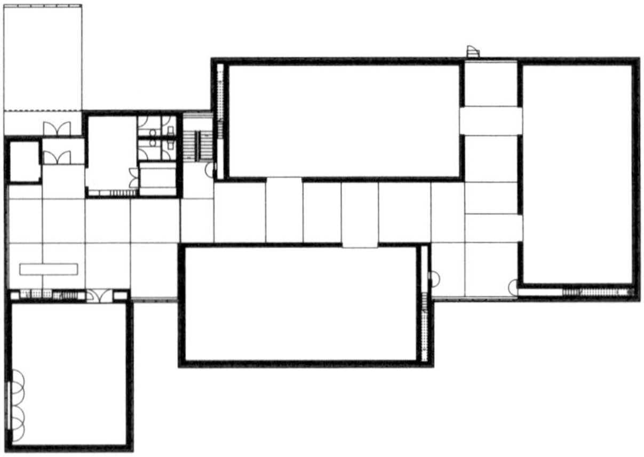

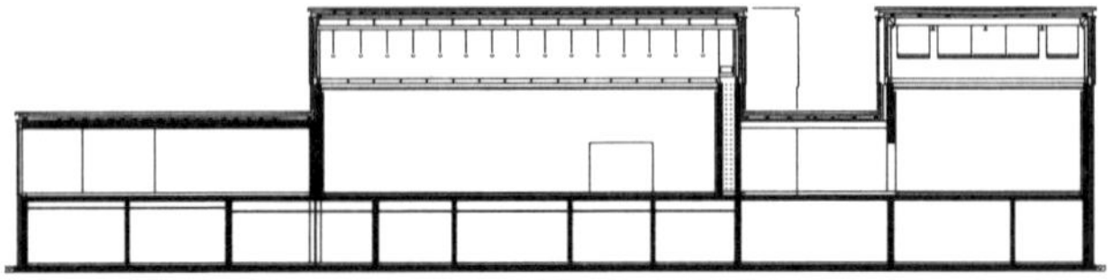

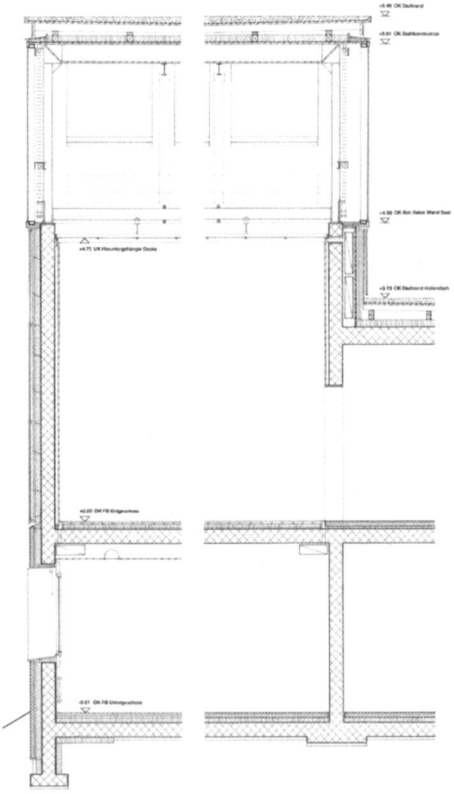

(Opposite left) Gigon/Guyer.
Kirchner Museum, Davos, 1989–92.
Detail section through cladding
and service zone

(Opposite top right) Gigon/Guyer.
Kirchner Museum, Davos, 1989–92.
Ground floor plan

(Opposite bottom right) Gigon/Guyer.
Kirchner Museum, Davos, 1989–92.
Longitudinal section

(Above) Gigon/Guyer.
Kirchner Museum, Davos, 1989–92.
Different glass conditions

(Right) Gigon/Guyer.
Kirchner Museum, Davos, 1989–92.
Side view

local urban pattern.[17] The plan describes a cluster of distinct volumes, similar to houses in a settlement. This association is reinforced by the internal concrete finish, which renders the core of the building as an internal street, a place for social interaction.

This memorable plan is tantamount to an original typology in which two complementary types, circulation and gallery, are defined in contrast to each other. Shadow begets light, the cave begets the cella. At the time of its publication, this plan created a critical sensation. For Marcel Meili, the composition represented "a total rupture with the traditional hierarchy of type, leading to an almost perfect balance between [enclosed] spaces and their extensions".[18] The new typology challenged not only established conventions, but also a contemporary emphasis on monad-like buildings, generating instead a "difficult whole" through the dialectical relationship of its parts.

The right plan

The Kirchner Museum is conceived under the sign of the right angle. The halls, rectangular in plan and section, are rotated by ninety degrees in relation to each other. This plan organisation raises the issue of what may constitute an appropriate formal gesture. The orthogonal geometry that dominates the composition has a double value. Firstly, it pertains to the withdrawal from formal expression seen to best complement Kirchner's art. Secondly, it follows a cultural and urban pre-requisite.

The right angle thus fulfils several roles. It provides a rational, pragmatic tool for organising the design and also constitutes a contextual reference, reiterating Davos's version of modernity as geometry. It supplements Kirchner's Expressionist art, to which it provides a neutral background. At a more general level, it can be seen as subscribing to a typically Protestant cultural incentive, in which all departures from the norm are strictly justified. The architects indicate their full awareness of this layering of meanings:

> The lighting section, the climate and the structure of the existing buildings in Davos demand the orthogonal [...]. The choice of the [Kirchner Museum] geometry is solely dependent upon the concept. And yet in our culture we feel closer to the orthogonal – it can be more directly employed and realised.[19]

Gigon / Guyer justify their use of the right angle through the alignment of conceptual discipline to a more general fondness for orthogonal geometries. Cultural, functional and conceptual requirements are brought into play to justify all aesthetic decisions. The implication here is that everything is rationally accounted for; that the contradictory requirements of programme, context, and construction are seamlessly and gracefully reconciled in the built object.

---

17 Gigon and Guyer, 2000, p. 24.

18 Meili, "Ein paar Bauten", 1991, p. 27.

19 Gigon / Guyer quoted in Adam and Wang, 2000, p. 11.

Gigon/Guyer. Kirchner Museum,
Davos, 1989–92. Circulation space
opening towards the galleries

However, there are aspects to the project that escape the conceptual purity of the plan, especially in relation to topography. The museum's lower level, housing ancillary spaces, is partly buried in the slope of the site and is revealed on the outside as an extruded concrete plinth with narrow windows (corresponding to the offices). This part undermines the non-hierarchical organisation of the main volumes and the dominating grammar of glass surfaces. The section's conceptual clarity falters somewhat at this point, where the horizontal plane well-suited to theoretical speculation gives way to the actual topography. This part of the design reads as an unwanted residue, resulting from the application of an abstract concept to the concrete situation.

Theory embodied

At the time of its conception, the Kirchner Museum was making an ambitious statement about the museum type. In the early 1990s, the proposition of art spaces characterised by material neutrality and formal restraint was a novelty.[20] The project rejected the prevalent model of over-expressive art spaces that could be found, for example, in the museums of Richard Meier or James Stirling. Instead, the galleries followed the curatorial stipulations of artist Rémy Zaugg for formal and material simplicity. The dialogue with artists rather than architects instigated a resistance to formal gestures, which left a strong imprint in Swiss architecture at the time. Like Herzog & de Meuron, Peter Zumthor and Peter Märkli, Gigon / Guyer's museum architecture proposed an alternative to the international mainstream.

This position reinforced the role of concept over and against individual impulse. As long as the internal logic governing all design moves is infallible, buildings can present themselves as unapologetically autonomous. Thus the design effort is directed less at the mediation of the surrounding situation than at a mediation of all problems set by context, programme, and technique.

The Kirchner Museum's logical resolution and pragmatic justification of every aesthetic decision point to the exercise of conceptual control over the creative gesture. Despite various typological references to factory and exhibition architecture, the use of glass is primarily a methodical grammar of material surfaces. The building is conceived as "a light-machine to illuminate the interior with even, controlled, diffused daylight".[21] By externally displaying its technical character, it demonstrates the inherently modernist aim of generating a new kind of museum. Rather than an urban institution organising a section of town, the museum offers itself more anonymously, as one of the dispersed attractions along the Promenade. The existing park acts as a buffer zone, allowing the building to be viewed in isolation, with mountains as a backdrop.

The Kirchner Museum displays an exemplary correspondence between idea, form and material; at the same time, the

---

20 The studio designed by Herzog & de Meuron to Rémy Zaugg's specifications (Mulhouse, France, 1995–96) featured "calm, almost meditative proportions", recessed skylights and plain surfaces. This constituted the prototype for their subsequent art spaces in the Tate Modern and other projects. See Mack, 2000, pp. 146–155.

21 Annette Gigon in correspondence with the author, 6 May 2009.

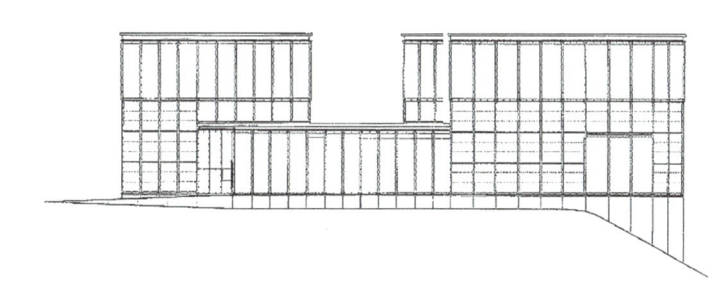

(Top) Gigon/Guyer, Kirchner Museum, Davos, 1989–92. Entrance

(Middle) Gigon/Guyer, Kirchner Museum, Davos, 1989–92. Cross section

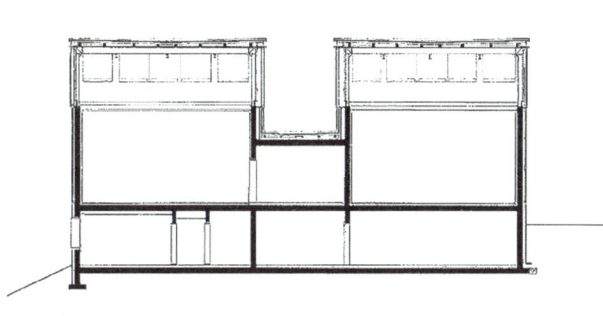

(Bottom) Gigon/Guyer, Kirchner Museum, Davos, 1989–92. West elevation

proportional variations, occasional outward views, and organic circulations escape the conceptual discipline. These particulars stand witness to a more poetic impulse, restrained and all the more valuable.

Kirchner's paintings of Davos revealed the drama of human limits hidden beneath simple, seemingly naïve observations of place. As a parallel, the seemingly simple volumes of the museum raise unanswerable questions about the autonomy of architecture.
It could be that artist and architects were animated by similar ideals – directness, purity, lack of subterfuge – yet used opposite strategies to attain them.

At one level the galleries, top lit but mostly without outward views, suggest an intense, overriding focus on art. The claims of the locale have been assimilated under climatic and light conditions. The awkward relation to topography reinforces a sense of disengagement with the actual urban situation; the museum standing in its park illustrates the modernist idea of prisms
in the greenery.

At another level, in this location the nature of contemporary urban territory is itself brought into question. The Davos Promenade is constituted like an Alpine version of the Vegas Strip, in which the requirements of *civitas* are subsumed under economic interests and individual desires. In this compromised situation, the illusion of a retreat into architecture appears as the seductive and difficult alternative. It is, nevertheless, an illusion. As the museum gardens have come under the threat of commercial development, the building's aesthetic and conceptual unity seems no longer unassailable. Faced with an implacable market logic, the fragility of architecture stands revealed.

Gigon/Guyer, Kirchner Museum,
Davos, 1989–92. South elevation showing
windows to the basement offices

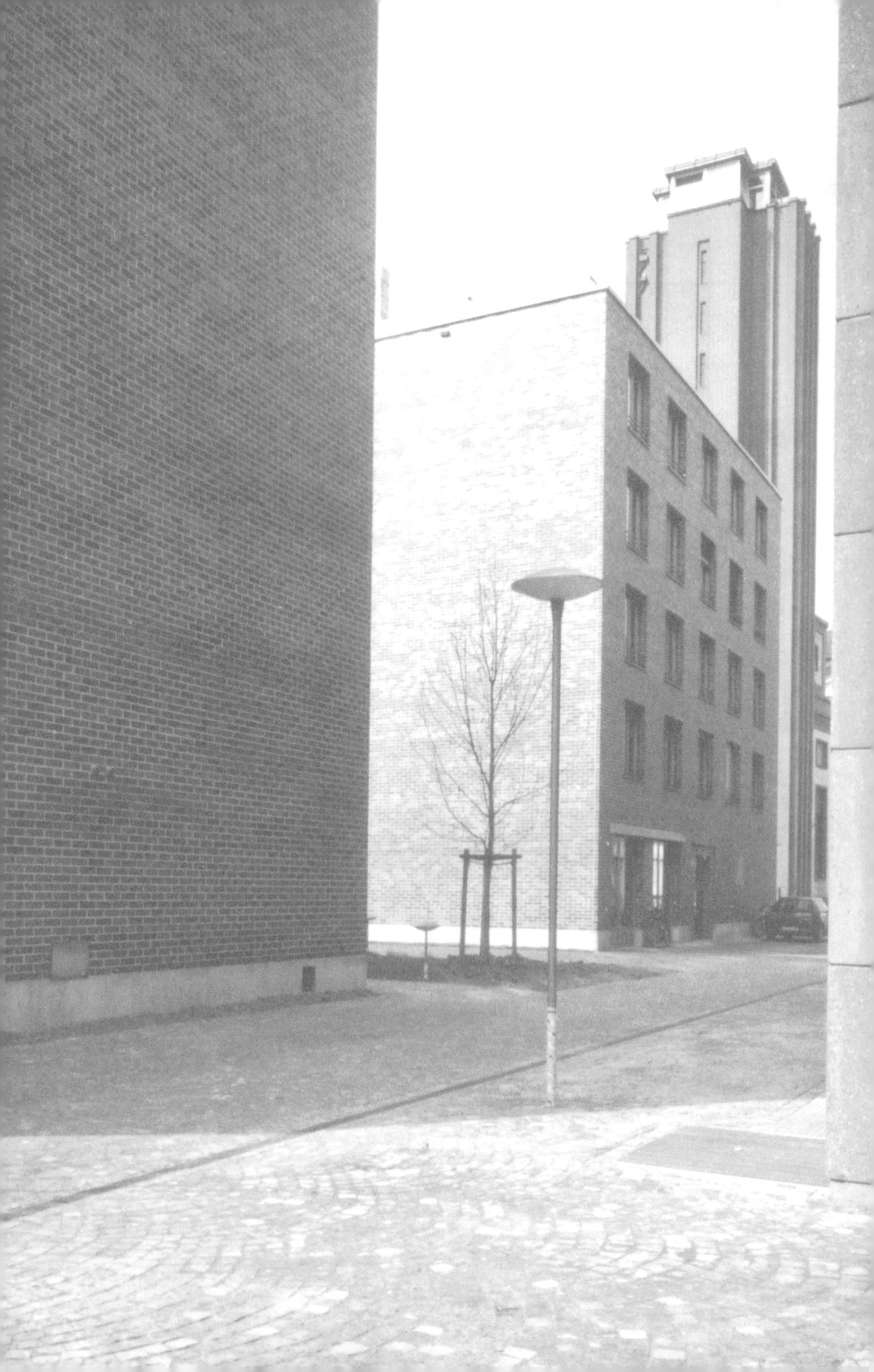

Diener & Diener
Housing and Office Buildings
Warteck Brewery, Basel
Project 1991–93,
Realisation 1994–96

At the Warteck Brewery, Diener & Diener oversaw the change of an entire urban block from light industry to residential and cultural use. Almost two decades of building experience lie behind this project, which represents a mature stage in Diener & Diener's urban-oriented output. Much of this work consists of housing and commercial premises, the largely inconspicuous yet omnipresent buildings that make up a city. Two intertwined issues are examined here: firstly, the overlap of interests and conflicts typically arising in an urban situation, especially with regard to regeneration; and secondly, the manner in which the architect's professional position informed the scheme in its practical and political context.

About Basel
Among Switzerland's cities, Basel preserves more than others the character of a city republic, distinct from the rest of the territory. This cultural feature is supported by an exceptional political situation: the canton Basel Stadt coincides with the commune, creating a powerful administrative apparatus. This small territory has attracted global industrial corporations, particularly in the domain of chemistry and pharmaceutics.

This situation is rooted in the city's history. Beneath the picturesque appearance of the medieval centre and the modern growth around it lie social and artistic infrastructures that make Basel unique. The bourgeois city, which Romain Rolland described in his novel *Jean-Christophe*, is still perceptible here: a place whose wealth is hidden behind an appearance of modesty and orderliness, whose hard-working, discreet elite wields considerable influence. Rolland's fictional portrait of turn-of-the-century Basel depicted

> an old town, full of intelligence and vitality, but also full of patrician pride, self-satisfied, and closed on itself. A bourgeois aristocracy with a taste for work and the higher culture, but narrow and pietistic, was quietly convinced of its own superiority […]. These influential houses, possessing fortunes generations old, felt no need to show off their wealth. […] Millionaires

dressed like humble shopkeepers, they spoke with their own raucous dialect, and went conscientiously to their offices every day of their lives.[1]

Rolland's description recalls his contemporary Max Weber's association of Protestant work ethic and capitalism, in which "the power of religious asceticism provided [...] sober, conscientious, and unusually industrious workmen".[2] Even a century later, Basel retains in its deeper cultural recesses much of Rolland's and Weber's society. Its eccentric position in Switzerland, closeness to Germany and France, and strategic position on the navigable portion of the Rhine have determined a particular historical development, from which its unique characteristics arise.

Perhaps Basel's most striking trait is the juxtaposition of a strong humanist tradition and a sophisticated bourgeois elite. Historically, the same wealthy families have long dominated the city's business and academic circles, with the result that economic and intellectual life remained close, even interdependent.[3] Art, collected for centuries as a sound investment, is still viewed as an economic as much as a cultural asset. The number and stature of Basel's art collections, outstanding for a city of its size, the grand scale of the annual art fair confirm this pragmatic understanding. Art is not only a spiritual means to achieve social well-being, but also a significant contributor to the city's wealth.

Basel is at the same time metropolitan and quaint, home to both the avant-garde and the conservatives. Its economic and cultural internationalism is underlined by rigid social structures. Lionel Gossman has seen here a "judicious mixture of principle and pragmatism, individual enterprise and social cohesion, adaptation to the new and fidelity to the old".[4]

The city's architecture reflects this oscillation between cosmopolitanism and conformity, openness and inwardness. More than art, the political status of architecture lays bare the tensions between individual creative impulse and responsibility to the common realm. Basel's *Stadtbildkommission* controls, as the name suggests, the image of Basel as an exemplary, design-conscious city. The *Kantonsbaumeister* (city architect) wields considerable power in determining which schemes get built and how.[5] The public is culturally informed and politically engaged. The local industrial giants use art and architecture to maintain a sophisticated, generous public façade. Urban strategies, while largely favourable to conservation, encourage new development. All this explains the high status that contemporary architecture enjoys here, but also its acute self-consciousness.

Backgrounds
Diener & Diener's buildings create a quiet yet impressive counterpoint to Basel's more assertive landmarks. They form much of the city's background, some blending in to the point of invisibility, others standing out on account of their highly

---

[1] Romain Rolland, *Jean-Christophe* (1903–1912), quoted in Gossman, 2000, p. 105.

[2] Max Weber, 2001, p. 120.

[3] Gossman, 1994, p. 67.

[4] Ibid., p. 92.

[5] Carl Fingerhuth, Basel *Kantonsbaumeister* from 1979 to 1992, supported the practices of Diener & Diener and Herzog & de Meuron (amongst others) at the crucial early stages of their careers.

composed elevations. These projects ambivalently function as both dwellings and architectural artefacts, individual statements of authorship and anonymous records of contemporary urban conditions. The engagement with modest but pervasive architectural programmes such as housing and commercial premises demonstrates an interest in the ordinary, social aspects of architecture. This is due both to Roger Diener's training and to the circumstances of his practice.

As a first-year student in ETH, Diener missed Hoesli's *Grundkurs* by opting instead for a pilot studio run by sociologist Hermann Zinn. He was introduced to architecture as a form of social research, for which street interviews were deemed more important than the project's formal resolution. Later on, in Luigi Snozzi's studio, Diener encountered a political, city-oriented stance parallel to Rossi's typological research. Students were encouraged to see themselves as "critical responsible beings capable of political thought and action".[6] Snozzi taught design as a means to understand reality and articulate a political urban sphere:

> Architecture is closely linked to social life and, at the same time, to nature. Fundamentally, it is a universal, permanent collective fact, of which the most advanced expression is the city, a natural part of man. The city, seen as an expression of history in form, becomes the principal point of reference for all design.[7]

Snozzi's understanding of architecture subverted its autonomy; social and cultural patterns were translated into form. The focus was not so much on buildings as objects, but on their meaningful engagement with their situation. This attitude remains clearly imprinted on Diener's own design work, in which "the object, the building, is no longer the focus. [...] Rather, the issue is one of recreating within the context of a specific site (*territorium*) a design in which values that guarantee human existence are exposed".[8]

If Diener's training is one determining factor, the other is his orientation in practice. Having joined in 1976 the office established in 1942 by his father, Marcus Diener, Roger Diener gained early access to medium and large-scale urban projects. Despite their intrinsic modesty his early designs, primarily urban housing and commercial schemes, were received by critics as radical works, attuned to the poetics of the ordinary.[9]

This programmatic orientation has developed in Diener's practice a particular sensitivity towards the anonymous. It is significant that the work is usually presented as a collective output of several long-term collaborators, under the umbrella name of Diener & Diener.[10] This shared dimension shifts focus from individual authors to what they have in common. The decisions are jointly deliberated, and the resulting buildings convey a level of common experience.[11] This architecture displays political and urban

6 Snozzi quoted in Diener, 1994, pp. 25–31.

7 Ibid., p. 27.

8 Ibid., p. 25.

9 See Diener and Diener, 1987.

10 Notable long-term collaborators before 1993 included Wolfgang Schett, Dieter Righetti, Jens Erb and Andreas Rüedi.

11 Diener and Righetti, 1991, pp. 71–72.

ambitions, representing collective rather than individual creative interests. Its statement of intent has been the creation of backgrounds for events, rather than eventful objects.

Negotiations: project history

The Warteckhof project should be seen as a manifestation of this ethical substrate. The site is located north of the Rhine in Kleinbasel, the more working-class, culturally diverse part of the city. Its history is tied to that of the local Warteck Brewery, set up in 1870.[12] The plant, completed in 1938, had grown as an insular conglomeration of industrial and commercial buildings, in contrast to the conventional nineteenth-century perimeter blocks to the west of it. Its chimney and water tower, engraved on the city skyline, became a Basel landmark.

After the brewery's closure in 1991, the site was intended for change of use, with partial demolition and the addition of residential buildings. A first scheme, developed by architect-contractors Suter + Suter as a perimeter-block masterplan, encountered strong public opposition and brought about the listing of several existing buildings. The second scheme, by Diener & Diener, replaced the perimeter organisation with a series of distinct objects within the depth of the plot. The plan added two substantial developments to the listed buildings, one commercial and the other residential. The existing industrial buildings were fitted as an applied-arts cooperative, a shrewd gesture supported by authorities and local community alike.

To compensate for the cultural use, the developers densified the rest of the site. The project's variations between 1991 and 1993, in which the office building became more compact and the housing layout denser, highlight a juxtaposition of interests – the developer's search for profit, the conservationists' concern for the industrial patrimony, the city's social and cultural ambitions, the community's resistance to change. This multiplicity of claims could not be sustained by the perimeter block solution requested by the urban development plan. Diener & Diener's proposal for an insular arrangement had to be submitted for local parliamentary approval as well as to the public vote, obtaining the final go-ahead at the end of 1993.

These protracted negotiations illustrate a political flexibility rooted in pragmatism. To a foreigner's eye it seems remarkable that the scheme was allowed to transcend planning stipulations, demonstrating the appropriateness of a different approach in its specific conditions. Warteckhof also illustrates how political, cultural and economic negotiations helped crystallize the architectural scheme. The interplay between artistic coherence and social relevance confirms Diener's declared trust in the competence and maturity of public decisions.

The concern with complex urban conditions and the resistance to unilateral solutions reflect a realist attitude. There seems to be an overlap between the interest in real conditions, the practice's

---

12   See Jenzer Bieri, 2007.

(Top) Diener & Diener,
Administration Building, Hochstrasse,
Basel, 1985–86

(Middle) Diener & Diener,
Apartment Building, Elsässerstrasse 57,
Basel, 1996–97

(Bottom) Diener & Diener,
Office Building, Kohlenberg,
Basel 1992–95

expertise in social housing, and its support in left-wing circles:

> We [Diener & Diener] are on the shopping list of socialist planners. We are not the first choice in the search for the 'Praline', that one beautiful building. […] We are always concerned with the complex region of the city. I guess our political links lead towards this type of urban issue.[13]

13 Diener, 2005.

Here, politics are shown as the fundamental ground of architectural endeavour. Thus constituted, the urban background constitutes a perceptible dimension of collective will. Architecture seeks a wider relevance than any "praline", or aesthetic accomplishment, could achieve by itself. It is therefore a contradiction that this idealistic proposition has become associated with a brand. Inevitably, Diener & Diener's work has acquired value on an international market animated by private interests rather than social principles. Nevertheless, their architectural output steers away from this situation through an assessment of reality as arising from practical processes.

Towards "the general form"

Diener & Diener's approach has been sustained by an evolving intellectual and theoretical framework. The early buildings, like Hammerstrasse (1978–81) and Burgfelderplatz (1982–85), reflected the different aspects of their sites: their façades mirrored their context, resulting in an overall heterogeneous appearance. In the heyday of Postmodernism, these projects reflected a vision of the city as a collage of fragments.[14] Later buildings at St. Alban-Tal (1985–86) and Picassoplatz (1987–93) illustrate an increasingly comprehensive reading of context, as if the site extended from the immediate urban topography to the city as a whole. This has resulted in the buildings' unified appearance and a growing tendency towards more anonymous physiognomies. According to Diener, "urban architecture should tend towards an expression open to various uses. For design, this generalisation means a renunciation of narrow typology".[15] As many of the projects are for mixed or speculative use, the notion of typology invoked here is morphological rather than functional – in other words, a matter of form.

14 Steinmann, 1991, p. 26.

15 Diener and Righetti, 1991, p. 77.

Martin Steinmann has articulated how important "the general form" is to Diener & Diener's work.[16] As direct site references are subsumed under the building's neutral expression, the appearance of "general forms" veers towards abstraction. The retreat from context-related gestures implies in this work a conscious level of autonomy: "we attempt to create a certain distance from the place by giving our buildings a more general form".[17] The search for general representations of an urban essence renders the buildings familiar, yet detached, ghost-like, with a deadpan expression against the everyday bustle.

16 A long-term personal and working relationship with Diener & Diener has allowed Steinmann to become a critical spokesperson for the practice. I use Steinmann's comments on Diener & Diener's work as equivalent to their own, as they often arise in conversations between them.

17 Diener and Righetti, 1991, p. 77.

This level of generalisation can render the building unobtrusive, simply a background for everyday events. At the same time,

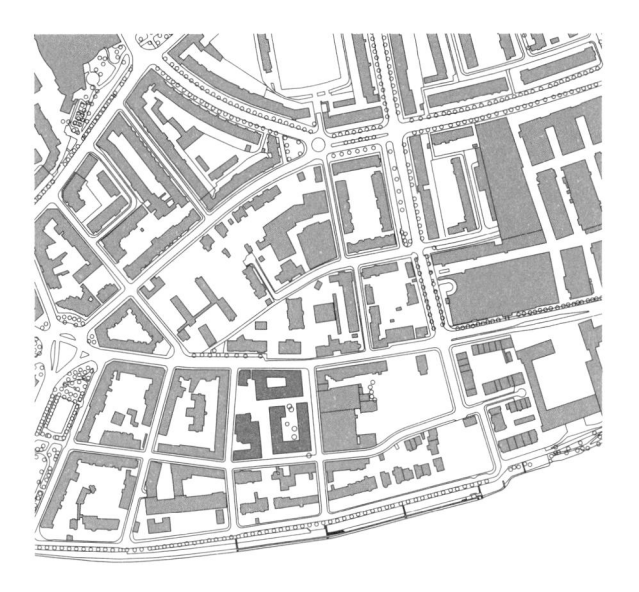

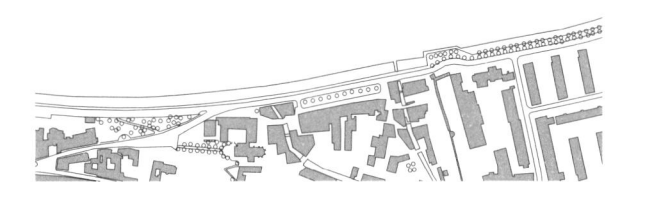

(Top left) Diener & Diener, Warteck,
Basel 1992–96. Site plan as built

(Above) Diener & Diener, Apartment
Buildings, St. Alban-Tal, Basel 1985–86

(Middle) Diener & Diener, Administration
Building, Picassoplatz, Basel 1987–93

(Bottom) Diener & Diener,
Apartment Buildings, Hammerstrasse,
Basel 1978–81

it impacts on its visibility as an architectural statement. The withdrawal into neutral expression therefore requires compensation: firstly, through the introduction of subtle yet definite authorial gestures, like the precise composition and proportioning of elevations; and secondly, through the creation of meaningful relations between buildings.[18]

The interest in planning and urban strategy confronts here the interest in buildings as autonomous elements within the city. Diener's understanding of planning is intrinsically architectural: "town planning attains its essence in those situations when it can bring a place into order with one house".[19] The acknowledgement of current economic and social fragmentation means that urban order is seen as a function of buildings and relations between them. Steinmann has coined the term "constellations" to denote these relational configurations of buildings.[20]

The notion of constellation is partly aesthetic, partly pragmatic, considering buildings as inhabitable environments. This explains Diener's oscillation between abstract notions like type or urban form and the concreteness of "houses", defined as "that which is general, […] that which is urban".[21] Diener has re-focused the work from theoretical abstractions to "things that are as normal as the 'house', and thus, as concrete, linked with experiences we have made from these things".[22] This conforms, roughly, to the passage from type to model represented in Rossi's "analogous architecture".

From the house to the city

The notion of "constellation", in the sense used by Steinmann, implies the reciprocity between houses and the spaces they demarcate. The Warteckhof project is such a "constellation". The block consists of four distinct elements, two existing buildings and two new. Within the open block, each has its defined character, while belonging at the same time to a larger composition, determined by its shape and position in relation to the others. The overall arrangement, reinforced by August Künzel's landscaping, defines spaces of movement and pause, outside rooms and corridors, protected corners for encounter and openings towards the ensemble. The composition is indebted to the distinction, characteristic of modernist planning, between solids and voids and circulation and green spaces.

Like a portrait that reveals the sitter's hidden traits, the scheme identifies and exacerbates the character of the neighbourhood. It renders visible a century-long transition between closed perimeter blocks, typical of the nineteenth-century city centre, and the peripheral fragmentation of twentieth-century developments. Within the block, the new buildings appear themselves as miniature representations of closed perimeter buildings. At the same time, discreet passageways lead inside the block to a network of possible through-routes, leading to a correspondence between the interior and exterior of the site.

---

18 See Diener and Steinmann, 1995.

19 Steinmann, 1995, p. 10.

20 Ibid., pp. 12–14.

21 Ibid., p. 14.

22 Ibid.

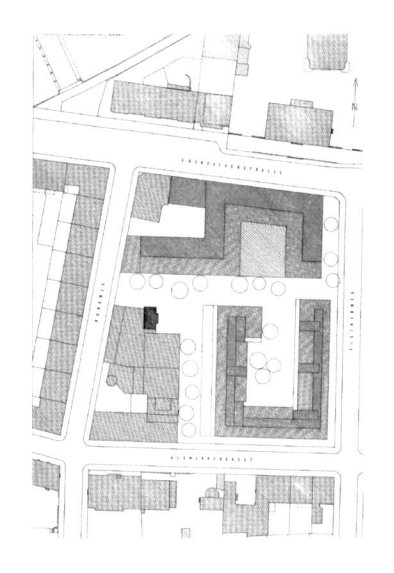

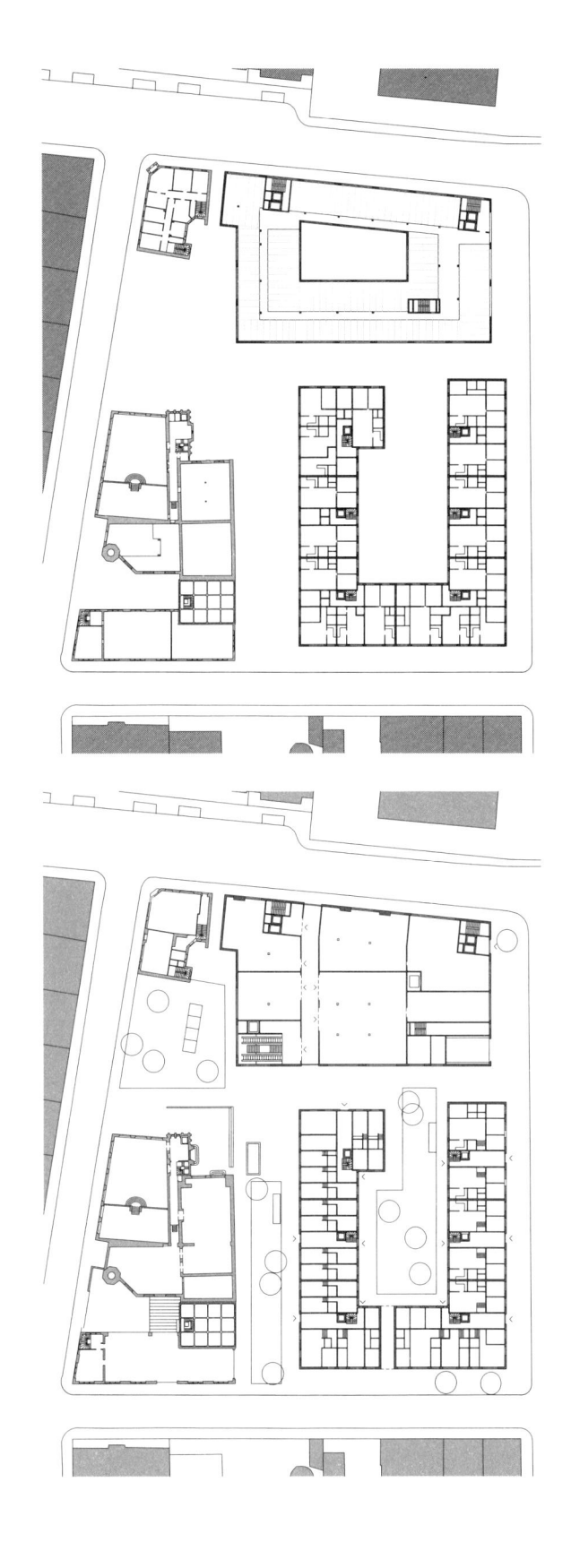

(Top left) Diener & Diener. Warteck,
Basel 1992–96. Site plan, project 1991

(Top right) Diener & Diener. Warteck,
Basel 1992–96. General plan, typical
floor as built

(Bottom right) Diener & Diener. Warteck,
Basel 1992–96. General plan, ground
floor as built

23   Diener and Steinmann, 1995, p. 64.

The correlation between building and city is primarily formal. The architects extracted from the original brewery the principle of "layering of large volumes and their differentiation with facing masonry".[23] This was then applied to the new buildings, determining a composition across the site in which access and views are manipulated to suggest densification. Both new buildings are subject to discreet formal adjustments, which override the internal logic of the plans to develop relations with the surroundings. Subtle variations from the typical U-shape give the apartment building a courtyard, both sheltered from and open to the rest of the block. The offices' geometry is slightly distorted to align with the street; a small projecting wing extends towards the listed corner building, visually implying a continuous street front. These small and tentative gestures, which in another context would seem disconcerting, are highly intentional and raise the plan to the level of aesthetic composition.

The visual layering of volumes, the mixture of old and new, and the framing of views are all compositional devices associated with the Picturesque. The discreet breaks from regularity, subliminal in actual experience, aim to recreate the typical effects of urban transformation. However, rather than being left as diachronic residues of piecemeal growth, they are brought together in a synchronic whole. Rather than the product of casualness or pragmatism, the new configurations are meant to convey architectural unity.

The dialectics of convention
We have seen how, in Warteckhof's overall plan, the use of simple volumes is counterbalanced by a refined relational composition. The same strategy of generality and difference extends to the use of materials and constructional techniques. Ordinariness is only the point of departure – conventions are only adopted in order to be adapted. What is familiar or appropriate in terms of its wider urban relevance doubles up as a subtle affirmation of artistic individuality. Thus the project is grounded in a dialectics of collective intelligibility and individual gesture, of typical objects and exceptional design – one could say, a dialectics of convention.

This is perhaps most apparent in the contrast between the two new buildings. They dominate the site and engender a vivid typological dialogue, into which the older buildings only marginally intrude. Their programmatic complementarity of housing and office is represented at the level of morphology (closed and open), materials (concrete and brick), and physiognomy (free and grid façade).

At a morphological level, the apartment building approximates an elongated quadrangle with one side removed, surrounding a planted courtyard. In contrast, the deep plan of the office building conceals an internal courtyard at first floor level. This *hortus conclusus* is inward-looking, a planted surface that doesn't detract from its primary role of bringing light and air into the building's core.

(Top) Warteck Brewery before development

(Bottom) Diener & Diener. Warteck,
Basel 1992–96. View within the block

The contrast between the two types is set up by the façades' materiality and tectonic expression. The office block recalls the "general" image of the modernist commercial façade, a leitmotif of Diener's work in Basel. It is clad in grey-green concrete blocks similar to the Fides Building (1988–90), where a conventional cladding system had its panels staggered to convey a self-supporting status.[24] The apartment building is clad in red engineering brick, in tribute to the old factory complex. Chosen for their lack of expressive texture, these materials deflect attention from themselves to allude to the bourgeois industrial city. The tonal complementarity of greenish concrete and reddish brick amounts to a metaphorical grey, the grey once identified by Heinrich Tessenow as the colour of town.[25]

The recourse to precise but ordinary construction techniques and materials renders the work contextual, both in the narrow sense of relating to block, street, neighbourhood, but also in terms of its capacity to evoke the city through the adherence to general types. At the same time, the neutral façades present themselves as abstractions of the convention. They are familiar, yet different – a condition that sets them apart.

The buildings' complementarity extends to their façades. The residential elevations are treated as matrices of openings, their varying widths articulating the difference between rooms. Thus the apartment layouts are almost readable on the façade. In contrast, on the office façade the regulating order is horizontal. The windows are expressed as narrow strips, their staggered arrangement akin to a brick bond. The centrifugal movement that results is witness to the speculative, open plan behind the façade. The difference in treatment implies programmatic differences: the fluidity of commercial rental space as opposed to the ordered seriality of stacked flats. And yet, both types refer to façades that are anonymous and ubiquitous in the city.

This neutrality follows an early modernist principle, advocating restraint for the sake of urban decorum.[26] At the interface between collective and individual realms, façades are understood as primary vehicles for conveying generality:

> The traditional aspect of façades – walls punctuated by windows – remains a determining element. […] It is not a question of evoking specific meanings through the material and its use; instead the outside wall must drive home the primordial aspect of the building, putting it in touch with the urban space. In the best case scenario the façade seems so obvious and discreet that it can be said to belong just as much to the city as to the building.[27]

One can identify in these words an appeal to timelessness, implied in the appeal to the "primordial" building. And yet, the façades are embedded in the historically specific imagery of

---

24 Diener and Righetti, 1991, p. 75.

25 Steinmann, 1995, p. 14.

26 Adolf Loos: "The house should be discreet on the outside, its entire richness should be disclosed on the inside" (*Vernacular Art*, 1914). Heinrich Tessenow: "Externally, we cannot be general enough" (*Die äussere Farbe unserer Häuser*, 1925).

27 Diener quoted in Lucan, 2001, p. 38.

the industrial city. The brick façade has two points of reference, the neo-classical apartment building and the modern factory. The wall-to-window ratio creates a tectonic ambivalence between masonry and concrete frame, nineteenth-century and modern constructional conventions.

Through formal reduction and a minimum of incident, Diener's work seeks to achieve a "synthetic image" of the city.[28] The Warteck elevations pertain to continuity with the urban realm; and yet, their rhythms and proportions create a systematic skin wrapped around the volumes. They suggest the concern with an abstract version of city, less responsive to the actual demands of orientation or differentiations between front and back.[29] The shifting windows and proportional variations are poised halfway between casual features and deliberate gestures. All variations are sufficiently subtle to preserve the intrinsic typological familiarity of these elevations. Nevertheless, their laconic expression remains ambivalently poised between convention and its transgression.

Normative dwelling

According to the architect's description, the apartment plans were "strictly laid out according to the regulations for subsidised housing".[30] The project offers a clear example of the normative being adapted to an architectural aesthetic concept. The picturesque composition of the overall footprint is counterbalanced by the disciplined apartment layouts. Regulations provide the objective basis that justifies the extent of compositional manoeuvres, the defining parameter of internal organisation.

To what extent this statutory order is advantageous is open to discussion. The same housing regulations became the basis for providing the minimum necessary when, under commercial pressures, the number of flats had to be increased. The earlier scheme (1991) displayed a different clarity of plan, with respect both to apartment layouts and structural efficiency. A median core of services, including lifts, ran along the entire length of the plan, determining inside the flats the separation of private rooms facing the courtyard and living areas facing the street. Generous circulation cores were placed in each corner of the quadrangle, and continuous balconies provided on the west and south-facing elevations.

The 1993 scheme lost, along with the external galleries, some of this initial ordering. The internal layout is more irregular, but not in a deliberate or picturesque manner. The cores, at almost half the original size, are less evenly distributed and the staircase configurations appear compromised. The bedrooms are now aligned to face north and east, rather than opening on to the quiet courtyard. Having lost the defined core of services separating the public and private rooms, the flat layouts became dependent on the introduction of in-built furniture modules to define the different territories.

---

28 Steinmann, 1995, p. 14.

29 This condition is specific to Warteck, in response perhaps to the buildings' need for self-definition in the spatial continuum of the block. Earlier Diener & Diener buildings, for example the housing projects at Hammerstrasse and Riehenring, respond to different site conditions with typologically different elevations at the front and back.

30 Diamond and Wang, 1992, p. 102.

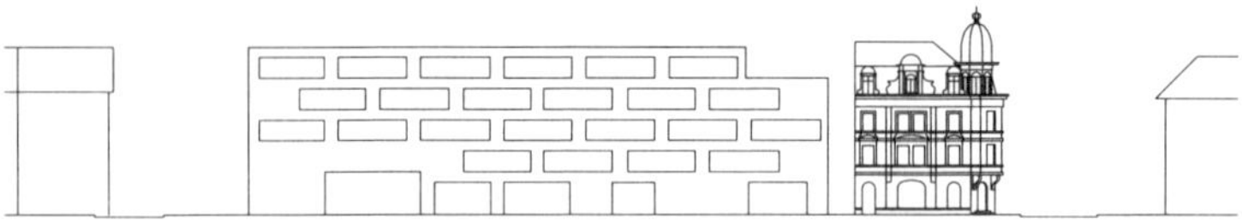

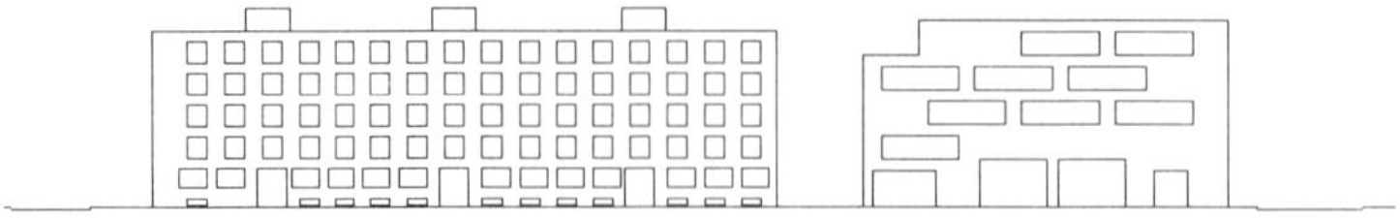

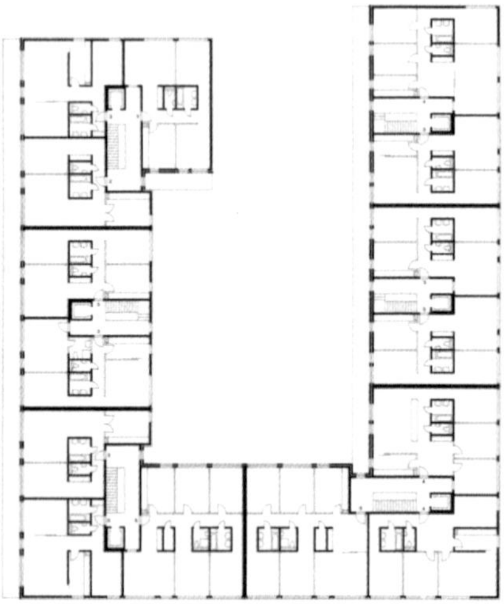

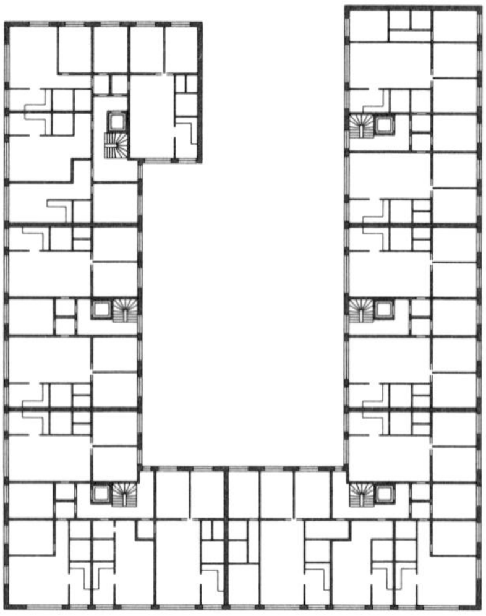

(Opposite top left) Diener & Diener.
Warteck, Basel 1992–96. Elevations

(Opposite middle right) Diener & Diener.
Warteck, Basel 1992–96. Plan, apartment
building, project 1991

(Opposite right) Diener & Diener. Warteck,
Basel 1992–96. Plan, apartment building,
project as built

(Above) Diener & Diener. Warteck,
Basel 1992–96. Façade of the
apartment building

These are small changes in the overall scheme, and the sense of compromise is muted. Nevertheless it is notable that the design aspect most affected here is the internal quality of private and common residential areas. While intended to safeguard standards, housing regulations can also represent the legal obligations for minimum acceptable provisions against which profit, rather than design, may be measured.

The appeal to housing regulations entails a balance between idealism, market realism and social welfare. This work references the modernist principles that governed the emancipation of the working classes. The principles of *Existenzminimum* form a rationalisation programme, covering everything from hygiene requirements to the restoration of human dignity. For Hannes Meyer, regulations represented the basis of societal order:

> The ABCs of socialist architecture in a planned economy are composed of norms, types and standards. We normalise dimensional requirements to typical space and typical equipment. We organize these typical elements as standard organic building entities for the socialist praxis of life.[31]

31 Hannes Meyer, "Über marxistische Architektur" (1931) quoted in Hays, 1992, p. 104.

In building the city from the apartment upwards, Modernism brought about the inversion of an urban order traditionally centred on public and sacred institutions. As the private unit became a "temple", so collective urban order gave way to an aggregate of individual aspirations. Later on this programme became statutory, and its potency as an avant-garde political ideal downgraded to a routine obligation. By invoking the regulatory power of statute, Diener re-enacts the modernist inversion of the traditional architectonic order.

Regulations serve to place architectural gestures under the control of a common order; the withdrawal from individual manipulation legitimises the built form. In this respect, the move is not so different from Zumthor's decision to follow the perimeter walls of existing Roman ruins in order to create their protective enclosure. This strategy relies on an order already inscribed in the project's situation to arrive at its final physiognomy, although both projects later depart from this primary determination of form. If, for Zumthor, authorship is established through the tectonic resolution of the buildings' skin, for Diener it is located elsewhere: in determining specific urban strategies, spatial relationships between buildings or between openings on the façade. However different, the two approaches converge on a belief in external appearance. The strategy of manipulating typological conventions constitutes a creative statement; the individual buildings represent both the general rule and its transformation.

Diener & Diener. Office Building,
Kohlenberg, Basel 1978–81. Interior

Between autonomy and participation

Warteck re-articulates a modernist leitmotif, the dialectical tension between individual creative gesture and deference to collective norms. The urban block is conceived as a miniature town, in which buildings stand in for general types. The architecture openly acknowledges the "reality of the construction site" and the urban policies shaping the everyday. At the same time, the compositional control exercised over both plan and elevations suggests that the ultimate aim is not full participation in urban anonymity, but differentiation from it.[32] The building's elevated status is made apparent in its laconic expression.

For Diener, "reduction means limiting ourselves to the few things that are necessary [in order] to control the effect of the spaces".[33] This interest is present even where all other tools of authorial emancipation are discarded: "there is often nothing left in our architecture except spatial effect".[34] The architecture tries to preserve its collective intelligibility (an ethical orientation), while articulating an artistic statement of individuality.

The collective dimension is preserved through the interest in types understood as general forms. Diener's discourse refers to types in the modernist sense of *objet-types*: objects or configurations that invoke universal values through form, independently of their practical context. Types are seen to represent "fundamental human experiences: the vertical window, the horizontal window, the door – they all relate to people".[35] At the same time, types are available as a formal repository modulated through variation. The work resorts to a field of types – door-type, window-type, cladding-type – that can be accessed and imported at will.

This application suggests that type is primarily understood as form. The architecture proposes a conception of order in which life is measured metrically, and practice is translated through geometry. The systematic façades demonstrate this displacement from dwelling to formal consistency. The universal experience of wall-with-windows is formulated as a gridded skin, an all-over field of openings unresponsive to the different aspects of the site, which sets the buildings apart as objects.

Since the mid-1980s Diener & Diener's buildings have been photographed as empty rooms, examining the windows as types projected against the city. This kind of study reinforces the view that the universal experience of dwelling is interpreted formally. "We apprehend a room thus represented", Diener wrote, "as we would a character in a neo-realist painting: for example we recognise the city dweller, who through the type he embodies illustrates several characteristics of his existential condition. These traits convey an independent message. His personality is on another level of perception than the one available to us".[36]

Such studies of empty walls extract the general from the particular and avoid narrative content, declaring a melancholy

[32] See for example Diener and Righetti, 1991, p. 75.

[33] Ibid., p. 77.

[34] Ibid.

[35] Ibid., p. 78.

[36] Diener, 1989, p. 38–39.

Diener & Diener, Warteck,
Basel 1992–96. Interior

[37] See Diener and Diener, 1987, pp. 93–98; Barbey and Diener, 1989, pp. 65–73; Carrard, Diener, and Dubuis, 1998, pp. 52–63.

condition. They imply a sense of isolation, perhaps the result of representing the city through framed, fragmented views.[37] At the same time, the rooms corresponding to these windows are less examined. Are they empty, white rectangles of space? Default solutions rising from regulations and building constraints? Too modest to be scrutinised by architects and critics? It is not clear whether views of the furnished rooms, filled with bourgeois memorabilia and kids' toys, are perceived to be invasive of privacy, or aesthetically compromised. Would they prove a reality of occupation misaligned with the architect's taste and the city's control over its public image?

Warteck represents a modern urban condition, according to which the inhabitants' private lives are kept beneath quasi-regimented façades. The overall regularity makes it part of the city, responding to a demand for dignified and appropriate dwellings. The geometrical composition of width variations or window placements is an ambiguous recognition of the inhabitants' individuality. Like the city, the buildings are shaped by the polarity of collective decorum versus personal emancipation.

The town's responsibility to provide decent homes, the architect's ambitions for emancipatory dwellings, the political and economic process through which they are provided – all these have created a mixture of laws and rights, responsibility and concern, economy and notions of home, individual values and market generalities. Under these conditions the apartment has become the *locus* of several layers of reality, some related to spiritual values, others to economic aspirations. Such realities impact upon the nature of home and the modalities of its decorum. From everyday issues of maintenance and cohabitation (cleanliness, parking or storage) these modalities can be extended to neighbourly relations, social calls, estate administration and childcare provisions, which qualify modes of life in Basel and contemporary urban Switzerland.

Warteck's problematic cannot be easily redressed in design. The dialectic of convention and innovation, poised between abstract city and actual house, represents perhaps the most potent form of negotiation between architectural autonomy and the claims of context. It reveals the limits, but also the potential of architecture in the tangle of social aspirations and market interests, preservation and development, which make up the post-industrial European city.

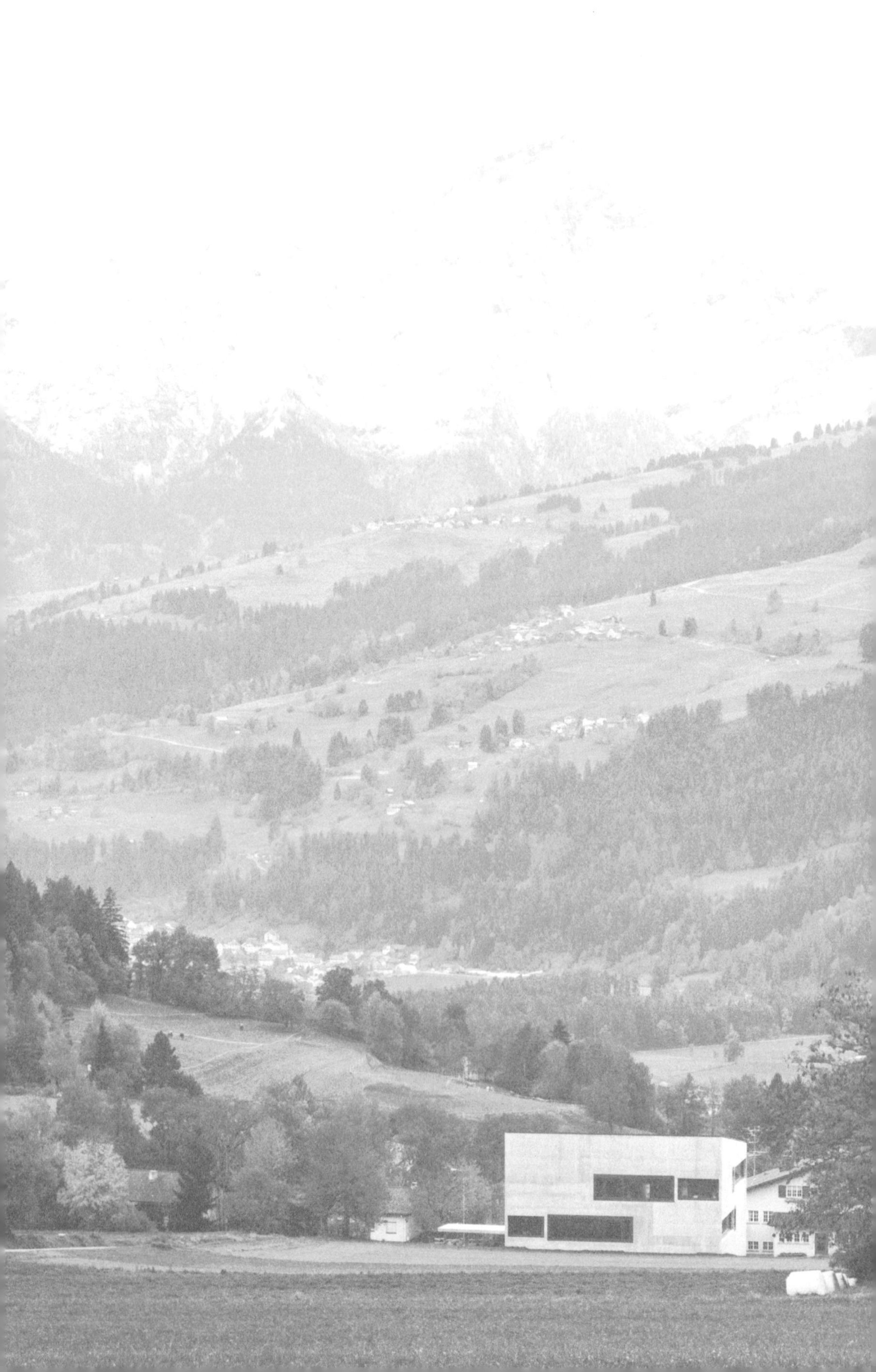

Valerio Olgiati
School Extension
Paspels, Graubünden
1996–98

This small school building, located in a remote mountain village, illustrates a similar tension between architecture as an individual artistic statement and as container of collective meaning. A freestanding concrete cube, set in a sloping field above the village, the building bears no relation to the local vernacular. It seems intended for a figure-ground composition with the Alpine landscape. This presupposes an architectural autonomy that is, nevertheless, undercut by its role as a functioning school.

This school extension (widely referred to as the Paspels School) represents both a communal institution and an architectural destination. It is accessible to occasional visitors, yet without openly catering for them. The locals are ambivalent towards the professional interest provoked by their school. They are partly proud of it, partly indifferent to all the fuss. The building has been preserved since completion in almost pristine condition, as stark and uncluttered as envisaged by the architect at design stages. This raises questions regarding its status in its cultural setting. Is this sense of preservation due to the locals' respect for their own institutional asset, or to its outstanding architectural status? Is this building primarily a school or a monument, and if the latter, what kind of monument? The present case study aims to address this cultural questioning.

Valerio Olgiati (b. 1958) grew up in nearby Flims, and moved his practice back there a few years after the Paspels School had been completed. Son of architect Rudolf Olgiati, he was trained in the ETH *Analoge Architektur* studio alongside Andrea Deplazes, Christian Kerez and Quintus Miller, amongst several significant others. Partially affected by analogue theory, Olgiati nevertheless departed from it in radical ways, so his work cannot be assessed in relation to it. His formal status as local Graubünden architect is equally misleading, even though it was a precondition for taking part in the Paspels architectural competition. Olgiati works and teaches worldwide, and even his local buildings reflect a strong international outlook.

The Paspels School, Olgiati's first significant building, established the autonomous level to which he has adhered since. The conceptual discipline that organises this institution, and which determines its object-like qualities, will form the bulk of this examination. However, the project's circumstances highlight its actual dependence on a concrete practical context.

The setting

Swiss school architecture embodies a mixture of civic and artistic ambitions. Switzerland's educational values are grounded in an enlightened rationalist tradition, postulated by Jean-Jacques Rousseau and Johann Heinrich Pestalozzi and later upheld by Jacob Burckhardt. Educational tendencies are identifiable in the Swiss literary heritage, through the key figures of Gottfried Keller and Friedrich Dürrenmatt.[1]

At a political level, education was a primary aim of the 1848 Confederation; the Polytechnikum, the first grand Swiss institution, was conceived as a symbol of national unity. On the other hand, the emphasis on communal autonomy has led to a decentralised educational system. Federal stipends for building schools are managed at communal level, and the architectural competition system supports a situation where the communities' cultural aspirations are met by the architects' professional ones.

In Graubünden, where the topography makes architectural efforts all the more compelling, there was a significant investment in school building in the 1980s and 1990s. Schools were seen as a kind of secular chapels, each new project a typical manifestation of a genre and at the same time unique in itself.[2] The school in Paspels stands out from this production, partly due to the architect's unwillingness to compromise and partly because of the locals' tolerance of its artistic ambition. Olgiati has acknowledged that the project's circumstances were acutely dependent on "certain constellations in Paspels, on the people who supported it politically, in the [competition] jury and later on".[3] Indeed, despite the regional proliferation of modern schools, this building's acceptance in the sub-Alpine rural community is little short of a cultural miracle.[4]

Situated in the Domleschg valley, Paspels is a small dispersed village surrounded by cultivated lands. Historically the inhabitants were farmers, but in the last hundred years many of them took seasonal employment in the Alpine tourist industry. Cantonal industrialisation generated new jobs and brought a sense of stability besides affluence. Although Paspel's population has increased overall, urban attraction is keenly felt and farming is in decline. These conditions account for the inhabitants' quasi-urban "open-mindedness", and their tolerance towards religious and cultural differences.[5]

Paspels is the only educational provider in the valley. Its school complex, dating back to 1940, was expanded in the 1980s. In 1996, anticipating an increase in student numbers, the commune organised a competition for an extension to the school precinct. The site was located at the north end of the village, on a plot facing the existing school buildings and surrounded on three

---

1 See Sorell, 1972, pp. 23–31.

2 For example, Bearth and Deplazes's schools in Alvaschein (1991), Tschlin (1993), Malix (1994), Vella (1997–1998), and Zillis (1999); Jüngling and Hagmann's school in Mastrils (1992–1993); Conradin Clavuot's school in St. Peter (1994–1998) and Gion A. Caminada's school in Duvin (1995).

3 Olgiati, Interview 2006.

4 See Tewsen, 1999.

5 Ibid., p. 2.

(Above) Valerio Olgiati. School, Paspels, 1996–98. View from north-west

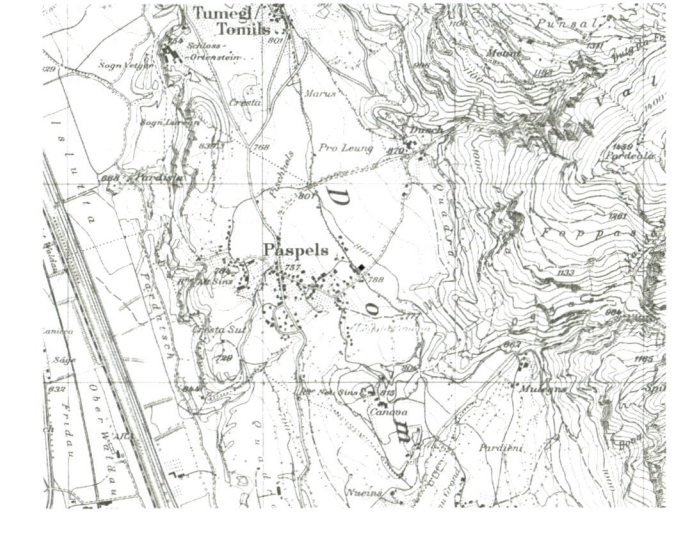

(Right) Valerio Olgiati. School, Paspels, 1996–98. Site plan

sides by agricultural land. The marginal position assigned the extension to the cultivated fields rather than to the settlement.

This final condition was fully exploited by the winning project, conceived as a singular volume in the landscape. While other competition entries had proposed low, sprawling schemes, Olgiati's scheme stood out as a three-storey compact cube, leaving much of the site untouched. Interestingly, its artistic merits – immediately grasped by the architects on the competition panel – were reinforced by the locals' more pragmatic considerations.[6] The commune's president, a farmer, valued the scheme for its economy of agricultural land.[7]

To an extent, the radical appearance of the winning scheme alarmed the community and it is probably due to the president's authority that the dissenting voices remained a minority. The controversy over the "style" of the new building brought to the surface dormant tensions between the Catholic and Protestant citizens, between conservatives and reformers.[8] One aspect that helped the project in the long run was its peripheral position, well away from the central village church. Ultimately the building gained public support for the same pragmatic reasons that had enabled its selection in the first place: its functionality, simplicity and careful use of land.

Another marker of the project's efficiency was its cost, which remained surprisingly low if one considers the expensive materials and exacting manner of its execution.[9] Early in the tendering process it emerged that, despite ambitious architectural specifications for polished in-situ concrete and solid bronze fittings, the costs remained average. This turned out to be a direct, if unintentional, consequence of the design. The building's compact volume meant that its external surface – the most expensive component – was smaller than for a lower, more elongated form. Thus the compactness that had appealed to jury and community alike was also responsible for maintaining the building within budget. This discovery impacted on Olgiati's formal tendencies, and many of his subsequent projects are variations on this theme of cubic volume.[10]

Finally, the scheme was also efficiently run at an administrative level. While subjected to communal scrutiny in the early stages, once past the popular vote the project was safeguarded against local interference. Client duties were delegated to one formidable individual, construction administrator Edwin Riedi. Riedi mediated between commune, canton and architect, ensuring that all stipulations were acted on quickly and decisively.

In conclusion, the existence of this remarkable building in Paspels is due to the particular configurations of the competition jury and client body. These unique circumstances serve to shed light on less specific themes: the empathy between architect and professional members of the jury, made possible at the level of a shared knowledge of ETH theory, and communal political

---

6   The jury included members of the Paspels administrative council and three local architects: Rudolf Fontana, Valentin Bearth and Beat Consoni. Although both Fontana (b. 1941) and Bearth (b. 1957) were trained at ETH, they belong to different architectural generations; Bearth was attuned to the issues of architectural autonomy through his diploma work with Dolf Schnebli (1983). His familiarity with the 1980 ETH theory allowed him to appreciate Olgiati's scheme on its own terms.

7   Tewsen, 1999, p. 2.

8   In this context, "reformer" is a historical term referring to the supporters of Graubünden's political reorganisation in the 1860s. Reformers were usually Protestant. For more information on the rapport between Protestants and Catholics in Graubünden see Barber, 1974, pp. 213–220.

9   Including professional fees, construction and fit-out, the school cost was precisely average among Graubünden schools built between 1996 and 2006. The total cost as indexed by the cantonal building department on 1 April 2006 was CHF 555 per m^3 (calculated to SIA norm 116).

10 Olgiati, Interview 2006.

organisation, assigning decisions to a minimum number of motivated and informed individuals.

Once the brief was satisfied, the points of agreement between commune and architect were limited to quantifiable elements – budget, area surfaces, and timetable. The question of beauty, in which communal interests meet authorial freedom, has remained meanwhile as mysterious to the Paspels citizens as to everyone else. Read against the Alpine backdrop, the school's abstract form represents the juxtaposition of distinct cultural outlooks. The project's essentially cosmopolitan aspects are read against a rural setting with conservative, traditionalist connotations.[11] The project reveals parallels with urban culture, but remains typical of its place, where the aspiration of constructional integrity is culturally embedded.

The School as autonomous unit

The building is conceived as an "indivisible whole" – a concrete cube in the landscape, roof sloping at the same angle as the ground.[12] In its physical context, its appearance seems dictated by private logic. The building's "obsession with totality" is first signalled on the elevations where two kinds of window openings shift position between floors, establishing a centrifugal motion and emphasising self-containment.[13] The entrance is the only exception to this dynamic composition, imposing a classical centrality. Its projecting concrete canopy and the doors, framed in heavy bronze, add a sense of ceremony.

Internally, the abstract concrete-lined hallways and familiar larch-lined classrooms are set in an intentional contrast. Their complementarity creates a closed system that is most clearly visible in plan. On the upper floors, the rooms are pushed into corners, defining a cross-shaped territory at the heart of the building. An office, smaller than the classrooms, allows one arm of the cross to widen out into a lobby opening outwards away from the village. The controlled positioning of elements and careful removal of detail give the interior a non-figurative, scale-less quality.

This central hall is the public focal point, a place assigned to the assembly of pupils. The large window frames views of cultivated land, the light changing with seasons and crops. The orientation towards nature emphasises the school's separation as a kind of private contemplative realm.

The overall conceptual unity is revealed through the complementarity of different elements, from the windows' typology and façade composition to the primary structure. The rooms are set within a clear perimeter boundary; they define the cruciform space at the centre of the building. The windows in the circulation spaces are flush on the outside, so as to provide seats on the inside; their ledges describe the wall's depth. The classroom windows, flush with the inside timber lining, describe the rooms' length, as if the plan were inscribed on the façades.

---

[11] Graubünden's responsiveness to contemporary architecture is discussed in the section "Construction culture in the Graubünden" (pp. 195–206).

[12] Olgiati, "School", 2006, p. 42.

[13] Bürkle, 1998, p. 68.

160

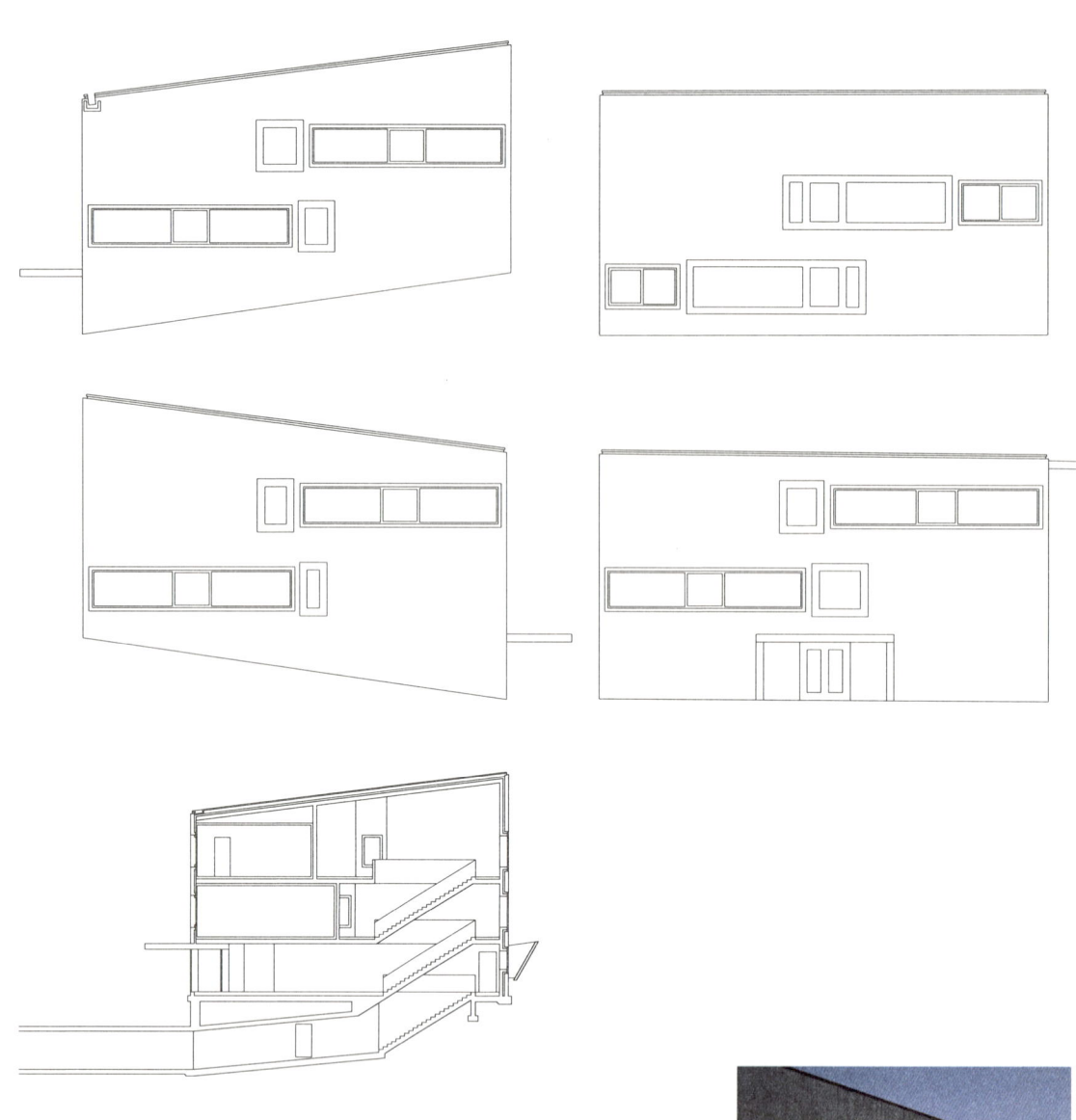

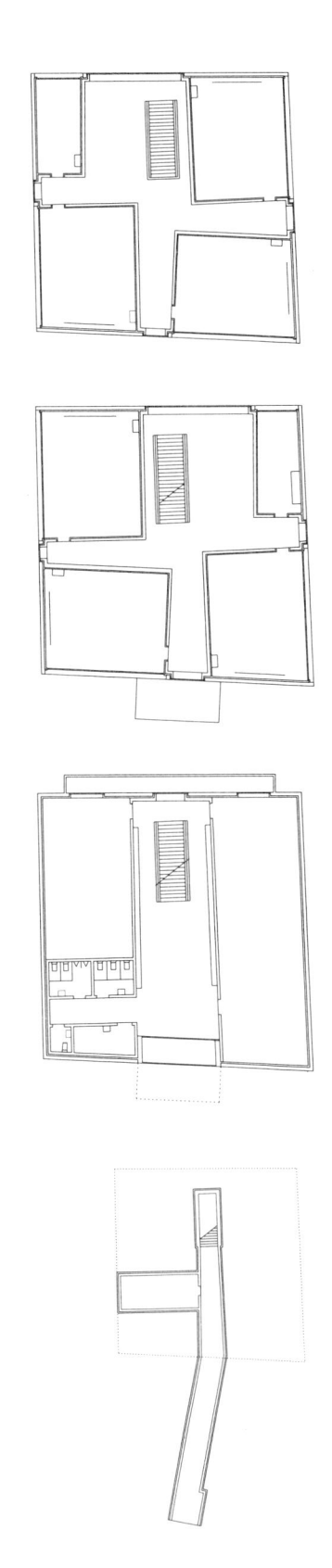

(Opposite top) Valerio Olgiati. School, Paspels, 1996–98. Elevations

(Opposite middle left) Valerio Olgiati. School, Paspels, 1996–98. Cross section showing the underground link to main school buildings

(Opposite bottom) Valerio Olgiati. School, Paspels, 1996–98. Entrance

(Right) Valerio Olgiati. School, Paspels, 1996–98. Floor plans

The structure is made of an outer shell and an inner system of walls and slabs that support each other. The drastic economy of means only allows a few elements for expression – the internal and external concrete surfaces, the timber-clad classrooms, the flush and the recessed windows. All these are tied up in the overall conceptual logic of the design, and reinforce its principles.

The result is not only volumetrically, but also conceptually compact. The only exception is the section, where the centric principle that governs the plans is upset by the underground connection to the old schoolhouse. While this tunnel was stipulated by the brief, its concealment under the ground suits the agenda of autonomy.

As a system of rooms grouped around an empty core, the plan betrays the need for a finite geometrical ordering. At the same time, its rational order is enriched by an irrational moment of deformation. The distortion of the perimeter has been informed not by site constraints, but by the author's dissatisfaction with the rigidity of the right angle. As a means of compensation, an intentionally arbitrary tug on the computer at one corner propagated inside the plan a general softening of angles.[14] The resulting spatial richness strips the corridors of an institutionalised reading, leading instead to mannerist perspective games. Thus the emphasis shifts from the conceptual reading of the plan to the building being experienced.

This need to counterbalance the rigidity of the rational concept with an irrational gesture recalls Rossi's appeal to analogical thought.[15] Having recognised the limits of conceptual ordering, the author has turned to pre-reflective experience as to a kind of meta-concept. The abandonment of orthogonality means that the standard functional and structural requirements were replaced with rules brought into play by a consistent plastic quality.

Conceptions of freedom

The building has been compared with a concrete "monolith", a boulder rolled down to the end of the village.[16] But to what extent is it actually monolithic? It is useful to note here Martin Tschanz's distinction between actual and allegorical monoliths, that is, between "a building like a stone that behaves like one" and one that only appears to do so:

> Monoliths in this [allegorical] sense are compact architectural objects which appear to be hermetic and reveal nothing of their content. They are stand-alone, often remote structures, […] objects without scale which have an imposing, characteristic, individual form […]. The design of the volume should suggest mass, which is mostly achieved by heightening a plastic deformation, preferably under the apparent influence of gravity or some other force.[17]

14 Ibid., p. 67.

15 For Rossi, analogical representation engenders a metaphorical type of deformation which, not unlike with the Paspels School, "affects the materials themselves and destroys their static image, stressing instead their elementality". See Rossi, 1996, p. 349.

16 Deplazes, 2005, p. 167.

17 Tschanz, 2005, p. 256.

(Top) Valerio Olgiati. School, Paspels, 1996–98. Typical classroom

(Right) Valerio Olgiati. School, Paspels, 1996–98. Interior lobby

At first glance, the Paspels School seems to adhere to the latter, representational category. Physically remote and materially homogeneous, the grey concrete cube could be a carved-out block. Nevertheless, this impression is contradicted by the modernist expression of the horizontal window openings. These *fenêtres en longueur* render the wall into which they are set as a membrane. Their shifting position reinforces the a-tectonic nature of the wall. The overall volume is indeed compact, but not heavy. The contradiction between materiality and fenestration, between the expectation of mass and its denial, is representative of a more extensive issue regarding structural integrity.

The constructional scheme is thoroughly integrated in the design concept. It is organised by two strands: the external presence of the abstract cube and, within this primary order, the complementarity between rooms and the cross-like space they define. The shifting wall positions and the wraparound effect of the façade have necessitated the structural binding together of walls and slabs into a structural whole. This has allowed solid concrete walls to be placed freely on the floor slabs, making possible the rooms' rotation from one floor to the next, and the elevational expression of this rotation.

Nevertheless, this conception of structural unity could only be sustained through concealing a tremendous amount of effort. The concrete envelope and inner walls are connected by high strength double-shear studs, which distribute the loads from the inside partitions onto the supporting outer shell. The structural discontinuity of internal walls has required the introduction of additional floor supports at the corners and longitudinal reinforcement to the concrete around the long windows.[18] These structural solutions are for the most part invisible, buried in the homogenising concrete mass. Ultimately, the building's tectonic unity is a matter of appearance.

The dichotomy between inside and outside represents a deliberate flaunting of both modernist and academic traditions. The Beaux-Arts theory requiring the congruence of actual structure and visual effect and the corresponding modernist dictum of "form follows function" are rendered equally irrelevant. It is not that Olgiati is interested in a deliberate falsification of tectonic expression, as with Herzog & de Meuron's Stone House. In the Stone House, the rubble wall and concrete frame were both presented as fictions, engaged in a perpetually open dialogue.[19] Conversely, in the Paspels School the very idea of tectonic integrity is rendered fictional.

The project signified to contemporary reviewers a radical "liberation of spaces".[20] The freedom of the plan can be understood in several ways – as liberation from structural restrictions, from orthogonality, from theoretical traditions. These categories are so disparate as to require more detailed examination.

18 Decasper, 2005, p. 334.

19 See Colquhoun, "Regionalism", 2009, p. 284.

20 Bürkle, 1998.

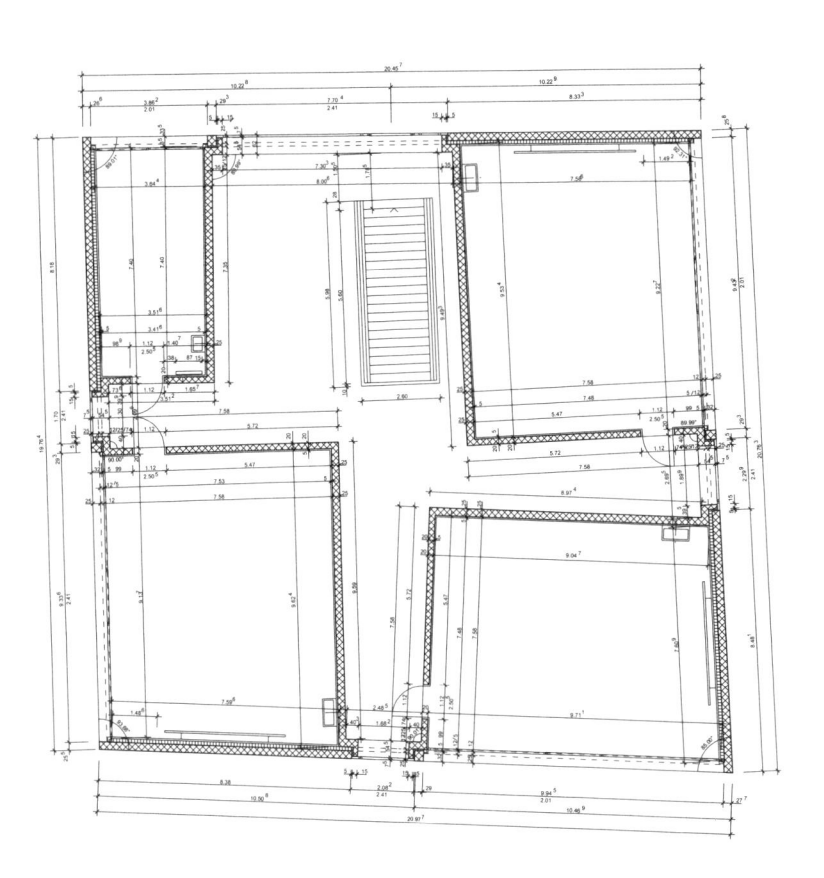

(Top) Valerio Olgiati. School, Paspels, 1996–98. Construction plan reduced from scale 1:50

(Right) Valerio Olgiati discussing the deformation of the Paspels School plan, Virginia Polytechnic Institute, October 2006

The free positioning of internal walls is essentially a version of the modernist free plan. However, rather than a column and slab system in which internal partitions merely divide the space, here the walls fulfil a structural and representational role. The practical problems of execution, the difficult integration of two interdependent structural systems, the in-situ construction, the invisible reinforcements demanded a highly sophisticated, technologically advanced approach. As Bruno Reichlin has observed, the geometrical departure from the right angle was also dependent on the new possibilities open to design through the use of computers.[21] Both the structural and geometric "liberations" thus reflect technological possibilities that are strictly of their time.

21 Reichlin, 2008, 122–123.

And yet, the school resists being projected as an iconographic statement about construction. Olgiati says relatively little about the school's actual building process. Once the concept has been established, one can assume that construction is so much part of the design as not to require additional energy. The investment in the processes and meaning of construction is less explicit.

This offers a clue as to Olgiati's attitude to the academic and modernist traditions. We have seen how the dichotomy between inside and outside, between appearance and reality, consciously undermines the principle of structural truth. Behind the solidity of concrete, one finds here an almost cheerful abandonment of the modernist expectations for structural integrity – an attitude indebted to the theoretical revisions of the 1960s and 1970s. Olgiati re-enacts, subliminally at least, Robert Venturi's validation of complexity and contradiction and his subsequent attacks on the moral connotations of structural truthfulness. The Paspels School explores no less than the architectural possibilities under which truth and deception can co-exist.[22]

22 The Baroque notion that architecture could concomitantly express truth and deception was revisited in Robert Venturi's *Complexity and Contradiction in Architecture*, 1966. See Forty, 2000, p. 290.

The School as a school
There is little to suggest that Olgiati's Paspels building is a school, even less that it is the extension of an existing one. There are two possible typological readings for the project, and neither of them is specifically educational.

The outer materiality and fenestration suggest a speculative urban type characterised by programmatic elasticity. In a city, obstructed by other walls and other windows, the memorable Paspels façades would be less visible. Their displaced openings would perhaps recall Diener & Diener's Kohlenberg office building (Basel, 1992–1995), whose power resides in the controlled distortion of urban anonymity. However, Diener & Diener's building addresses the city, and the position of its windows is subject to perception from specific viewpoints. By contrast, at Paspels the openings express an autonomous, internally predetermined logic. Only the south façade, facing the village, makes an exception by deferring to the civic realm and offering a point of entry.

A second typological reading is domestic. This is made possible by the timber-lined classrooms which, both in construction and atmosphere, follow the conventions of the *Stube (Stiva)*, the typical living room of Alpine dwellings. The classrooms appear immediately warm and intimate. The relative visual clutter of chairs and desks is familiar and counteracts the cold emptiness of the foyer, thus reinforcing the complementarity principle.

The referential spectrum is thus stretched between schoolness, urban anonymity and the local vernacular. Moreover, the building opens an interpretative compass that goes beyond functional, regional or historical specificity. With its interplay of elemental geometrical motifs – the cross and the square - the plan recalls primitive representations of the world or the city. This primordial urban reading is maintained by the interlocking of classrooms and circulation. Their contrast in terms of materials, colours, sounds and atmospheres invokes the dualities of private and public, external and internal spaces in a city. One tends to read the classrooms as houses around the piazza-like clearing of the lobby.

On the other hand, the two spatial types are fused together in a self-sufficient whole, risking art-like isolation. The possibilities of crossover are minimal. The doors are pushed out into the recesses of the plan, so that the central space remains essentially empty, and its potential urbanity is undercut by abstraction and separation. This is consistent with the building's ambivalent relation to the everyday reality of the village, and even with its graphic representation in the laconic line drawings produced by Olgiati's studio.

The Paspels School takes upon itself a double role as a lived-in place and architectural shrine. Its emphatic unity would be undermined in the heterogeneous fabric of a city. By inverting the expectations of the image-type, and by replacing urban anonymity with isolated monumentality, Olgiati's building reveals an enduring theme of German-Swiss architecture: the polarity of city and mountain. The building's "suggestively classical rise" above the village, its outer detachment and inner processional organisation point to a universal ambition.[23] The abstract interiors, the monad-like unity and orientation towards nature imply the search for a more profound meaning than that of its obvious use.

The school in Paspels has been conceived as a small temple in a natural setting; its ambition is intelligible beyond and despite its secular use. This perhaps explains the building's pristine state today; the respect, rather than casual familiarity, shown by the community. Given the nature of its programme, the building in use remains surprisingly deferential to its radical asceticism. That the dark walls of the hallways have never been covered with paint or colourful artworks suggests that the school's concept has been communicated to its users in a manner hardly conceivable elsewhere. The teachers have made positive remarks about the

23 Dell'Antonio, 1998.

[24] Bürkle, 1998, p. 68.

architecture's influence on pupils; the hardness of concrete and the enforced emptiness have apparently raised no qualms.[24]

As a building respectful of its surrounds, considerately economic and doing its job, the school elicits the villagers' respect at a practical level. However, the extent and character of this acceptance pertain to a deeper cultural connection. Alongside its artistic and educational goals, the school fulfils their more profound expectations for a meaningful civic gesture.

Valerio Olgiati. School, Paspels, 1996–98.
First pupils using the school, 1998

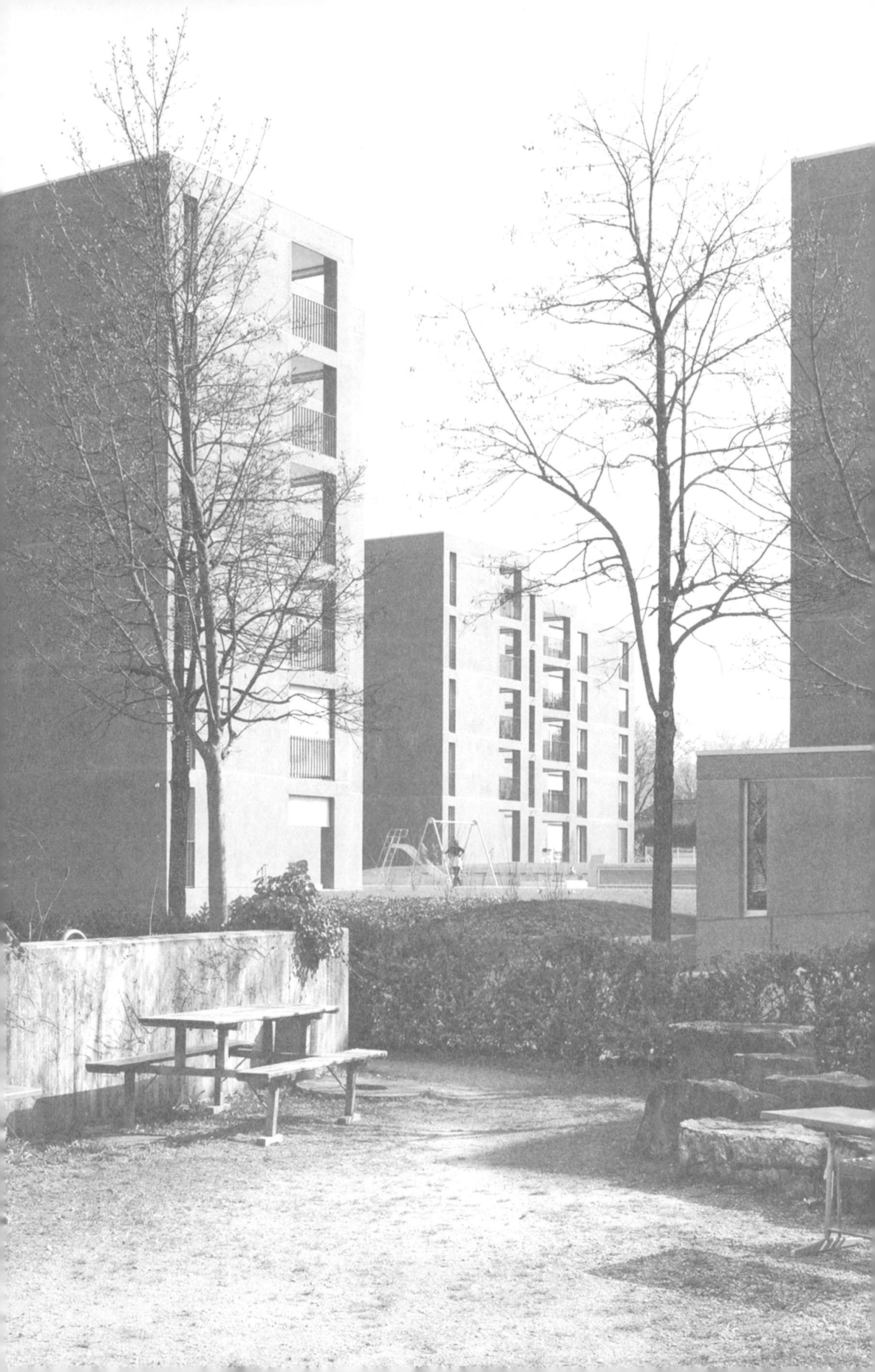

Von Ballmoos Krucker
Stöckenacker Housing
Affoltern, Zurich, Project 1997,
Realisation 2000–2002

By name, suburbia implies a relation of inferiority to the city. And yet, with the growth of polycentric conurbations, distinctions between suburbia and the actual city become ever more blurred. As the dense and tightly regulated city spills outwards, peripheral settlements and industrial outskirts become the focus of actual development. Suburbia is gradually moving away from simulations of inhabitable nature, towards simulations of urban territory.

The Stöckenacker housing development in Affoltern, outside Zurich, highlights the tension between the urban aspirations of suburbia and its status as marketable conception of nature. Designed in 1997 by the partnership of Thomas von Ballmoos and Bruno Krucker, the development connects two revisionist strands. Firstly, by concentrating on the cultural image of prefabrication, it provides a critique of post-war, medium-density housing estates. Secondly, it questions the established expectation of what suburban environments might provide for their inhabitants. This line of inquiry became particularly relevant in the late 1990s, at a time when the Zurich authorities announced plans to provide ten thousand new housing units within ten years, and suburban sites were set aside for redevelopment.

The Stöckenacker housing illustrates, not unlike the Kirchner Museum, the manner in which the theoretical issues formulated throughout the 1980s were received and interpreted by a new generation in the following decade. Apart from the actual building process, the architectural concept works to pull together the strands of construction, materiality and contextual deference into one indivisible whole. This case study explores how sophisticated concepts were relied upon to bring urban order to a suburban context.

Both born in 1961, Bruno Krucker and Thomas von Ballmoos belong to the transitional generation that studied at ETH after Rossi had left and before his theories had been re-evaluated in the *Analoge Architektur* studio. In the perceived vacuum between two strong theoretical paradigms, this generation took its inspiration from contemporary practice rather than from teaching studios. The early projects of Herzog & de Meuron, Diener &

Diener and Peter Zumthor instilled the kind of conceptual and tectonic ambitions that are clearly perceptible in the Stöckenacker development. Similarly, the brief provided a concrete context for exploring a wider intellectual theme. The design constitutes a commentary on ordinariness and ubiquitous construction processes, informed by a theoretical stance strengthened through teaching and research.[1]

City and suburbia

Studio Basel's research has pointed to a large area around Zurich where "the urban reality is repressed and papered over by a rural ideology".[2] Affoltern, a village caught up in urban growth, is a case in point, an intensely negotiated boundary between suburbia and the countryside. The project is located in Unteraffoltern, a suburban district planned in the 1960s according to the modernist model of multi-storey blocks floating in greenery. More recently, Affoltern has provided sites for several large-scale housing projects. With its eighty or so flats organised in three blocks, Stöckenacker was a relatively small predecessor of these developments.

This housing scheme, the winning entry in a competition held in 1997, was the first significant project of the practice. The client was a commercial partnership between a housing association and a private developer. Both parties contributed part of the land, with the remainder of the site leased from the city of Zurich. Therefore three administrative bodies, two private and one communal, were involved in the decision making process. Their different agendas are reflected in the variety of housing units and the different apartment configurations of the three, seemingly identical, blocks.

Construction started in 2000, and the delay had a significant impact on the choice of materials. Due to a change in building regulations, the single brick panel construction first envisaged had to be replaced with prefabricated washed concrete panels. It was less the material than the constructional principle – the use of prefabrication – that constituted the indispensable element of the design concept. For the purposes of this project, prefabrication was used as a conceptual tool for critically re-evaluating suburban living, in particular post-war housing estates.

In assessing the suburban setting, von Ballmoos and Krucker referred to the photographic series *Settlements, Agglomeration* (1993) by Swiss artists Peter Fischli and David Weiss. This study provides an ironic, David-Lynch-like commentary on suburban places, in which nature figures as partly ornamental, partly threatening. Similar to the places recorded by Fischli and Weiss, Unteraffoltern is "of an almost irritating normality".[3] The long low blocks are staggered and meandering, a vision of accessibility and safety lost in the vegetation. Such settings, on account of their ordinariness, are often seen by architects to contain the promise of a deeper intelligibility.

---

[1] The exchange between theoretical discourse, teaching and practice is central to the partnership. Von Ballmoos and Krucker were affiliated with a number of publications that make this exchange explicit – for example Krucker, Jenatsch, and Cavelti, 2005, pp. 138–159.

[2] "The Zurich Metropolitan Region", 2006, p. 612.

[3] Solt, 2003, p. 38.

Stöckenacker subscribes to this attitude by seeking to provide a dignified background for everyday life. The project's overall configuration and constructional strategy are determined by a critique of late modernist, prefabricated suburban estates. They set up a contrast with the existing pastel-coloured, rendered blocks and their vague orientation with respect to the street. The clearest manifestation of this critical strategy lies in the heavy-looking, dark material presence of the development. This signals the intention to create in a suburban environment a place with *gravitas*, an urban settlement.

Urban form

> That is the problem with Swiss boxes – you cannot put balconies on them.[4] **Bruno Krucker**

[4] von Ballmoos and Krucker, 2006.

The scheme comprises one five- and two six-storey blocks arranged in an L-shape, defining a garden plot away from the street. Concentrating the mass of the development on the margins of the site has created an incomplete perimeter block, with a communal green area at the centre. The living spaces open onto this shared garden through large covered balconies.

The provision of terraces posed a dilemma for the architects. There was no question in their mind of the inhabitants' need for private, external rooms, protected from the elements. However, while functionally indispensable, balconies impacted on the overall tectonic expression. Housing models with added-on balconies, "like metal cages, seemed unreal from an architectonic point of view".[5] Other recent projects had, under the current theoretical imperative of formal purity, dispensed with balconies altogether. In the end, von Ballmoos and Krucker hit upon a third option: staggered profiles that could incorporate balconies within the overall volume.

[5] Ibid.

It's worth noting that the consideration of precedents in the decision-making process bears the imprint of inherited theory. The architects did not conceive the project solely as determined by programme and urban situation, but also in relation to a set of typological references. On the one hand the contemporary canon proved to be an indivisible part of their research, pointing to the strong professional network of local influences and relationships. On the other hand, this discourse was itself subjected to muted criticism. Discreetly, Stöckenacker challenged the formal idealism of monolithic volumes.

The architects integrated instead all programmatic, formal, constructional and aesthetic systems into another concept: the exploration of interlocked L-shaped elements. Everything in the project - from urban configuration to the individual volumes, to the apartments' layout and the shape of each prefabricated element – falls under the formal discipline of the L-shape.

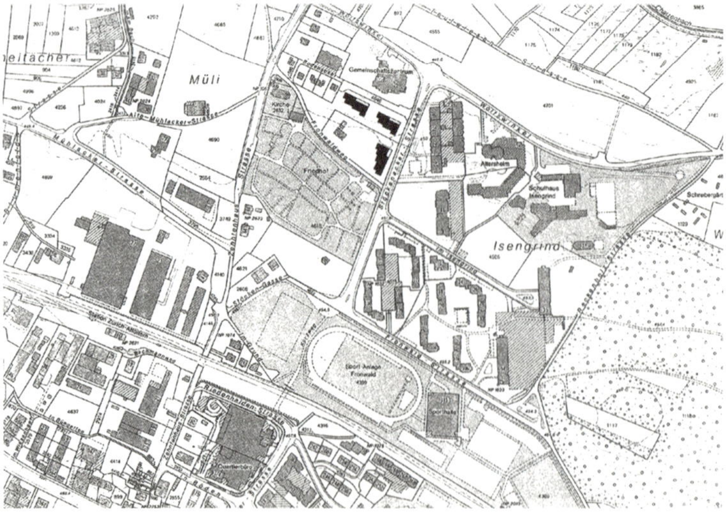

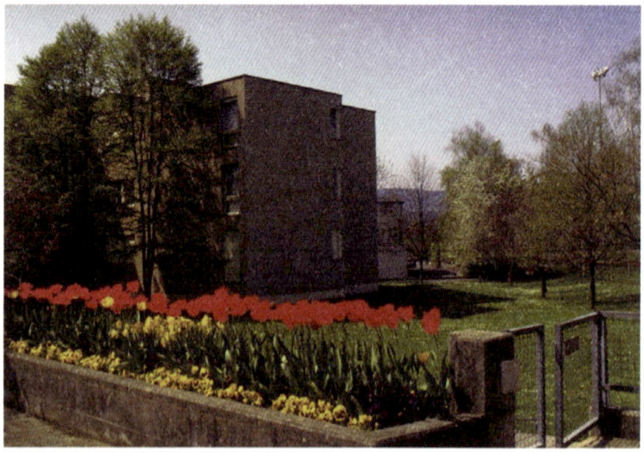

(Opposite top) von Ballmoos Krucker.
Stöckenacker Housing,
Zurich 1997–2002. Site plan

(Opposite bottom) Fischli/Weiss.
Settlements, Agglomeration, 1993

(Above left) Gigon/Guyer.
Housing Broelberg I,
Kilchberg Zurich, 1989-92

(Above right) Morger & Degelo.
Housing Müllheimerstrasse,
Basel 1989–93

(Right) von Ballmoos Krucker.
Stöckenacker Housing,
Zurich 1997–2002. Interior

At the larger scale, the blocks' positioning provides a feeling of enclosure. From certain angles the volumes seem to melt into one folded grey surface, a three-dimensional grid whose open and closed parts slowly emerge as neatly stacked pillars and walls. This sense of continuity serves to embed the buildings into their environment as one entity, rather than as a collection of disparate units.

In modernist housing, separate blocks have often been distributed in a regular or shifting matrix across the landscape. This emphasises the purity of concept over the lived-in quality of the masterplan. In contrast, Stöckenacker's more intuitive footprint is subject to an organisational strategy that only reveals itself through direct experience.

> An important aspect is that the blocks create an ensemble, a conglomerate by which we tried to make the three buildings operate as a *constellation*. Special to this conception of constellations is that they are only available through perception, not in the abstract.[6]

6 Bernet and Sommerhalder, 2002. Translation from original interview in German.

The architects' use of the term "constellation" alerts us to the creation of an urban typology, not dissimilar to Diener & Diener's work at Warteck. The "constellation" is intended to impact equally on the city and on the individual buildings that create the configuration. At an urban scale, it acknowledges urban order as pluralistic and contingent, but also seeks to act within this to create a new kind of coherence:

> The expression constellation [...] refers, in this case, to an assembly of houses. [...] The city coheres at a point where the houses create a certain form in the sense of a constellation [...] a recognisable form.[7]

7 Steinmann, 1995, p. 12.

Von Ballmoos and Krucker acknowledged a vivid interest in Diener & Diener's "strong" buildings, which through their presence could rearrange their surroundings. Stöckenacker is informed by the same notion of an assembly of buildings intended to create a finite, contextualised urban order. Where the project surrenders formal purity to programmatic demands, it compensates through the identifiable materiality of its components. The common architectonic language of the blocks is deemed more important that the uncharacteristic complexity of their plan arrangement:

> What happens at Stöckenacker is dependent on perception. [...] There are various viewpoints, and to understand the project you need time to move around and perceive the whole.[8]

8 von Ballmoos and Krucker, 2006.

The estate's claim to urbanity arises from its direct experience in location. The importance accorded to perception in understanding the ensemble is indebted to art – specifically,

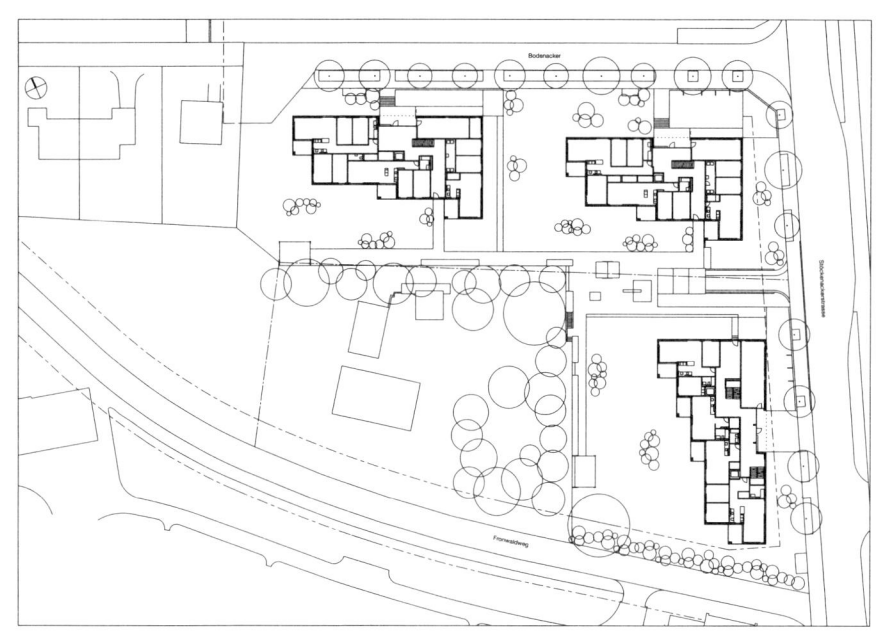

(Top) von Ballmoos Krucker.
Stöckenacker Housing.
Zurich 1997–2002. General plan,
ground floor

(Bottom) von Ballmoos Krucker.
Stöckenacker Housing.
Zurich 1997–2002. General plan,
typical floor

to the balancing of irregular shapes found in David Rabinowitch's collages. At urban scale, this strategy could be understood as picturesque. The project distances itself from the severe formal demands of the "Swiss boxes", reflected into regular, rational masterplans. One may imagine the architects' frisson at proposing the saw-tooth-footprint buildings, unequally distributed along two edges of the rectangular site.

Paradoxically, the graphic awkwardness of the plan leads to the impression of urbanity of the entire development. The blocks' arrangement provides the layered view characteristic of inner city districts. The apparent densification provides a dynamic contrast between the street and the park-like garden at the back. The open balconies towards this communal area establish a network of informal chats, benevolent nodded hellos and furtive looks to the neighbour's belongings, typical instances of private life in urban contexts.

This intimacy is counteracted by the formal severity of the proposal. The first photographs, taken in 2002, documented the newly completed project as a geometric exploration of the right angle under a clear sky. Without the everyday clutter of lived-in homes, the emphasis shifts to the discipline of stacked solids alternating with stacked openings, light and shadow, proportion and formal order. These issues shift attention to the second strand of the overall concept, the redemption of prefabrication.

Beyond prefabrication
Stöckenacker proposes a critical assessment of "prefab" suburbs and attempts to improve on this widespread, if often maligned, type of construction. Through a historical assessment of prefabrication, von Ballmoos and Krucker have connected the issue of detail with the overall appearance of a building and the general feeling of estates thus constituted.

The requirements for acoustic insulation and the limited scope for modular spatial configurations precluded the possibility of complete prefabrication. The floor slabs were poured in situ, followed by the assembly of precast wall panels and lintels, then the pouring of the next in situ slab. The optimal combination of construction methods doesn't detract from the considerable conceptual weight bestowed upon the design, formation and assembly of the self-supporting prefabricated façade. This approach is far from the matter-of-fact building process, originally envisaged for the efficient erection of vast estates without the need for qualified skill. Prefabrication has been so refined and calibrated as to rely entirely on the architect's control. It is viewed as a concept, whose revision in new circumstances and with the help of improved technology boosts, rather than undermines, the architect's status on the building site.

This process of reification began with a critical distancing from the conventions of prefabrication, which allowed the architects to establish a different formal expression:

von Ballmoos Krucker,
Stöckenacker Housing,
Zurich 1997–2002. View from garden

> We wanted to avoid the image of prefabricated social housing where the window appears as a hole punched in the middle of the panel. It always looks too small, [because] its size is restricted so as not to disturb the structural performance of the panel. The regular thickness of a prefabricated external wall panel is eight centimetres and you always see this line around the corner of the typical 70s prefabricated buildings, eight centimetres from the corner – it is a weakness, it makes them look like they're made out of card.[9]

9 von Ballmoos and Krucker, 2006.

As an alternative to standard prefabrication, the architects proposed solid elements of varying width, alternating with full-height windows, so that no continuous vertical joints would be visible. Special corner elements were developed in order to create an impression of weight.

> We sought to give a solid, compact view of the whole building. The corner elements were difficult to produce, six metres long and L-shaped to give an impression of solidity to the corner. They appear to be forty centimetres thick, solid slabs instead of the eight-centimetre actual thickness. We never adjoined one piece to another so you never get a vertical joint running the height of the building: they are always alternating with windows, and the position and width of the window is somewhat joined to the element and its dimensions. It was also easier to integrate balconies into this system of alternating openings and [solid] elements.[10]

10 Ibid.

The strategy that connects prefabrication and tectonic expression also frees the project from the rigidity of excessive repetition. The eye rests on the horizontal width variation of both solids and openings, born of an internal logic whose familiarity reassures. One feels able to approximate from the outside which spaces require just a slant of light – a bathroom, a storage area, a corner of the living room – those that can do with a door-width window – bedrooms, kitchen – and clearly distinguish those behind a full expanse of glass. This horizontal variation softens the ensemble, counteracting the discipline of vertically stacked elements.

Through its emphasis on tectonic correctness, the project brings into relief the modular nature of the elements. This sets up a tension between the buildings' expression as monoliths or as assemblies of parts. The assembly is made visually explicit on the façade. Mastic joints separate the prefabricated elements - grey in colour to match the concrete, but lighter and sufficiently wide to ensure the clear perception of each solid element in isolation, like toy wooden blocks. The project's sophistication results from

(Above) von Ballmoos Krucker.
Stöckenacker Housing, Zurich 1997–2002.
Prefabrication and assembly

tailored details, such as the indentations supporting the window lintels – delicate adjustments that reprise the consistent theme of L-shaped assemblies.

The strategy has important implications for the prefabrication process, whose complexity is greatly increased by the intricate invisible profiles of the elements. The detail drawings, as well as the film documenting the processes of execution and assembly, demonstrate the high level of labour skill on which the architects have been able to rely – the manifestation of Swiss tectonic culture. Through recourse to this cultural dimension, the process of prefabrication is recast in a different light.

Materiality

The project's urban configuration, formal expression and construction method were developed in relation to each other. The one independent element is the surface of the prefabricated elements. The estate's materiality is defined by dark grey concrete, textured by visible aggregate. The panels' finish is the most important variation from the competition proposal, and therefore the element on which the client had the most direct input through negotiation.

Despite tight budgetary controls, the clients decided to use the relatively expensive finish proposed by the architects. In the year that passed between the competition and detail design stages, new building regulations regarding energy requirements were issued, which the single-brick skin system first proposed in the competition scheme could no longer fulfil. Fortunately one client opposed the default low-cost solution of insulated render, used for the buildings all around. This gave rise to an opportunity to examine different construction techniques, in a search for an appropriate tectonic expression.

In the course of research, the architects dismissed pressed cement panelling as too flimsy, and double-brick construction as too expensive and fragile. A tour with the client around Zurich gave them the opportunity to propose washed concrete, used on 1970s buildings.

> There was a lot of communicative work, rather than simply construction development. Of course it's difficult to deal with regulations and client requirements, but this kind of resistance, or simply questioning, forces us to rethink the project and improve on it. With Stöckenacker, it also gave the client the chance to develop an awareness of construction. [...] The advantage was that the people really understood and identified with all aspects of the project. The entire committee was with it, having decided things with a certain consciousness of what they were doing.[11]

11 von Ballmoos and Krucker, 2006.

The architects' statement articulates a constructive, almost didactic relationship with the client committee. Under the change in circumstances, the design development brought mutual benefits. The consultation process led to the decision to invest in a more expensive, yet durable material, requiring only a small amount of regular maintenance in the long term. In turn, the material expression is perhaps the strongest character-building feature of the project, imparting a dimension of urban decorum that lends the entire estate an aura of desirability.

The clients were convinced to support this less obvious solution, whose efficiency only becomes apparent when measured against maintenance and repair costs. Their farsightedness contrasts the profit-driven culture that increasingly characterises building industries worldwide. Ultimately, it's not the architect's professional ambition that has the last word, but the client's pragmatic interest in lasting quality.

From the typical to the abstract, and back again
Stöckenacker manifests the same correlation of outer shape, internal configuration and construction strategy found in the other buildings examined here. The design concept is a smoothly jointed entity, taking into account all architectural and practical considerations. Its revisionist language can be identified at an urban scale, through the redemption of suburbia, and in detail, through the redemption of the prefabricated panel.

The original strand in this conceptual circuit is a critical understanding of suburbia that oscillates between marketing concept and the colonisation of nature. The buildings are inserted in their context by means of a controlled, structured "normality". Stöckenacker represents a radical separation between the landscape and the densely built urban settlement. At competition stage, the six-storey scheme stood out from other entries that spread density uniformly across the site. Stöckenacker's densification in turn releases more ground for landscaping. However, unlike its 1970s neighbours, the new estate provides a clearer sense of orientation and unity:

> We needed to create an urban edge or relation for the house itself, because a weak point of the 70s [housing] is that the houses swim in this green and you don't know how get inside. Another distinction was the effort not to separate the blocks but bring them together as one place, rather than as separate islands.[12]

This suggests a corrective approach to the modernist paradigm of high-rise dwelling in the green. The reinforcement of street edges and the radical separation of the "dense" front from the "garden" back recall the pattern of metropolitan perimeter blocks. The project is, ultimately, a hybrid between two distinct and often contrasting urban types.

12 Ibid.

At the same time, through its revision of prefabrication, the project claims to improve the ubiquitous profit-led, high-density developments, separated from urban life through half-hearted colour schemes and ill-conceived planning. The architects seek to endow such environments with dignity and depth. The ordinary is redeemed through a coherent concept, material presence, elegant proportions and detailing. Consequently, von Ballmoos and Krucker's analytical revision of prefabrication turns a banal type of construction into a refined accomplishment. As the design progressed, the projects' technological aspects acquired a certain autonomy and sense of priority, tending towards iconographical value.

This attitude towards prefabrication represents a covert critique of immateriality. Considerable energy is placed into developing the corner elements to appear as massive slabs. The façade configuration eliminates the need for vertical joints, which would essentially give the unsettling impression of collapsible, disposable buildings. The strong material character achieved by the rough washed concrete, in which colour is embedded rather than applied, illustrates the same intent towards materialisation, densification and the creation of an impression of weight. This intention betrays the same attraction for the monolithic encountered in many of the pure prisms known as Swiss boxes.

Stöckenacker's revisionist agenda and formal vocabulary are modernist in scope. The architects training and their continued involvement with ETH, through teaching and research, reveal a sophisticated knowledge of historical modernism.[13] The scheme continues in the respected *Siedlung* tradition established in Switzerland during the early twentieth century, and it can be seen to fulfil the Bauhaus ideal of the house-atelier as technological temple. This ideal sees art as a constitutive, indivisible part of the whole.

Housing is redeemed through the appeal to art. For this project the architects referred to Fischli and Weiss in the search for a defining atmosphere, to David Rabinowitch in the search for compositional principles, and to Jean-Luc Godard for cinematic parallels between the private lives and urban environment. This cultural horizon is a matter of lifestyle and of expectations attached to the architectural profession, particularly in Switzerland. Stöckenacker's balance of formal and programmatic interests has been influenced by this extra-curricular openness. The façades articulate a conflict between aesthetic credentials and typical dwelling, between the perfect form and an improved quality of life.

The ensemble has weathered well. Towards the street, the blocks preserve a closed, regulated appearance. Signs of inhabitation become more apparent at the back, where the flats open up towards the garden. To protect the landlords' aesthetic ambitions, lease policies restrict the possibility of closing the terraces. Even so, the balconies constitute the main possibility for personal

---

13 At the start of his career, Krucker worked as assistant in Arthur Rüegg's construction studio in ETH and co-authored an anthology of twentieth-century modernist case studies, analysed from a constructional angle. See Rüegg and Krucker, 2001.

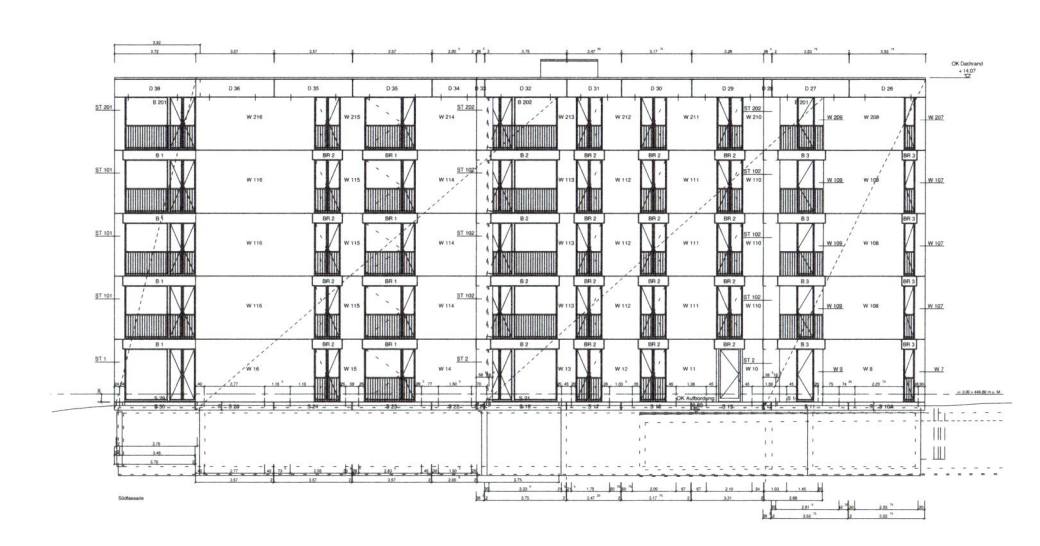

(Top) von Ballmoos Krucker.
Stöckenacker Housing,
Zurich 1997–2002. Terrace in use

(Middle) von Ballmoos Krucker.
Stöckenacker Housing,
Zurich 1997–2002. Elevation, construction
drawing showing panel assembly

display and differentiation. The geometric abstraction of the grid of openings and walls is counteracted by the typical presence of potted plants, bicycles and terrace furniture, which allow the project to soften into an ensemble of living, breathing homes.

Despite its proximity to Zurich, Stöckenacker's urban ambitions do not guarantee urbanity. Like other newer and bigger developments nearby, it is a small metropolitan island, creating its own idealised reality in an undetermined environment. This indicates architecture's limitations in relation to the wider potential of long-term, large-scale territorial policies.

At the same time, through its fastidious prefabrication, the project claims more than constructional integrity. By providing a monolithic and permanent estate instead of the ephemeral house of cards normally associated with prefabrication, the architects provide a commentary on the life of the inhabitants. This amounts to an ethical proposition projected on issues of appearance. And yet, the expression of monolithic simplicity is achieved with great effort at detail level. The façades' tectonic clarity is dependent on complicated moulds and a high level of skill, which are ultimately incompatible with mass fabrication. Like a latter-day Bauhaus ideal, Stöckenacker allows architects and craftsmen to infiltrate the factory and the construction site. The higher cost of the product is justified through the fulfilment of both a civic and a personal need for dignified, lasting dwellings.

Backgrounds II

3.00 ▼

2.80 ▼
2.60 ▼
2.40 ▼

2.30 ▼
2.10 ▼

The Background
of Practice

How neatly, how safely, how trimly, how solidly, how seriously, how spotlessly, how conscientiously, how tastefully, how tidly, how thoroughly, how seriously and so on they build in this country.[1] **Max Frisch**

1 Frisch, 1982, p. 213.

In Switzerland, construction is not just a means to an end. Notwithstanding its importance in the international modern movement as a whole, here the material aspect of building has always been given special emphasis. While historically, in Germany, France or Russia such inclinations tended to imply Marxism or philosophical materialism, in Switzerland construction has been less ideological. The "materialist" tendencies of Hans Schmidt or Hannes Meyer were not fundamentally carried into the local experience of Modernism.

One indication of the Swiss concern with building is the abundance of site photographs circulating in the media. Continuing the early modernist tradition of documenting heroic stages of construction, such photographs are not only factual accounts of a building's assembly; they have a kind of representational value. In the early twentieth century the images of steel structures awaiting completion symbolised a new age, in which social problems would be resolved through industrial production. Since the 1980s the technological promise was replaced by a poetic appreciation of construction, often tied in with evocative close-ups of material surfaces. The value of construction has shifted to an appreciation of detail and material texture – both, in different ways, claiming a close engagement with concrete reality.

But although conceptual and constructional strategies enjoy a high level of exposure, other less palpable stages of a building's realisation are seldom on display. The decisive whisperings between competition jurors, the public consultation and popular vote, the procedures for fund raising, planning approvals, cost control, the collaboration between architect and client – all these are somehow implied in the process, and go without much mention in the critical discourse. The domain of the architect's experience that balances agendas, expectations and personalities is generally seen as ancillary to the creative process and ultimately separate from it.

The practical context is thus dismissed as potentially compromised, the site of confrontations between the creative imagination and an imperfect reality. Occasionally circulating as anecdotes or apocryphal stories, mostly undocumented, the ordinary situations of design nevertheless constitute the concrete framework for each building. The planning and building regulations, the commissioning process, the collaborative nature of design and client expectations are factors which constitute the deeper common context in which all practicing architects are engaged, regardless of status and individual position. This practical context of actual dependencies and concrete situations underlines the intellectual dimensions of Swiss architecture. And yet, looking at the minutiae of practice doesn't yield any universal methodologies. Every project brings to light different aspects of architectural practice, it remains subject to individual circumstances. The architects' resistance to the blanket term "Swiss architecture" is partly in recognition of this individuality.

To an extent, the production is directly influenced by a common set of cultural and political circumstances. Projects are measured against the common yardstick of federal commissioning processes, the architect's professional status, and the state of the construction industry. Even where participants hold little in common, the practical context constitutes a shared ground.

Despite the particulars of programme, context and approach, several of the case studies presented in this book originate in similar circumstances. Let us consider for example the museum in Davos, the school in Paspels, and the housing in Affoltern, all first buildings in their architects' careers. Firstly, all acted as statements of intent, articulating the architects' emerging positions. The need to position oneself with respect to the professional discourse goes back to the shared theoretical context. And yet, the need for such a positioning results from the belief in architecture's ethical dimensions. Secondly, these projects were commissioned through invited competitions, and the winners were chosen despite being virtually unknown at the time. Thirdly, the architects' assumed lack of building experience didn't prevent them from developing sophisticated construction strategies, well controlled during realisation. This suggests, besides the adherence to certain professional standards, the existence of enabling administrative procedures and a cultural status of construction that are quite particular to the Swiss context.

Among European architects, the Swiss competition system is commonly cited as a remarkable advantage. It allows young practices to compete for work alongside more established architects, and to reach potential clients in a manner that is free of

(Page 190) Bearth & Deplazes
studio, Chur, 2010

(Above) Franz Fueg, Portmann House,
Hessigkofen, 1964, photographed
during construction

(Bottom left) Peter Zumthor,
Thermal Baths, Vals, 1990–96,
Stone cutting

(Bottom right) Bearth & Deplazes,
Meuli House, Flasch. The building
site as a still life

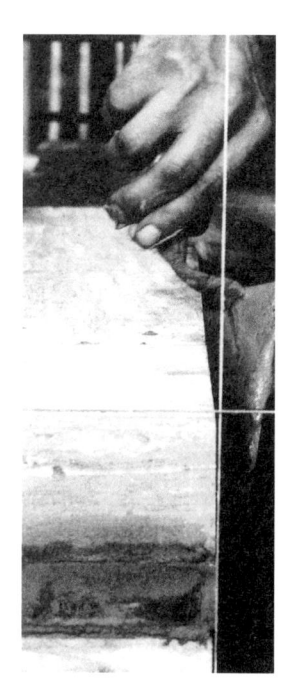

prejudice. It provides some degree of transparency with regard to public commissions, and it preserves the professional respect accorded to architects. Competitions are closely regulated by professional bodies, and the constitution of the jury panel is pre-determined so that architectural members are usually in the majority. This ensures that architectural quality is upheld, alongside political or economic considerations.

High production values are also commonly cited as characteristic of Swiss architecture. For Swiss professionals working abroad, the low expectations of other construction cultures often leads to vexation. Conversely, for foreign architects, the status accorded in Switzerland to construction – and indirectly, to the profession – has led to an idealisation of the local conditions for architecture.

Swiss practitioners are sceptical of such external enthusiasm, and with good reason. For one thing, each project entails an effort that this level of generalisation tends to trivialise. For another, the stereotypes regarding architecture and construction are actually misleading. The situation increasingly reflects a global, profit-led, contractor-led approach to construction, which drastically limits the architects' role and possibilities for expression. An implacable economic logic affects Switzerland, together with the rest of the world. As the practical conditions become less local and less quality-oriented, the full impact this has on the architectural profession is yet to be gauged.

In these circumstances, projects like those we have examined have already acquired a historical specificity. In the last decades of the twentieth century, they illustrate a reliance on construction skills and on the architect's control over the building process. Even when there is an acceptance of tolerance, accident and weathering, this implies a no less deliberate decision regarding the expressive potential of the material and available construction techniques. The buildings' formal or intellectual elegance is matched by the elegant integration of construction in the overall concept, the exercise of all possible control in the process of realisation.

Marcel Meili sees the high expectations of construction quality in the architecture of the 1980s and 1990s as linked to its search for "presence". The theoretical developments examined here coincided with the beginning of radical changes in the profession and construction industry. As a reaction, the works sought to demonstrate "the clarifying, unifying, and stabilizing force of architecture (and of the architect) in the building process".[2] Rigour is thus not simply culturally conditioned; it is a statement of authorship, a kind of defence mechanism. Constructional precision articulates a resistance to changing global conditions. Swiss architecture at the close of the twentieth century is not a seamless continuation of earlier construction or cultural traditions, but represents the architects' response to a worldwide threat to these traditions.

2   Meili, 1996, p. 25.

The sense of permanence that accompanies well-built buildings is not simply a matter of cultural heritage. The Swiss value accorded to construction is the complex inheritance of local crafts traditions, the engineering aspirations of *Neues Bauen* and the *Werkbund* synthesis of craft and industry. Within the profession, the architects' attitude to construction has been affected by theoretical developments since the 1960s; a substantial know-how has been propagated through the training of technicians, supported by an extensive apprenticeship system. Outside the profession there are economic factors to consider, such as the scarcity of land for development and the nature of Swiss industrialisation. There are also cultural specifics, namely the Protestant work ethic and the demands of a knowledgeable, affluent client base.

Each of the case studies discussed earlier relates differently to the construction industry and local construction cultures. On the basis of location, programme and execution, the projects present very distinct facets of Swiss architectural practice at the end of the twentieth century. In sum, they suggest that there are no "typical" conditions, just a series of parallel and ever-changing realities in which architecture operates. This section addresses the Swiss context of architectural practice, but not through a systematic analysis of the full spectrum. Instead, three aspects have been singled out for discussion: the cultural status of construction in the Graubünden; the federal dialogue between architectural training and associated trades; and finally, the professional status of the architect.

Construction culture in the Graubünden

Graubünden architecture is not illustrative of the wider conditions of Swiss praxis. It operates as a system within a system – indeed, architects from other cantons are as intrigued by it as are architects from other countries. What attracts attention is the responsiveness of this rural, mainly conservative canton to radical contemporary architecture. This rapport can be explained in two ways. Firstly, building quality constitutes a common ground that mediates between architects and the communities they serve. Secondly, as a consequence of its dominant tourist industry, Graubünden's character displays inherent urban traits.

The school in Paspels, the Kirchner Museum and the Schutzbauten in Chur all figure on the allegorical "metro map" compiled by Andrea Deplazes and Valentin Bearth in 2004.[3] The map shows around one hundred new projects built in the Graubünden between 1988 and 2004, presented as though they were stations on a metropolitan transport map. The proliferation of new buildings conjures parallels between the actual remote topography and an imaginary urban network.

Bearth and Deplazes's metaphor continues the established discourse that likens Switzerland to a city, presenting architecture as a force of thoughtful territorial densification. The notion that the

[3] Wirz, 2005, pp. 16–17.

mountainous topography shelters an urban nature helps explain the strength of Graubünden's modern architecture.

Studio Basel developed the idea that, due to the influence of tourism, commerce and economy, Alpine culture is beginning to approximate metropolitan life. Meili's essay "Is the Matterhorn [a] City?" examines the emerging perception of the Alps as being "urban".[4] Until relatively recently, agriculture, tourism and industry had coexisted in balance. The mountains remained a physical obstacle to everyday routes, preserving a metaphysical aura of untamed nature. With the gradual burrowing of strategic infrastructural tunnels, the hollowed-out mountains have acquired a new status. Under the accelerating conditions of a global market, the Alpine regions are now dominated by tourism:

> The Alps are marketed as a variation of the city within a different context but also as icons of compensation. […] The Alps can no longer possibly embody the mysteries of nature as an alternative to urban living. […] Valley topographies have now become the mountainous settings of an oversized, urban scale: a kind of metropolitan staffage, comparable to the silhouette of Manhattan.[5]

This metaphorical flattening of territory is partly responsible for the emergence of an architecture that combines rural and urban referential horizons. The demand for art, in the service of cosmopolitan tourists and commuters, is juxtaposed to the architects' desire for projects that are both appropriate in a local context and relevant for a wider professional discourse. Thus the "underground map" of new architectural monuments is not to be read as a paradoxical emanation of mountain culture but, as put forward by Bruno Reichlin, as the expression of an ultimately urban pluralism.[6]

At the same time, this urbanity is not equally distributed, but restricted to those locations that can sustain it. It acts as a factor of further demarcation between Alpine urban structures such as resorts and well-connected villages, and rural "fallow lands" which are isolated, depopulated, and predominantly agricultural.[7] At stake in the muted conflict between urban and rural realities is the inherent character of place.

The tensions between factors of urbanisation and traditional impulses define the new architecture. On the one hand this production is supported by a theoretical discourse that is non-specific, international in character; on the other, in practice it responds to conditions typical of Graubünden. These include a certain landscape (mountains as topography and/or backdrop), local construction and lifestyle typologies (*Strickbau, Stube*), material palette (timber, stone, render). Added to this, small communities support social mechanisms that allow the inhabitants' direct input on projects. These mechanisms are

4 Marcel Meili, "Matterhorn", 2006, pp. 919–926.

5 Ibid., pp. 921–924.

6 Reichlin, 2002, p. 134.

7 "Alpine Fallow Lands, Alpine Resorts", 2006, pp. 876–885.

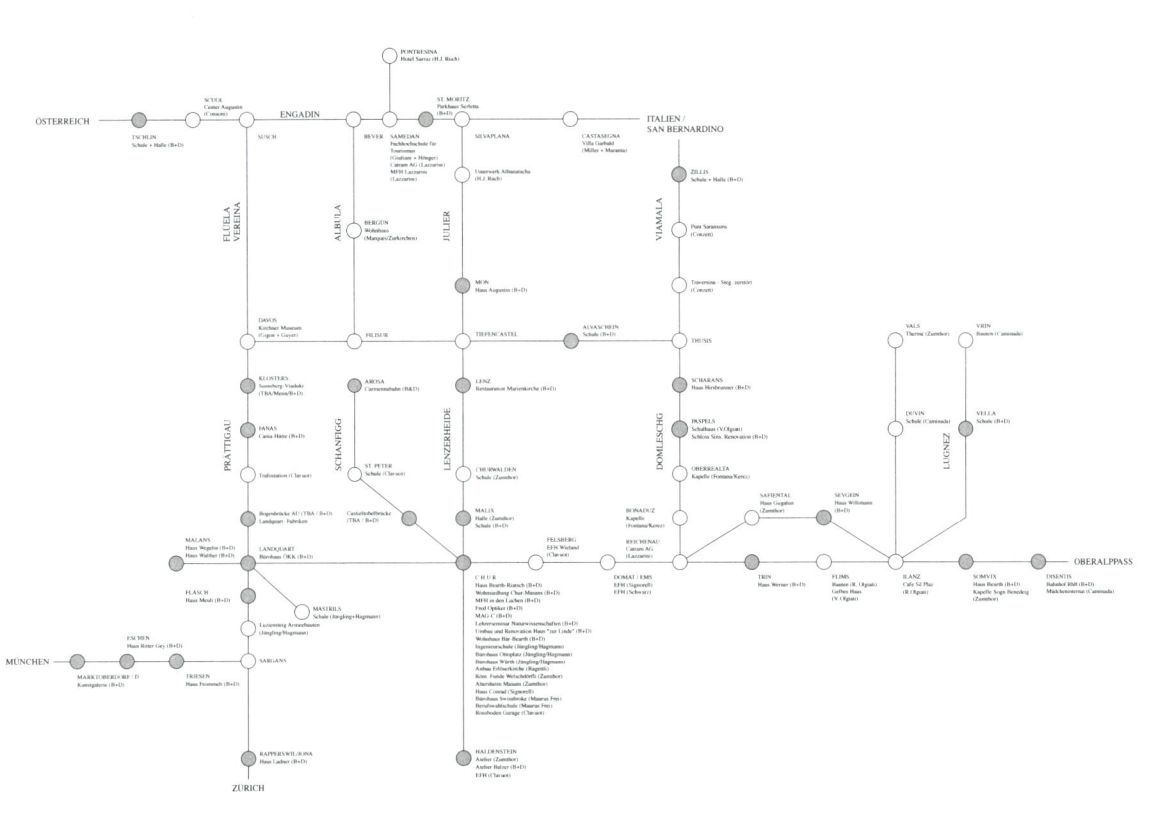

(Above) Bearth & Deplazes. Metro Map
of Graubünden architecture, 1988–2004

(Right) *2G* no. 14, *Building in the
Mountains*, 2000. Cover

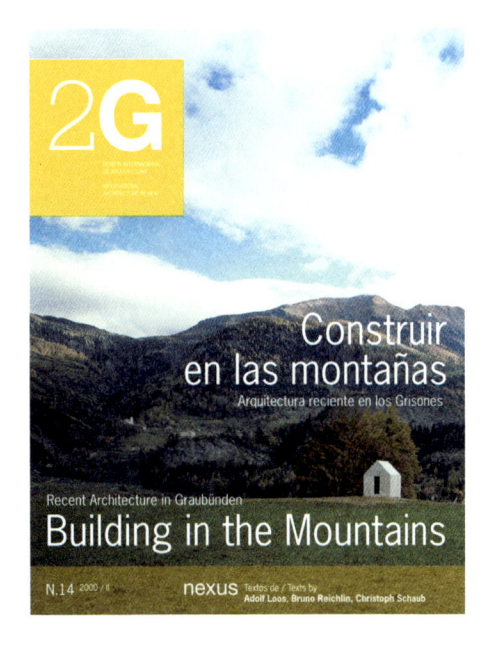

enabled by the collaborative mentality that has for centuries ensured people's survival in this challenging environment. These specifics affect the processes of design and production, and thus impinge on the architectural and construction culture of the region.

(a) The implicit ideals of Graubünden construction

> Our situation has a certain anachronism, something specific to the Alps – some things are still possible because the economy is organised in a certain way. [...] You work more or less with the same people.[8] **Jürg Conzett**

8   Conzett, 2006.

In spite of its radical reputation in architectural journals, some aspects of Graubünden architecture tend towards the archaic. This is explained by the local exercise of direct democracy, craft traditions, and the coexistence of different cultures in a small territory. The Paspels School points to the paradoxical quality of an architectural culture which conflates urban and rural horizons.

New buildings highlight the tension between a community's traditional values and a modernisation that is perceived to threaten these values. Historically, the same tension was apparent in the power struggle between canton and autonomous communes. The heterogeneity of Swiss constituencies challenges the federal ideal of an equal distribution of resources.[9]

9   Communal identity is established on account of type of political organisation; position within a canton; linguistic, urban, religious and topographical characteristics; finally, the degree to which the commune is modernised. See Diener et al., 2006, pp. 251–280.

10 *Porträt Kanton Graubünden*, 2007.

In the mountains, the decentralisation is more extreme. In 2006, fifteen per cent of Graubünden communes had less than one hundred inhabitants, with almost fifty per cent counting between one and five hundred inhabitants.[10] Topography dictates which communes benefit from economic development or transport infrastructure and which are compelled to survive through agriculture. A commune's capital depends on circumstantial factors like accessibility, tourist potential and the availability of natural resources: stone, timber, water, energy. The lack of such assets impairs the settlement's economic viability.

In this context the commune's struggle to retain political autonomy, sometimes in adverse environmental or economic conditions, comes with responsibility towards its citizens. The construction and maintenance of schools, roads and bridges account for most of Graubünden's items of communal expenditure.[11] In spite of cantonal and federal subsidies that support traditional yet less lucrative means of life, particularly agriculture, their redistributive efforts cannot counter a process of selection, an economic survival of the fittest, on which the commissioning of public architecture depends.

11 Barber, 1974, pp. 220–223.

In architectural matters, the Graubünden culture of direct participation presents both advantages and drawbacks. Traditionally, citizens were directly responsible for the implementation of communal decisions. As Benjamin Barber

12   Ibid., p. 271.

wrote, "a vote for a new common building meant building it [...] a contract entered into by the head to put the body to work".[12] Modernisation has relied on external specialists for the provision of fundamental and expensive necessities like new roads or schools. The relationship to outside architects can easily be charged, as the commune's attempts to retain control clash with the architect's personal and professional ambitions.

The most typical aspect of the Paspels project was perhaps the organisation of the initial competition. Both judges and competitors were predominantly architects with local connections. This reflects a long-standing tradition of working within the local economy and with local people – with known quantities as it were. On the other hand, the personal nature of the enterprise suggests that individual reputations impact on the project's commissioning and development. The Graubünden modern commissioning displays a quiet but consistent preference for indigenous practices.

One of the more revealing examples of this phenomenon is Gion A. Caminada's string of projects in and around his native village of Vrin. This remarkable series consists of infrastructural insertions (telephone booth, workshops, stables, slaughterhouse), private houses, and a mortuary chapel. Together these structures amount to an experimental body of work for a remote commune, stubbornly protected from modern developments. In fact, the scope of Caminada's long-term project differs little from the remedial work or insertions that occur in any built environment, at times without any architectural input. The buildings make a virtue of their pragmatic, everyday nature. Yet their architect enjoys an international standing and some of his most utilitarian interventions have acquired an uncanny aesthetic dimension.

Caminada belongs simultaneously to the communal and professional spheres, to the local carpentry workshop and ETH Zurich. His architecture, which a cursory glance would distinguish from the historic fabric merely through the lighter shades of new timber, expresses a delicate balance between local appropriateness and wider appeal. The materials and techniques are recognisably vernacular, yet claim a modern aesthetic through the buildings' abstract volumetry and façade treatment.

Caminada's established position in Vrin would suggest that personal loyalties customarily take precedence over federal or international professional criteria. However the advantage of being local doesn't guarantee the work, it simply makes it a possibility. Caminada testifies to the complex, long-term tactics necessary to secure building approval:

> For a project that is out of the ordinary to be accepted, you have to talk it through countless discussions. At the outset, too, there tends to be a certain negative reaction. If this is likely to result in a conflict, then you have to take

> a step backwards. You have to make sure the conflict is properly defused before going on with the project. In order to achieve this objective, you have to have a great number of one-to-one conversations with different people, and also a lot of meetings. This whole process can take several years. Nevertheless [...] it is the most fruitful stage of a project that you want to carry through.[13]

[13] Caminada in interview, Schaub, 2002, p. 137.

While an urban project is steeped in the anonymity of large-scale policies and invisible interested parties, here individual involvement is indispensable for eventual approval. Moreover, communal ratification does not just fulfil a formal statutory requirement, but imbues the architecture with civic *gravitas*. The connection between village culture and the formal typology of the architectural object involves both architect and users.

> A building in a small village like Vrin always has a social value. [...] In order to appreciate what architecture is appropriate for Vrin, you have to be receptive. It is essential to understand and develop the [existing] structures. [...] A project has to fit with the place.[14]

[14] Ibid., p. 139.

A less clear precondition for the project "fitting in" is that the architect is also, to some extent, subject to public approval. It is in the nature of young careers to depend on personal ties, be they familial or professional. Implicitly, each emerging practice is ascribed a certain operational territory, sometimes for the duration of its career.

This is certainly applicable not only to Graubünden, or to Switzerland for that matter. But here, such territorial connotations are particularly visible. For example, given the proximity of Basel to Zurich, it seems remarkable that the great majority of Herzog and de Meuron's works in the first fifteen years of practice concentrated in Basel, while their concerted efforts to break out of their hometown did not target Zurich, but seemingly anywhere else in the world. Herzog & de Meuron's internationalism doesn't signify a lack of interest in operating in Basel, but merely in enhancing the scale of their local operations. Similarly, Diener & Diener's early work was also mostly based in Basel, although later on their operational territory expanded throughout Europe and beyond.

This is not to say that architects from elsewhere in Switzerland or from abroad are prohibited from building in an area in which they do not reside. On the contrary, the higher the level of artistic consciousness, the more opportunities for outside practices there are. The greatest number of commissions still stems from winning invited competitions or competitive bids. However, an architect's presence on initial shortlists is subject to less transparent criteria, just as the completion of the competition

(Above) Gion A. Caminada,
Slaughterhouse and stables, Vrin, 1994–2000

(Right) Gion A. Caminada,
Mortuary Chapel, Vrin, 2002

201

project is subject to political pressures, financial viability and statutory approvals.

In Graubünden, the popular vote for public commissions sometimes reflects the fault lines of communal micro-politics. The public visibility of one's vote sometimes adds pressure on the individual voter. And yet, it is important to recognise that the apparent favouritism displayed in the commissioning process, based on local or tribal ties, is not the result of cynical corruption but the logical conclusion of a centuries-old culture of personal interaction and responsibility.[15]

The more the architecture appeals to a greater audience than its actual users, the more the choice of architect rests in the balance. A thermal bath attracting tourists is an economic success, but when the building claiming extra-communal status is a school, a care home for the elderly or a private house, different tensions come to the fore between visitors and locals. This partly explains why some communities prefer unchallenging collaborations, freeing the actual projects from the constraints of a radical artistic vision and making them more available to pragmatic interests.

The Graubünden culture of strength and stubbornness, bred by the harsh Alpine environment, tends to radicalise this choice. In some communes, international appeal is bound to raise suspicions or unleash defensiveness more than it would in a metropolitan environment. The more the architect insists on a particular unassailable vision, the more he risks being labelled, in a culture focused on economic survival, with the ambiguous accolade of "artist".

(b) The consequences of craft culture

The idea of a local craft culture is one of the long-standing myths of Swiss production. The expression "Swiss-made", and the expectation of quality it implies, is as much a marketing construct as a factual phenomenon encountered in everyday situations. This expectation is so ingrained that it is often left in the background of an architect's preoccupations. The smoothness of actual detail is far less the focus of design than conceptual smoothness.

Explanations as to the existence of a particular form of perfectionism vary, but its existence is uncontested. Peter Zumthor sees this phenomenon as the product of an "Allemanic culture" of making things (indebted to the German *Werkbund* as much as to any local predetermination).[16] More specifically, according to Martin Steinmann, the claim of unostentatious excellence is a by-product of Protestant culture.[17] Marcel Meili sees it as the emanation of a non-urban culture, a society of farmers and artisans "closely linked to that which is done by hand".[18] The proto-industrial economy was supported by watch-making, textiles, and chemistry: trades that relied on quality as a marketing concept.

---

15 See Barber, 1974, pp. 237–274.

16 Zumthor, interview with author, 2006. The German *Werkbund* was created in 1907 with the aim of improving the quality of mass-produced items. At the time, Anglo-Saxon culture was seen as the more successful model for design in the industrial age. See Colquhoun, 2002, pp. 57–61.

17 Steinmann, 2004.

18 Meili, interview with author, 2006.

Meili links the expectation for quality with the rural aspects of Swiss industrialisation, brought about by the availability of natural resources like water and energy. Even where industry was located in cities, these were small by comparison with other European cities, and retained a specific character. Historically, production in small communities has enabled matters to be conducted on a personal level, creating an incentive to work well. It can be argued that the specific patterns of non-urban social interaction – affecting the way business is conducted, as well as people's attitude to their own work – have focused responsibility on the individual, who is accustomed to direct participation in communal matters. The claim of individual responsibility for the attainment of communal goals has had direct repercussions on the way people work and view the product of their labour. In any particular place, the available skills create specific configurations based on this general model. In Graubünden, such configurations have been operating at three levels.

Firstly, it is possible to identify an informal network of long-term professional associations between architects, engineers and contractors, stretching across several projects. Olgiati's collaboration with site architect Peter Diggelmann and structural engineer Patrick Gartmann, Caminada's work with local carpenter Simon Alig, or Jürg Conzett's association with Peter Zumthor or Jüngling Hagmann are all such examples. Secondly, even in cases where the working relationship has ended, a sense of historical connection remains between one-time collaborators; the experience often impacts subsequently on design. Valentin Bearth, Dieter Jüngling and Andreas Hagmann all worked in Peter Zumthor's office during the 1980s; Conzett was among Zumthor's earliest collaborators. Such connections bring long-term, mutual benefits. For example, through his employees Zumthor became more acquainted with the ETH discourse. In turn, in Zumthor's studio several partnerships between former collaborators were forged. Thirdly, the Graubünden is characterised by a particularly strong craft culture. There seems to be more overlap of expertise between various aspects of design; it is hard to determine where the architect's work ends and the engineer's or craftsman's begins. Zumthor's work is informed by his joinery training; Conzett demonstrates in his own work aesthetic ambitions that go well beyond structural efficiency, and so on.

Since the 1990s, such local collaborative networks have felt the pressure of federal and European legislation, and of an economic search for profit. The emerging tensions are at some level the consequence of urbanisation. Stipulations for competitive tenders, while beneficial in terms of project costs, endanger the fragile structure of personal relationships on which the local construction culture depends. It is increasingly recognised that the general model imposed from above, which has spread more rapidly in urban areas where administrative issues are more anonymous, reflects negatively on the architect's professional status and, as a result, on construction quality.

An aspect of the Graubünden economic model which has direct architectural repercussions is the local availability of timber and stone. Having led to the creation of a particular vernacular, embodying a vast amount of traditional construction knowledge, these materials continue to dominate contemporary production. Caminada's buildings in Vrin are, almost exclusively, variations on local *Strickbau* techniques. His material choices fulfil at once the iconographic demands of the commune and a pragmatic principle of sustainability:

> The question I asked myself was how we could make use of that heap of stones that were apparently of no value. These […] had accumulated over the course of years, the product of excavations, the building of roads, the demolition of old buildings etc. I set out to create the foundation wall of the slaughterhouse with this material. The stones began to take on a different aesthetic, a totally different look.[19]

19 Caminada in interview, Schaub, 2002, p. 137.

Within the local self-administrations, what would elsewhere count as a costly way of building becomes not only affordable, but sometimes the best option. For example Zumthor's Therme Vals stonework, which would have been prohibitively expensive elsewhere, was available and accounted for within the commune's own economic system rather than at market value. Like Caminada, Zumthor sees this not just as common sense but as an act suffused with artistic intent, supporting the unity of the overall concept:

> Layer upon layer of Vals gneiss, quarried 1,000 metres further up the valley, transported to site, and built back into the same slope […] within its homogeneous stone mass [the building] still retains a clear sense of the strongest of the initial design ideas – the idea of hollowing out.[20]

20 Zumthor, 1996, pp. 11–12.

Graubünden's craft culture of stone and timber is matched by the trained skill of working concrete. The extensive construction of roads, bridges and water dams in the area has engendered a modern iconography, as recognisable as the local vernacular. Thus, when Olgiati chose to build the Paspels School in concrete, this was not necessarily interpreted as a statement of opposition to the typical cultural heritage, but an alignment with another of its aspects. Pragmatically, it made at least as much economic sense as one of the traditional materials. At a practical level, the client representative could apply his own technical expertise, acquired on the water dams, to set the high standards of the school's finishes.

Where architectural production is oriented towards craft, the architect tends to exercise more control over the production processes. Zumthor's early timber projects depended on his formation as a cabinet-maker, not only on the local availability

Swiss factory in a rural setting, 1914

of carpentry skills. In his case vocational training was used self-consciously, affecting not only his architectural output – timber buildings conceived as precious furniture pieces – but also his overall professional persona.

The link between craft culture and high-quality construction is not exclusive to Graubünden. It is the consequence of a particular feature of Swiss education, the apprenticeship system.

Fachhochschule and ETH: between craft and theory
In the international imagination, Swiss crafts traditions retain an almost medieval, guild-driven character. This stereotype is contradicted by the actual existence of a cross-cantonal training network, which is modernist in spirit. Kurt W. Forster remarked that Swiss architecture is characterised by a paradox rooted in its political context. The training of architects is conducted at a federal level, whereas practice – as we have seen in the case of Graubünden – is regional.[21]

After high school, the majority of German-Swiss pupils complete a period of professional apprenticeship and additional trade courses, including some that lead to architectural qualifications. The theoretical instruction provided at federal level by ETH and other academic institutions is paralleled in a network of vocational schools. The most established among these are the *Fachhochschulen* [colleges of applied sciences, formerly known as technical colleges] but there are other institutions, such as the Basel School of Design, from which Zumthor graduated. The options and course combinations available for architectural training in various cantons make it difficult to generalise on the nature of this kind of instruction. Historically, the *Fachhochschulen* have provided a practice-based professional background, enabling a widespread grasp of craftsmanship and construction know-how.

The *Fachhochschulen* are not exclusively Swiss. They also exist in Germany and Austria, suggesting an affinity with *Werkbund* and Bauhaus principles. In the early decades of the twentieth century, the Bauhaus sought to bring together artist and craftsman through the common aim of building. This aim had social democratic reverberations, but failed to challenge the political and economic realities of capitalist production.[22] The apprenticeship training required for vocational courses implies an interdependence of architecture, craft and industry similar to the earlier modernist model. For example, Zumthor's training in the Basel School of Design in the 1960s displayed a stronger connection to modernist principles than ETH did at the time.[23]

The polytechnic bias of ETH means that here too practical application is essential. The attention devoted to construction and technical modules in the early years is on a par with design. As at the Bauhaus, construction seeks an artistic dimension, but the role of industry in achieving it is more ambiguous. The teaching of elements that comprise the strictly constructional or industrial

21 Forster, 1997, p. 4.

22 Schwartz, 1996, pp. 1–6.

23 Zumthor, interview with author, 2006.

field of knowledge is ultimately subordinated to the artistic unity of the artefact.

This belief is expressed in Andrea Deplazes's preface to a manual of construction techniques: "Only in conjunction with a concept […] the initially isolated technical and structural fragments are at once arranged to fill a consummate, architectural body".[24] Conceptual coherence is meant to redeem the object from the menial status of the simply manufactured. This ambition is not dissimilar to the redemption of the everyday from sheer banality, which Swiss architecture seeks through its interpretations of typical forms and ordinary environments.

In the past, the cultural ecology of the *Fachhochschulen* in relation to ETH suggested the existence of two complementary forms of building knowledge, one based on practical experience, the other on theoretical background. Swiss architectural production in the 1980s and 1990s was moulded by the convergence of these educational models, one steeped in the most involved form of practice, the other more theoretical, tinged with a conceptual bias.

More recently, the *Fachhochschule* ethos has been questioned by an increased demand for courses in the ETH fashion, often led by ETH-trained architects. Underlining this phenomenon is an aspirational ambition with complex social, economic and cultural causes. The downside is a diminishing pool of architectural technicians, which threatens the delicate complementarity of intellectual rigour and technical know-how still recognisable in the Swiss architecture of the 1990s. As technical expertise is increasingly outsourced to contractors, the architects' role in construction and, by extension, their professional status, are now in a state of flux.

The architect's professional status

The earlier case studies are symptomatic of the attitudes towards construction perceptible in the architectural profession at the end of the twentieth century. The projects of Herzog & de Meuron, Diener & Diener and von Ballmoos Krucker offer critical commentaries on construction in certain conditions, from an updated vernacular to the more industrial production associated with typical urban and suburban environments. Peter Zumthor's attitude is more involved, tending towards a Romantic appreciation of craft. Gigon and Guyer earnestly reprise the modernist motif of Davos architecture.

In the case of Olgiati's Paspels School, the issue of construction is perhaps least explicit. The expectation of good building is incorporated in the culturally high production values, just as the engineered details that sustain the building are concealed within its emphatic mass. Olgiati's disinterest in the representational aspects of construction is consistent with his decision to subcontract out the project's administration and site supervision. This signals a separation of architecture's technical aspects from

[24] Deplazes, 2005, p. 10.

its artistic dimensions, although not a total one. The architect is fully aware that "various respective relationships between architect, construction supervisor, clients and craftsmen are necessary to build well".[25]

The Paspels School was built between 1997 and 1998. Fifteen years earlier, when Herzog & de Meuron were planning the Stone House, their equally radical artistic ambitions had been supported by in-house technical knowledge. The project's drawing archive reflects a dual design process.[26] On the one hand the initial sketches, fragments of perspective views and painterly colour studies, notes scribbled all over, emphasise a conceptual side. On the other hand the construction drawings, also drawn and annotated by hand, translate the concept into building terms. The two kinds of drawings signify two interdependent areas of expertise. As representations of architectural authorship, they acknowledge the collaborative and multi-layered nature of design.

Despite their distance in time, in both Olgiati's and Herzog & de Meuron's case there is no question of their constructional know-how. The architects exercise confident control over the building site. However, the two situations show the existence of fault lines between design and production, and their gradual separation into distinct spheres. The change in representational techniques and the increased dependence on computer drawing seem to assist this separation.

In time, this is bound to affect the role of the architect on site and the expectations regarding professional duty. Historically, the Swiss architect's status bridged the intellectual and practical aspects of design. The professional indemnity insurance still covers the management of site works, on the grounds that the architect exercises control over the trade sub-contractors. In this respect the construction model differs from Britain or the US, where managing roles are assigned to main contractors. The prestigious quality of Swiss construction is related to the architect's close contact with all trades and the exercise of control over every aspect of the production, from design to completion.

The intellectual aspirations of design, partly articulated in theory, have been exercising steady pressure on this professional role. The implicit preference for creative design has led to the practice of subcontracting administrative duties and site supervision. The recourse to technical architects, within an architectural firm or sourced from a different company, becomes a desirable option.

A special situation is presented by Peter Märkli's Zurich practice, which is split into two physical entities: the anonymous studio in which the practitioner works virtually alone, and a medium-sized production office that sees projects through construction. This could be seen to epitomise the distinction between a creative elite and the majority of architects that form the interface with the building industry. The misalignment between Märkli's unique creativity and the standard requirements of architectural practice

25 Olgiati, 2008, p. 43.

26 The archive was published in Mack, 1997, pp. 59–63.

is adjusted within the larger production office. This example reveals the claims made by praxis on personal artistic agendas, and stands witness to the different kinds of knowledge and skills necessary to bridge initial design and completion stages.

At the moment, the nature of architectural competence hangs in the balance. As long as professional education still enables an overlap between artistic-theoretical and more practical kinds of knowledge, there will be architects who can span the spectrum necessary for the high level of practice customary within Swiss architecture. The more professional training favours the artistic-intellectual over the practical aspects of architecture, the more future generations will relinquish control over the building processes, at the expense of construction quality. This would create more of a levelling between Swiss and other national construction industries.

It is difficult to trace the extent to which the polarisation between "designers" and "builders" comes from within the profession, or in response to external pressures. It is certainly consistent with wider parallel phenomena – the reliance on computers for conveying information, the speed of technological development, the emergence of managerial roles in the construction industry, the increasing complexity of professional indemnity, the economic demand for profit. There seems to be a clear link between this professional fragmentation and a greater participation in the global economy. As architects operate abroad, they become reliant on the technical expertise of local practices. The author provides a design brand for export; outsourcing, as in other industries, becomes the norm.

Resistance to these developments is only possible on a small local scale and within a limited time-span, as was shown in the case of the Graubünden. Just as the idea of "Swiss-made" quality has been turned into a marketing tool, so, too, the cultural resonance of Swiss construction can no longer be taken for granted.

Thematic
Interpretations

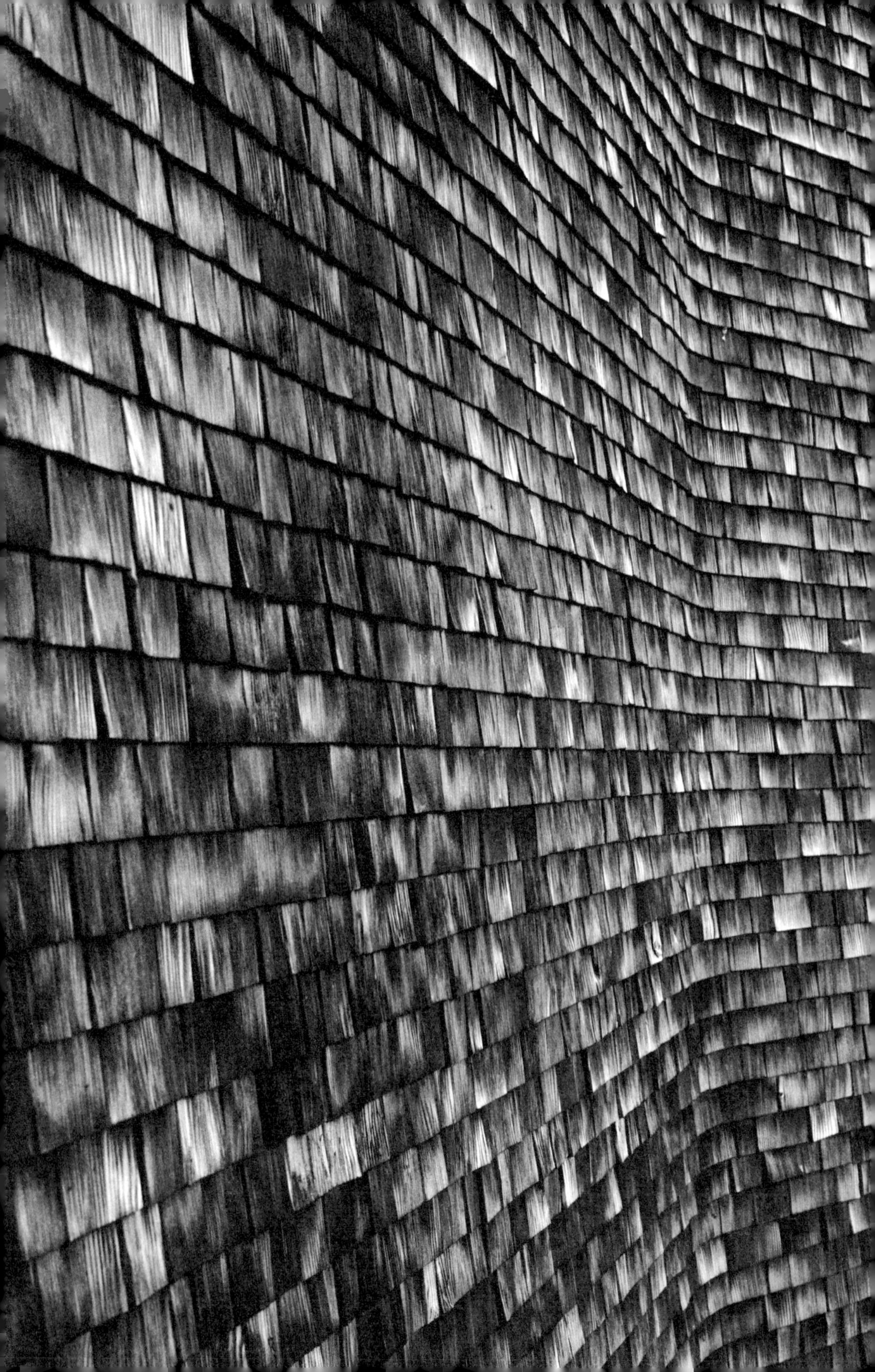

Towards a Swiss Model

> To let reality be felt and intellectually confronted [...] we feel this to be a political necessity.[1]
> **Herzog & de Meuron**

[1] Herzog and de Meuron, 1992, p. 143.

The case studies gathered above under the rubric "Forms of Practice" rely, to a greater or lesser degree, on conceptual coherence. They illustrate a theoretical spectrum that was formulated during the 1980s, then disseminated and interpreted during the 1990s. The Kirchner Museum represents, perhaps most clearly, the moment when its themes were radicalised and enriched, adding new dimensions to the discourse. Gigon / Guyer's insistence on endowing an idea with materiality places them somewhere between Herzog & de Meuron's cerebral approach and Zumthor's tangible constructs.[2] In the Kirchner Museum neither dominates the other; rather, the abstract and the concrete are set in a dialectical relationship. Design begins from an examination of reality "as it is", and architectural additions are conceptually articulated. This self-imposed discipline accentuates the object-like qualities of surface and material.

[2] Annette Gigon interviewed in Adam and Wang, 2000, p. 8.

At some point, the projects stop deferring to rational decisions and stray into a private territory of biographical memories, impressions and atmospheres. The acknowledgement of sensuous materiality and associative images brings to the argument a more limited order, which is often in counterpoint to the complexity of the context.

Wilfried Wang identified in Gigon / Guyer's work the paradoxical qualities of "normality and irritation".[3] This observation may be extended to other Swiss projects concerned with readings of reality ordered by abstraction. The resulting qualities of architecture tend towards the production of "artefacts". The architects' interest in ordinary environments and their wariness of monuments, modernist or otherwise, result in the design of buildings that in fact become monuments, albeit of a different kind. The projects draw upon a common referential repository that spans from concrete, physical traits of buildings to less tangible considerations. This provides the opportunity to identify, despite the surface heterogeneity of Swiss production, some deeper shared themes.

[3] Ibid.

Likeness

One way in which projects adapt themselves to their surroundings is through formal similarity. References to the existing are taken up deliberately, in order to endow the new forms with older meanings. The cubic volumes of the Kirchner Museum are factory-"like", Zumthor's studio in Haldenstein is stable-"like", the Schutzbauten in Chur, shed-"like". Similarly, Diener & Diener's work in Basel builds upon an established imagery of urban housing or speculative commercial buildings.

The theme of likeness is ambivalent. While suggesting kinship between two or more entities, it also acknowledges that they are different from each other. The architecture examined here oscillates between fitting in and standing out from its immediate context, between subscribing to a conventional image and stating its (artistic) individuality. The eccentric, coloured elevation of Herzog & de Meuron's Blue House (1979–1980) stands among the earliest, most didactic demonstrations of this duality.[4]

The allegiance to ordinary forms has become part and parcel of ETH theory. It echoes the intention of Rossi's analogical architecture, formally rehearsing deeply familiar models like factories, urban galleries, or houses.[5] In the Swiss production, the focus on humble types reflects a concern with culturally relevant, ordinary models. The scope of formal analogies first established in the 1980s was extended throughout the next decade. The removal of detail and the formal distortion of the original models led to the creation of a new imagery, in which only the most essential or typical elements have been preserved.

Bearth & Deplazes's projects in Graubünden villages illustrate this tendency. The school in Vella (1994–1997) duplicates the double-pitch roofs of the neighbouring houses but eliminates characteristic details (projecting eaves, perforated timber decorations). It establishes a distinctive modern identity through its formal abstraction, through the subtle shading of the render, recalling the modernist white façade, and the geometric asymmetry of the window reveals. The deformed perimeter of the Willimann-Lötscher house in Sevgein (1998–1999) has created a loose lozenge-shaped house with starkly different aspects on its narrow and wide sides. Both school and house are unified in their appearance through the consistent application of material, render and respectively vertical timber boarding, to all elevations. Render is a camouflage material, which effectively "renders" houses indistinct from their built environment. However, timber has a more ambiguous role, suggesting that formal or typological likeness is closely related to another shared motif: the painterly expression of material.

---

4 The Blue House in Oberwil used an ordinary brief (suburban house) as a vehicle for extraordinary architectural ambitions. See Mack, 1997, pp. 26–31.

5 See Rossi, 1996, pp. 348–352.

(Above left) Herzog & de Meuron.
Blue House, Oberwil 1979–80

(Above right) Bearth & Deplazes.
School, Vella, 1994-97

(Right) Bearth & Deplazes.
Willimann-Lötscher House, Sevgein, 1998–99

Active surfaces, abstract interiors

The projects studied here tend towards an "over-all" appearance, characterised by wrapping the cladding material around the entire volume.[6] In Herzog & de Meuron's Stone House as in Zumthor's Schutzbauten, the quasi-unprocessed quality of natural materials gives rise to associative meanings pertaining to an archaic, traditional, humble quality. Both projects acquire a rudimentary, yet skilled, hand-made character, intensified through the weaving of small-scale elements into large unarticulated surfaces. In contrast, at the Kirchner Museum the processes invoked are exclusively industrial. The impersonal character diminishes the narrative possibilities of the material and renders the glass surface more obdurate, bringing attention to itself.

The focus on material illustrates a wider tendency of matching the simplicity of form with the visual intensification of its surface. This applies, beyond the present cases, to buildings as diverse as Peter Märkli's La Congiunta, Valerio Olgiati's Yellow House (Das Gelbe Haus) in Flims, Herzog & de Meuron's Signal Boxes in Basel or Zumthor's Thermal Baths in Vals. Steinmann has attributed special significance to this emphatic sensuousness. For him, it represents a "shift in the *recherche architecturale* from things as meaning, to things as experience".[7] That is to say, the interest in the material's painterly character replaces more referential imagery, like that used during the early 1980s. Once literal contextual quotations were deemed too unstable, they were replaced with synthetic interpretations of context, in the form of a unified material appearance.

This strategy results in the self-sufficiency of buildings related to, yet detached from, their surroundings. The painterly façade takes attention away from the building's place in the city, creating a tension between its autonomy as an artefact and its participation in the everyday. For example, despite a grammar of openings suggestive of masonry construction, the Stone House is not about walls, but about surfaces. The stone is treated as a species of wallpaper, not unlike the a-tectonic concrete volume of the school in Paspels. The material surfaces of the Schutzbauten pertain primarily to the act of their making and only partly to the existence of a local, timber-oriented craft culture. At the Kirchner Museum, the glass skin is key in conveying a self-referential quality; at its most contextual, it offers an abstract reading of local light conditions.

The Warteckhof and Stöckenacker developments make relatively less of a virtue of their materials, yet they maintain a sense of overall wrapping. Stöckenacker's grey concrete has an iconographic significance, its sombre tone conveying urban dignity. In the Warteckhof, the elevational compositions pertain to the rhythm of anonymous urban façades, and the choice of brick and concrete reinforces the urban imagery.

[6] Annette Gigon interviewed in Adam and Wang, 2000, p. 7.

[7] Steinmann, 1994, p. 11.

(Page 212 and top left) Peter Zumthor.
St. Benedetg Chapel, Sumvitg, 1988–89.
Shingle cladding

(Middle left) Peter Zumthor.
Thermal Baths, Vals, 1990–96.
Stone cladding

(Top right) Herzog & de Meuron.
Signal Box Auf dem Wolf, Basel, 1989–94.
Copper strip cladding

(Middle right) Peter Märkli.
La Congiunta, Giornico, 1989–92.
Concrete wall

(Bottom right) Valerio Olgiati.
The Yellow House, Flims, 1998–2000.
Painted façade

The abstract interior is the internal equivalent of the wrap-around cladding; it presents a similar intensity of surface treatment. If the "over-all" façade surface underlines the building's autonomy, on the inside the "over-all" folded surface emphasises the spatiality of rooms. The abstract interior retains at least some dependency on the needs of inhabitation. In the Stone House the abstraction remains restricted to the outside; internally, the white plaster walls define more or less conventional rooms. The Schutzbauten's permeable timber skin is visible on the inside, but at low level it is concealed behind a black cloth that allows internal display.

In contrast, in the Kirchner Museum, the cave-like circulations are defined by surfaces that reject conventional definition as walls, ceilings or floors. These concrete surfaces contribute to the creation of poignantly empty spaces, characterised by concrete folded surfaces. A certain lineage of such all-concrete interiors may be recognised, from the Kirchner Museum to Peter Märkli's La Congiunta (1992), Olgiati's Paspels School (1996) or Christian Kerez's Forsterstrasse apartments in Zurich (2005). Adapted from public to private projects, the provision of abstracted interiors is at odds with the programmatic needs of dwelling.

This material strategy is not restricted to concrete. The layered stonework of Zumthor's Thermal Baths in Vals (in effect the facing of a concrete-masonry composite) is likewise used to create a unified interior, reinforcing the concept of spaces carved into the mountain rock. However, when floors, walls and ceiling are all clad in timber, like in the classrooms of the Paspels School, the effect is opposite. The interiors provide a typological reference to the traditional *Stube*, but the domestic connotations are tempered by the reductive and precise detailing of timber surfaces.

Parts and whole
Another common feature is the adoption of non-hierarchical spaces as a substitute for the conventional duality of rooms and corridors. Through its omission of corridors, the Stone House translates an idea of wholeness in terms of geometric coherence. If the traditional house is often configured as a corridor-less plan with a hollow core, with a main room doubling up as hallway, here the cross wall's central position pertains to a contrary condition. The configuration is primarily based on a graphic correspondence between plan and elevation. The rectangular rooms figure on the symmetrical plan as equivalent, if unequal, spatial compartments.

A different relationship between rooms (as parts) and plan (as a whole) occurs at the Kirchner Museum and the Paspels School. Both plans describe a condition similar to the Stone House, with equivalent rooms pushed into the corners. However, the central cross that separates the rooms of the Stone House has been expanded into a defined spatial entity. This results in a different kind of equivalence, between complementary spatial types. The quasi-modular galleries and classrooms are embedded into a looser spatial configuration, which serves as a connective circulation space or foyer.

(Top left) Gigon/Guyer.
Kirchner Museum, Davos, 1989–92

(Top right) Christian Kerez.
Apartment Building Forsterstrasse,
Zurich, 1998–2003

(Middle) Peter Märkli.
La Congiunta, Giornico, 1989–92

(Right) Peter Zumthor.
Thermal Baths, Vals, 1990–96

[8] See Lucan, 2001, pp. 126–129. This typological understanding indicates the degree to which Swiss architecture re-interprets its own precedents, and not only anonymous traditional, historical Modernist or contemporary international models.

The plans of these three buildings have acquired an independent value of their own. They operate almost as graphic signs that can be adapted to different situations. In a late overview of this period of Swiss architecture, the plan drawings of the Stone House and of the Kirchner Museum were selected to represent two characteristic typologies, denoted respectively as "corridor-less" plans and "constellation" plans.[8] Both types are concerned with revising the idea of corridor, whether it is widened to become a distinct room or squeezed out altogether. The bourgeois convention of the corridor as a subservient space is thus subverted by the search for more direct spatial relationships. The problem is transferred to the anxious tension between the building's overall resolution and the appropriate expression of its constituent parts.

Within this field, the room for interpretation is vast. In the Paspels School, the classrooms placed in each corner of the original square create a cruciform central lobby, similar to the loose configuration of the Kirchner Museum circulation. In both projects, the corridors are given a rough concrete finish to convey their condition of being "outside" the inhabited rooms. They are rendered less visible than the actual outside, which is entirely determined by its dignified presence in the landscape. Rather, the internal connecting spaces are seen as abstract generalisations of "room", somewhere between containers and multi-purpose environments. In contrast to the Kirchner Museum, in Paspels the duality of enclosed rooms and enveloping corridors is subsumed within the compact overall volume. The emphasis on the unified perimeter is similar to that of the Stone House. The school project can be seen, in this sense, as a synthesis of the two earlier plan typologies.

The architectural currency of type-configurations raises questions about their proliferation as geometric abstractions of urban order. The Paspels School is intended as a monument, conveying urbanity in the pastoral setting. The Kirchner Museum, as an interpretation of the urban structure of Davos, turns a process of piecemeal growth into a serial, modular version of town. Warteckhof, another established example of the "constellation" typology, extends the ambiguity from the one building to an entire urban block. The flowing spaces between buildings create an internal cohesion within the block and establish its connection to the city. The ensemble acts like an urban landscape, setting a tension between the project's individual aesthetic and the collective conventions of the urban continuum.

Rectangularity

The Kirchner project is characterised by the deliberate avoidance of expressive gestures. In the early 1990s, Gigon / Guyer stated that they needed "an occasion in order to break out of the orthogonality".[9] Their formal reticence purported an ethical basis, not dissimilar to Herzog & de Meuron and Zumthor's rejections of "arbitrariness" circa 1988.[10]

[9] Annette Gigon interviewed in Adam and Wang, 2000, p. 10.

[10] Herzog and de Meuron, 1992, p. 144; Zumthor, "A Way of Looking", 2006, p. 16.

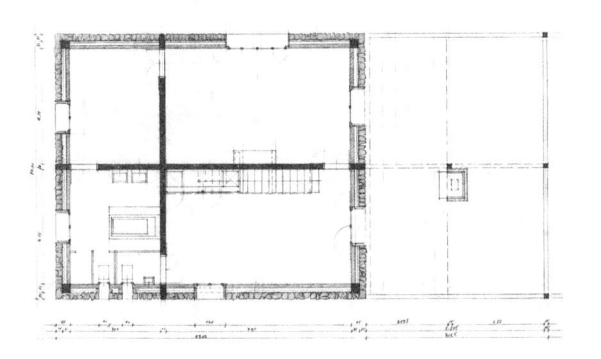

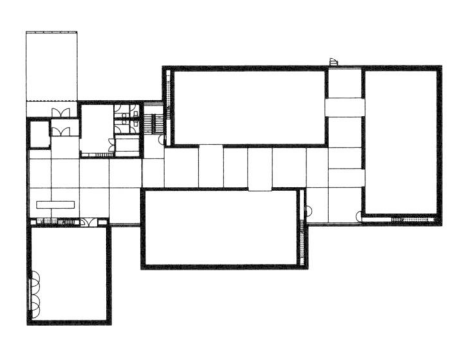

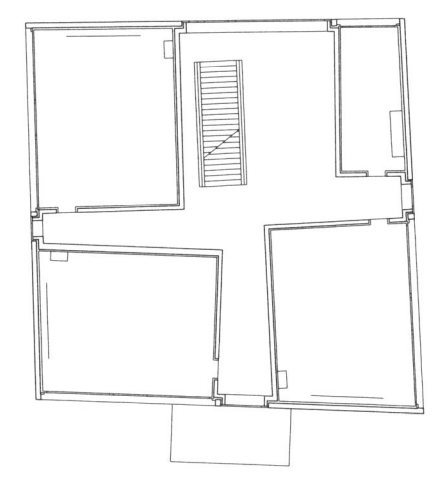

(Top left) Herzog & de Meuron.
Stone House, Tavole, Italy, 1982–88.
Plan, ground floor

(Top right) Gigon/Guyer.
Kirchner Museum, Davos, 1989–92.
Plan, ground floor

(Above) Valerio Olgiati. School,
Paspels, 1996–98. Plan, first floor

The assumption here is that the orthogonal is not arbitrary. The right angle is seen as neutrality itself, a cultural symbol that integrates the building into its real context. Unlike other design devices, the orthogonal lays claim to a kind of inexhaustible universality. It simultaneously represents a blank canvas, radical reduction, normality, and the rigidity of academic convention.

Using rectangularity as a geometrical expression of ordinariness gave way in the late 1990s to a more open attitude, making the virtues of rectangularity or non-rectangularity a function of each project's circumstances. Herzog & de Meuron's passage from an early preference for the orthogonal to later forays into freer forms may be gauged from the differences between the Basel Signal Boxes. Despite their equivalent sculptural presence amidst railway tracks, they differ formally. While the first Signal Box (designed 1988–1989) is a mute rectangular prism, the second (designed 1994) is vertically twisted, creating an impression of instability. Nevertheless, this formal gesture remains indebted to orthogonal order. It has been justified as "correcting" the trapezoid shape of the footprint, determined by site conditions, to become a rectangle at the top floor.[11]

11 See Mack, 2000, p. 83.

Zumthor's Schutzbauten make a formal opportunity out of their reliance on the perimeter of the existing ruins. The architectural decision consists of following this irregular footprint, rather than creating an individual formal gesture. In the Vals Thermal Baths, where the forms were carved out of shapeless rock, Zumthor has fallen back on the passepartout of rectangularity.

The Paspels plan was determined by the slight deformation of an original square – never by more than five degrees – in order to remain almost imperceptible and thus avoid overly expressive connotations.[12] This deviation introduced an irrational moment into the rigid geometric plan. Here arbitrariness and disorder have the subversive intentionality of Dada art, as does the broken pillar in the Yellow House (1995–99). And yet, Olgiati's form-making strategies vary from one project to another. I have shown the formal predilection for compact and cost-effective cubic volumes as originating with Paspels. In later projects, Olgiati has appealed to "objective" factors in order to justify formal departures from the cube: planning stipulations (Condominium, Chur, 1999) or structural efficiency (University of Lucerne, 2003).

12 Olgiati, *Interview*, 2006.

The interplay of reason and subjectivity is symptomatic of a wider ambivalence between claims to objectivity and what constitutes an architectural gesture. The objective common ground results from the observation of existing patterns and the adherence to established conventions. The mark of individuality goes back, as one would expect, to more subjective readings of context.

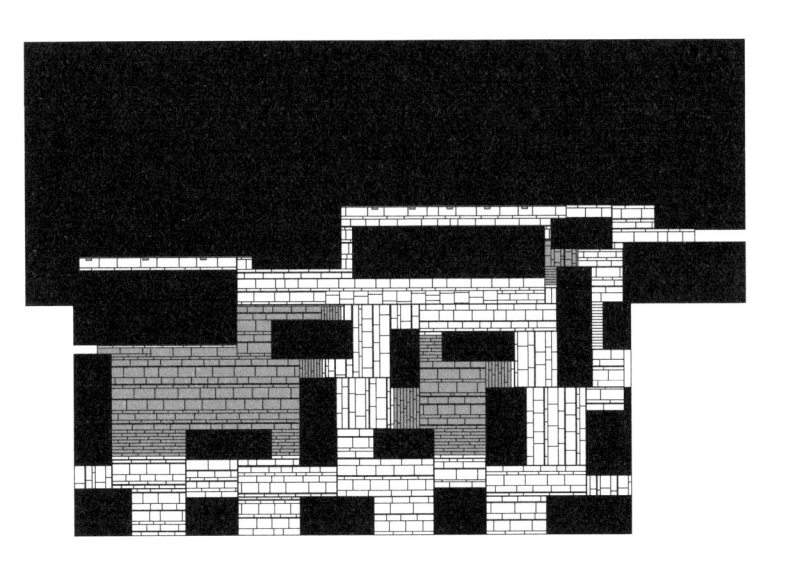

(Top) Peter Zumthor.
Thermal Baths, Vals, 1990–96. Plan

(Above left) Herzog & de Meuron.
Signal Box Auf dem Wolf, Basel.
Project 1989, realization 1991–94

(Above right) Herzog & de Meuron.
Central Signal Box, Basel.
Competition 1994, project 1995,
realization 1998–99

Presence

The categories through which a possible Swiss model has been considered have been so far tangible parameters, pertaining to material and form. Attached to this tangibility is a generalised search for architectural "presence" or "effect".[13] These are aesthetic categories, pertaining to a contemplative mode and removing the subject from the claims of past and future existence. During aesthetic contemplation, the viewer is absorbed into the moment; history seems to stand still. The perception of the object takes precedence over its intended use, and its connection to the world is severed by the fixation on intrinsic physical qualities. As Minimalism would have it, objects cease to accept meanings being reflected upon them and declare themselves as self-sufficient, complete and autonomous.

The timelessness of aesthetic moments is an undercurrent of the Swiss discourse. The autonomy of objects, a leitmotif of late Modernism, was illustrated in Rossi's theories around typology as much as in his analogical revisions. Rossi pursued in his architecture the effect of his childhood Sacri Monti: "the stasis of timeless miracles, tables set for eternity, drinks never consumed, things which are only themselves".[14] The Swiss architects have found a similar sense of stasis elsewhere: Zumthor in everyday objects, buildings and their atmospheres; Herzog & de Meuron in an intellectually controlled architecture; Diener & Diener, in general types and the appeal to realist art.[15] The recourse to art, whether as the architect's justification of design or the critic's interpretation of it, represents a search for stillness. The architecture more or less succumbs to the aesthetic ideal of isolating the subject in the "perceptual vacuum" of the moment.[16]

Certainly the discourse is careful to differentiate between architecture and art. And yet, it doesn't fully recognise that the autonomy of artworks is itself fictional. Just as the aesthetic experience of timelessness during the contemplation of art doesn't mean that time actually stops in the gallery, so the art object's claim of self-referentiality is undercut by an inevitable referential horizon.[17] Its meaning always refers to something beyond its own form and material. Karsten Harries once observed that minimalist objects "do not so much grant presentness as they signify it. Signifying presentness, they mean a secularised grace".[18] Presence, in turn, cannot be equated with an aesthetic experience removed from the practical sphere – all the more so in the case of architecture.

For Swiss architecture around 1990, the reaction against Postmodernism created a gesture of negative intervention, a retreat into silence against the background *muzak* of market culture. The search for a specific presence and the aspiration to timelessness can be read in these projects as forms of resistance. They belong to the horizon of artistic autonomy in modern capitalist society. The adherence to this horizon declares architecture's removal from the everyday, to a level purified through intellectual or constructional coherence.

---

13 For example Steinmann, 1994, pp. 8–24; Steinmann et al., p. 9; Diener and Righetti, 1991, pp. 77–78.

14 Rossi, 1981, p. 5.

15 Diener, 1989, pp. 38–39; Peter Zumthor, "A Way of Looking", 2006, p. 17; Zaera, 1993, pp. 21–22.

16 Zumthor, "A Way of Looking", 2006, p. 17.

17 Valerio Olgiati acknowledged this impossibility by including a "golden picture" by Helmut Federle in his "Iconographic Autobiography" (2006). For him, this painting represents the recognition that "one is incapable of managing to free oneself from references". Federle's painting is paired with a "white picture" by Robert Ryman, representing "the hope of managing to free oneself from references". The pairing of the two abstract paintings, one depicting "everything", the other depicting "nothing", represents a fundamental dialectic in Olgiati's work. See Olgiati, "Iconographic Autobiography", 2006, p. 141.

18 Harries, 1989, p. 31.

Peter Märkli, La Congiunta,
Giornico, 1989–92

CopyQuick
CopyQuick
CopyQuick
CopyQuick
IMPORT
PARFUMERIE
Oettinger
Tobacco-Center
CIGARES
CIGARES

Notions of Resistance

Rather than identifying a consistent Swiss discourse through a common set of themes or values, it is easier to do so on the basis of the themes and values it rejects. Many of the architects' pronouncements in the late 1980s and early 1990s bear witness to a sense of defiance – in particular, through the common appeal to the notion of "resistance". Each architect ascribed particular meanings to this term; the general discourse is marked by the nuanced interpretations of a shared impulse.

"Resistance" is set in opposition to license, individualism and arbitrariness, all architectural manifestations of a wider cultural malaise. In the late 1980s, the architects positioned their work as a reaction to the stylistic strategies of fragmented historical pastiche. Postmodernism and Deconstructivism were seen to pertain to a sort of moral decadence, a visual equivalent of consumerism. For Zumthor, the opposition to this mainstream celebration of relativism implied a higher moral ground:

> In a society that celebrates the inessential, architecture can put up a resistance, counteract the waste of forms and meanings, and speak its own language.[1]

[1] Zumthor, "A Way of Looking", 2006, p. 27.

A similar statement, made at the time by Herzog & de Meuron, reflects more explicitly an ethical ambition:

> We are against arbitrariness because it always serves to dismantle resistance, an aesthetic political resistance to simple consumerism, to the dizzying speed with which this consumer behaviour has to be maintained by new picture material. Our *moral-political* resistance to this arbitrariness is also related to a fear of being pulled into the current ourselves […] a fear of being ourselves degraded into guises.[2]

[2] Herzog and de Meuron, 1992, p. 144.

(Opposite) Diener & Diener, Office Building Kohlenberg, Basel, 1992–1995

The best position to define reality and cope with it was through the return to the medium of architecture. The reaction against "being degraded into guises" was to reveal those bases of the profession that constituted an incontestable truth. The problem was determining exactly what these bases might be; and the subsequent lack of consensus might have stemmed from the range of possible interpretations.

The negative moment illustrated by the retreat into "presence" signals the rejection of an established canon. Over time however, the object of the rejection changed. In the 1960s, autonomy was invoked in order to avoid the dissolution of architecture into related disciplines; in the late 1970s architects reacted against restrictive typological methodologies; in the 1980s, against a general formalist *laissez-faire*. At the turn of the twenty-first century the attitudes changed again, with more recent works embracing the all-pervading relativity. This suggests a kind of closed cycle, the attempt to avoid the very essentialism and self-righteousness that previous notions of resistance had created.

Postmodernism was itself a form of resistance against the abstracting austerity of modernist orthodoxy. And yet it propagated the same order as Modernism, albeit with a changed imagery. Eventually, both Postmodernism and the Swiss reaction against it come down to a continuation of Modernism; the former hidden, feigning indifference, the latter more explicit, manifesting a restrained earnestness. Despite the Swiss project's cultural ambitions, the focus remained on form, which is a modernist concern. As Marcel Meili wrote:

> In opposition to the predictability and abstraction of the late modernist dogma, [...] we sought an architecture that could embody more general cultural significations. This could, we felt, be achieved through re-centring the project on issues of form, provided we integrated it with a more global understanding of the modalities of its "usage".[3]

[3] Meili, "Ein paar Bauten", 1991, p. 22.

The main reason behind the rejection of Postmodernism around 1990 was that it represented a randomness of design decisions, bordering on the cynical. Herzog & de Meuron's "moral-political" distaste for arbitrariness is characteristic of this understanding. Objectivity, hailed as the stable ground, remained nevertheless vague, a matter open to interpretation. What it did provide was the motivation for seeking architectural coherence in the territory between type and form.

Reduction as a form of resistance

Diener & Diener's creative output remains amongst the most concerted efforts to open the formal production towards the city. These buildings seek a universal intelligibility grounded in the transparency of type, their neutral physiognomy "an expression open to various uses".[4] Therefore, when exploring the issue of type-forms in the Swiss production, it is only right to start with them.

[4] Diener and Righetti, 1991, p. 77.

The withdrawal from overt expression represents a reaction against a lack of urban order. With the city understood as a "conflicting contradictory phenomenon without clarified logic", as Meili put it, "the indeterminateness and divergence of today's life robs the form of its reason".[5] In response to this condition, Diener & Diener reverted to "the most general form".[6] The architecture preserves its formal basis.

Diener's architecture emphasises reductive formal principles, spatial and visual relationships. Its autonomy acknowledges that an unselfconscious imitation of urban types is no longer possible. The architecture articulates neutrality as its own expressive means, abstaining from the proliferation of overly theoretical, abstract or arbitrary gestures. This observation applies to others, too. For Meili, formal reduction helps make sense of a confusing reality; it pursues silence above theoretical and advertising chatter:

> In a diffusive culture such as ours, there are only a very few devices available that can hold form together. In their subdued, nearly mute fashion, they speak to the last vestiges of a collective sensibility, as hopes for finding a common basis for active comprehension fail.[7]

In the 1990s, the various approaches of Swiss architecture converged on "reduction" as a kind of formal convention. The participating architects and critics set it up as a manifestation of a more fundamental resistance, a *rappel à l'ordre*:

> The reduction is, at last, a defence against the wild proliferation of meaningless and uncontrolled constructive connections.[8]

This restriction placed the accent on architecture as an ordering system from which all that is unnecessary was removed. The resulting formal simplicity emphasised relationships between elements, either at the small scale of detail and material or at the greater scale of urban intervention. A consensus emerged in the writings of Diener and Meili, associating reduction with the idea of architectural effect:

> Reduction means limiting ourselves to the few things that are necessary to be able to control the effect of the spaces. [...] There is often nothing left in our architecture except the spatial effect.[9]

> The restriction to a few, uninterrupted materials and their unusual application imply a search for effect almost exclusively in the evocative qualities of the materials themselves.[10]

---

5 Meili, "Luzernerring", 1991, p. 43.

6 Steinmann, 1991.

7 Meili, 1996, p. 24.

8 Ibid., p. 25.

9 Diener and Righetti, 1991, pp. 77–78.

10 Meili, 1996, p. 25.

> The formal material [...] is so discreet as to almost achieve the limit of indifference, the degree zero of significance.[11]

[11] Meili, "Ein paar Bauten", 1991, p. 24.

The use of reduction appears here to have an ambivalent value. On the one hand it stands for integrity. It seeks a hidden layer of truth beneath the formal manipulations and compositional incident that gain value in the market culture. On the other hand, reduction remains subject to notions of effect, which suggests it is viewed as an aesthetic category. This ambivalence recalls Le Corbusier's modernist oscillation between objective "truth" and subjective "taste", with similar consequences. It defines architecture as form, opening its understanding to the vicissitudes of concept, subjectivity and intuition.

From the type to the typical

The Swiss tendency towards formal reduction aims at appropriateness or, rather, at the avoidance of improper gestures. This implies anything from modesty and the voluntary acceptance of objective constraints, to a deliberate cultivation of the banal and the laconic. Whatever the underlying motivation, the concerns with objectivity and appropriateness are met in the artefact itself and its making. The buildings' systematic consistency suggests the dominance of a theoretical model, demanding intelligibility and coherence.

Alternatively, the entire assembly could be seen as an elaborate justification for "culturally-embedded" qualities of precision, control, quality, cleanliness. This interpretation doesn't stand, if only because such characteristics cannot fully represent a post-industrial European society. One might recall Max Frisch's fictional character Anatol Ludwig Stiller, the rebellious artist who viewed these qualities, typically recognised as "Swiss", with acute distaste. The artist stood, in contrast to an oppressive social apparatus, for depth, controversy, fallibility, a motif of life itself. For Stiller, the "blatant passion for material perfection, as manifested in their contemporary architecture and elsewhere", constituted "an unconscious substitute achievement" or the compensation for "spiritual compromise".[12] The stereotype suggests a fear of anything but bare objective facts, a concern for correctness. In design terms such concerns are satisfied by the application of rigour, harnessing the work's poetic impulse into a technical solution.

[12] Frisch, 1982, pp. 213–214.

If cultural stereotypes cannot be given exaggerated importance, it would be equally misleading to isolate Swiss architecture's preoccupation with form from the cultural patterns in which it has emerged. At some level, the stereotypical reflects the typical and offers some indications of the cultural values that are held in common. The *status quo* lies somewhere between stereotype and the professional reliance on architectural autonomy.

While architecture's formal focus is itself arbitrary, there are moments when the built works, over and against theoretical justifications, pertain to a deeper order. Can one read the typical patterns of the culture into what is done, despite the theoretical reliance on form? Or does the buildings' self-sufficiency and coherence amount to fiction, where context is no more than a version of museum culture?

The sphere of praxis that supports architectural production suggests a creative tension between architectural ambitions to arrive at the type-form and an equally ambitious pragmatic concern with realisation. Independently of the architects' agenda, things are built well because building well is part of local culture. The political need for public ratification, the dialogue with the construction industry, with professional networks and educated clients are processes that anchor the architecture in praxis. It is through practical considerations that architecture escapes the autonomy of objects.

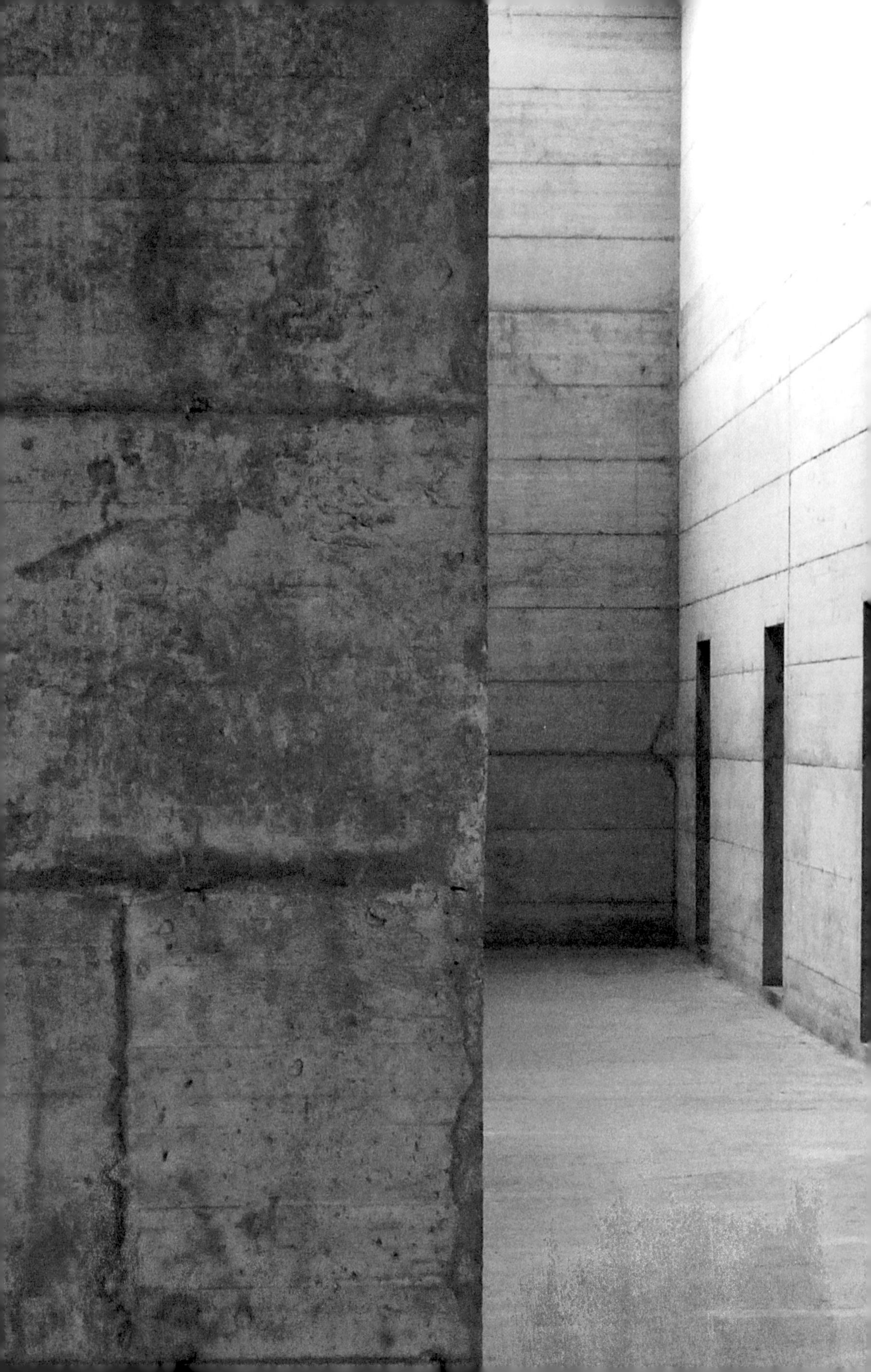

Degree Zero

The formal strength and material focus of Swiss projects invite, primarily, an object-based analysis. A first glance registers simple volumes wrapped in active surfaces – prisms whose skin is textured, patterned, three-dimensional, expressing tectonic or ornamental urges. The previous chapters sought to explain this treatment of forms and materials as a topic in itself. The present section is about the second glance. It hopes to introduce some of the meanings and messages implied, rather than expressed, in the accomplished artefact. Its theme is the reduced form.

The preference for simple, primary volumes suggests that obvious formal gestures have been carefully avoided. At the same time, many architects clearly delight in incident and use various means to imprint some specificity on the general *parti pris*. Almost anything may provide the basis for eventful irregularities: the pattern of natural materials and their weathering, geometric peculiarities imposed by site constraints, inhabitation, regulations, or structural efficiency. Whatever its cause, any formal transgression tends to be conceptually justified; even where the concept is mostly a cover for authorial licence, it still guarantees a kind of self-discipline. Thus it is not gestures that are avoided at all costs, but those gestures that are arbitrary, unaccounted for in the greater conceptual scheme.

In the absence of any justifications for visual incident, the default mode of Swiss architecture remains formal neutrality: the pure prism, the blank canvas. This explains why, in the early years of international exposure, this production was widely associated with a minimalist sensibility. Martin Steinmann presented this connection in experiential terms: in Swiss architecture, as in Minimal Art, the focus was on the object and the experience it engendered in the viewer. The connection to Minimalism was thus rooted in the aesthetic domain.

At the same time, however, Steinmann associated the Swiss works with the Pop subversion of market imagery, and the appropriation of everyday consumerist motifs in design.[1] He thus established a clear dialectic at work, between an almost solemn retreat into the form and materiality of the object on one side and the opening towards everyday images on the other. Each of these

1 Steinmann, 1994, pp. 8–25.

(Opposite) Peter Märkli,
La Congiunta,
Giornico, 1989–92. Interior

tendencies establishes its own distinct kind of reality: on the one hand the reassurance of concrete substance, on the other the domain of the familiar and the ubiquitous.

This dialectic suggests that the withdrawal from gesture witnessed in Swiss architecture has wider implications. Understandably practitioners remain cautious about associations between their work and Minimalism. They acknowledge the tendency for formal reduction, though never merely as a matter of aesthetic choice. The preference for recessive formalism could be seen in psychological terms, as a cultural disposition. And yet it seems to posit an attitude with respect to the world, which could be described as an ethical ambition.

The ethics of reduced form

Martin Steinmann saw in Swiss production a "search for a *degré zéro*, at which architecture would attain a new *presence*".[2] There is an obvious relation between the "degree zero" metaphor and this reductive sense of form, poised between abstraction and familiarity. Steinmann was not alone in finding a literary qualification for this tendency. The degree zero formulation has been, occasionally, used interchangeably with "empty sign", as in Peter Zumthor's ambition for buildings that "reach beyond signs and symbols", that are "open, empty".[3] These enticements seem to work on the strength of association, as if the implied meaning is to be grasped through allusion rather than definition.

The structuralist roots of the "degree zero" indicate its literary origins. Roland Barthes coined the term in 1957 to denote "a sort of basic speech, equally far from living languages and from literary language proper".[4] This primary, reticent mode of expression was to anchor the text in absolute and permanent values, as the "social or mythical characters of a language are abolished in favour of a neutral and inert state of form".[5] A minimum of incident would provide a clearing in the ever-growing profusion of ideas, materials, objects put forth by the market economy, which Walter Benjamin famously described as a perpetual addition of cultural debris.

The direct communication established through degree zero writing avoided the vagaries of subjective aesthetics. Through it the literary work would uncover an elusive essence, and be able to claim ethical status:

> If the writing is really neutral, and if language [...] reaches the state of a pure equation, which is no more tangible than an algebra when it confronts the innermost part of man, then Literature is vanquished, the problematics of mankind is uncovered and presented without elaboration, the writer becomes irretrievably honest.[6]

[2] Ibid., p. 24.

[3] Zumthor, "A Way of Looking", 2006, p. 17.

[4] Barthes, 1984, p. 64.

[5] Ibid.

[6] Ibid., p. 65.

The degree zero of art is in other words a guarantor of authenticity. Transposed to architecture, this pertains to the capacity to express through reduced formal means a fundamental dimension of human existence.

Nevertheless, Barthes was aware that this authenticity becomes relative as historical conditions change. The bourgeois consumption culture renders the degree zero only momentarily effective, without duration. The artwork's fate in the market culture suggests this gesture of freedom must inevitably return to the status quo which it first resisted:

> Mechanical habits are developed in the very place where freedom existed, a network of set forms hem in more and more the pristine freshness of discourse [...]. The writer, taking his place as a "classic", becomes the slavish imitator of his original creation, society demotes his writing to a mere manner, and returns him a prisoner to his own formal myths.[7]

The pursuit of the degree zero is therefore utopian. The authenticity that it seeks is unattainable; the wider conditions for communication are undermined by the established social order:

> Writing [...] is a blind alley, [...] because society itself is a blind alley. [...] The search for a non-style or an oral style, for a zero level or a spoken level of writing is, all things considered, the anticipation of a homogeneous social state; [...] there can be no universal language outside a concrete, and no longer a mystical or merely nominal, universality of society.[8]

In other writings, Barthes's parallel between writing and society expanded to commentaries regarding culture as a whole. The *Mythologies* essays (1957) presented culture as a self-renewing package of artistic emancipatory attempts and commercial constructs, offered as self-evident and natural values. This makes more explicit the debt to Ferdinand de Saussure's structuralist linguistics, indicating a belief in culture's readability as a system of signs.[9] Structuralist thinking performs, at a wider level, the oscillation between form and meaning manifested in architecture in the ambivalence of type, and with the same limitations.

The structuralist notion of language as a structure for the transmission of messages does not grasp its role in enabling understanding and communication. Similarly, the existing belief in the deep structures of culture is inhibited by the idea that culture can be understood scientifically, according to epistemological criteria of certainty. The question raised by Barthes's degree zero is therefore whether one can find a human language that is not embedded in its culture, or, in an architectural equivalent, an architecture conceived in abstraction from its circumstances.

[7] Ibid.
[8] Ibid., p. 72.
[9] See Allen, 2003, pp. 39–41.

The degree zero of architecture, understood as a distilled medium of primary forms devoid of compositional manipulations, is likewise a purely abstract proposition. Seeking authenticity as an end in itself is a corollary of instrumental thinking; it places architecture on a conceptual level, where the unselfconsciousness of "authentic" objects is itself unavailable.

Through the degree zero thematic, Swiss architecture is philosophically placed under the province of structuralism. Its debt to structuralist thinking could be traced back to the popularity of Barthes among ETH students during the 1970s, and to the semiology courses that Steinmann ran with Bruno Reichlin at gta at that time. This teaching was itself informed by Rossi's (and indirectly, Manfredo Tafuri's) attempts to apply Saussurian structural linguistics to architecture.

At face value, the constant and inevitable assimilation of ethical-minded, autonomous avant-gardes into the bourgeois cultural value-system also applies to the reductive trend in recent Swiss architecture. Indeed, the idea of cohesion within this particular phenomenon can only be applied to a brief period of approximately ten years, from around 1985 to 1995. Thereafter it becomes difficult to identify a common degree zero. Increasingly, the celebrated Swiss *auteurs* turned elsewhere in their research for personalised modes of expression.

An important characteristic of the Swiss discourse is that the quest for meaning ascribed to the degree zero is often reduced to a question of geometry. In 1988, Herzog & de Meuron stated their position as "a search for perception and meaning, a search of something hidden, something that is integral to nature [...] A search that must fail at the moment I believe I have found my geometry".[10] A set of forms is constantly assimilated to the currents of capitalism, thereby projecting the creator further on his search for self-definition.

While Barthes' literary model has proven stimulating for Swiss architectural production, it has determined for it the same limitations. Structuralism itself confused the commercial manifestations of market culture with the more fundamental and hidden dimensions of culture, declaring economic mechanisms as eternal arbiters of human existence. Architecture's outward dependence on these mechanisms makes its position all the more vulnerable.

Between culture as object and culture as sign
The direct equivalent of Barthes's degree zero in the visual domain is 1960s Minimal Art. In its effort to engage with reality, Minimalism was a compelling and paradoxical proposition. Its products embodied a philosophical resistance to the crisis of Modernism, as manifested through the obscure subjective references of Abstract Expressionism. Minimal Art proposed to counteract this crisis through the production of objects freed from any reference except to themselves.

[10] Herzog and de Meuron, 1992, p. 142.

To avoid any compositional or anthropomorphic associations, the artists shunned conventional artistic means (figuration, the canvas as window), mediatory devices (pedestals, frames, narrative titles) and materials (bronze, marble, watercolour). Minimal Art's materials were taken from contexts other than the gallery. Often "aggressively" industrial, they were formed into inert, solitary objects, close to what Clement Greenberg had deemed "non-art".[11] These objects stated their difference from the realm of representational aesthetics through their directness, declaring themselves as *objects* precisely in opposition to artworks.

Early on, Greenberg had remarked that Minimalism's claim to objecthood was fatally undermined by its reliance on a conceptual framework.[12] Nevertheless, his analysis was itself restricted to objects and their theoretical armature. The focus on corporeal interactions between viewer and object, as stated by Michael Fried in an apparent attack on Greenberg's critique, continued to overlook the deeper context for phenomena, suggesting that deeper meanings are located solely in this relationship.[13] These poles of minimalist critique are indeed closer then they may seem. The debates converge in the assumption that meaning resides in the art object and the gallery.

Marshall Berman identified two contradictory species of Modernism in 1960s culture: one "withdrawn" and the other "affirmative".[14] Barthes and Greenberg illustrate the former strand, whereby as a form of societal commentary art turns inwards, to its own terms of expression. As Greenberg wrote, "each art had to determine, through the operations peculiar to itself, the effects peculiar and exclusive to itself. By doing this [it] would narrow its area of competence, but […] make its possession of this area all the more secure".[15] One notes here a parallel with Cartesian epistemology – perhaps useful for certain conclusions in the sciences, but ill-suited to the domains of art and architecture. This positivism sought to determine the content of each discipline as an autonomous medium. Barthes returned literature to language, Greenberg restored painting to the flat canvas, and Aldo Rossi re-focused architecture on type.

The notion of architectural autonomy is a manifestation of "withdrawn" Modernism. It seeks a return to the essentials of the medium (form, type, material) as a common basis from which universal claims might be made. Nevertheless, this re-tracing of boundaries further undermines the fragile continuity of a fragmenting culture. In isolation, artistic gestures lose the potential richness that could arise from a more involved practice:

> An art without personal feelings and social relationships is bound to seem arid and lifeless after a little while. The freedom it confers is the freedom of a beautifully formed, perfectly sealed tomb.[16]

---

[11] See Greenberg, 1968.

[12] Ibid., p. 183.

[13] Michael Fried placed Minimalism under the rubric of theatricality. See Fried, 1968.

[14] Berman, 1983, pp. 29–30.

[15] Greenberg, 1992, p. 755.

[16] Berman, 1983, p. 30.

In contrast, "affirmative" Modernism found potential and beauty in the everyday, seeking to blur the boundaries between art and other domains of activity.[17] This set in motion the enthusiasm for a supposed "popular culture" that can be identified both in Pop art and architectural Postmodernism.

The term "popular culture" originates in anthropological studies of so-called primitive societies, attempting to understand scientifically those cultures not mediated by the elaborate conceptual apparatus of Western tradition. The term was imported into the arts in connection with the appeal to commercial imagery and advertising. The system of signs proposed by structuralist descriptions was adapted to readings of economic behaviour, allowing the cultural order to be perceived as a system. The iconography of the Vegas strip or the suburban Levittown, elevated to meaningfulness by Venturi and Scott Brown, mostly arose from the reading of individual desires, much like advertising. This cultural ambiguity traced the limitations of Pop; as Berman notes, "pop Modernism never developed a critical perspective which might have clarified the point where openness to the modern world has got to stop".[18]

One recognises in the formal strategies of 1980s Swiss architecture a debt to both these modernist variants, together with the attempt to filter out their shortcomings. The existing references to Minimal and Pop art reinforce this dependency.[19] The early works, responding to a complex context through multifaceted, heterogeneous designs, seem more concerned with the representational content of communicative "images". This is the case for example with Herzog & de Meuron's Blue House (Oberwil, 1978–79) and Photographic Studio Frei (Weil am Rhein, 1981–82), or Diener & Diener's Hammerstrasse I (Basel, 1978–81) and Burgfelderplatz building (Basel, 1982–85). From the late 1980s onwards, as illustrated by the earlier case studies, the production shows marked tendencies towards unified objects, characterised by their materiality and tectonic expression and pertaining to the totality of *Gestalt*.

Some autonomous objects of Swiss architecture display the framework of form and material, emancipated from context, characteristic of Minimalism. This connection needs to be addressed. Donald Judd's interest in "objectivity" led to the production of three-dimensional, unitary forms with an "obdurate" material identity.[20] The focus of his art was on the object as an assembly of directly expressed characteristics. "The thing as a whole, its quality as a whole, is what is interesting. The main things are alone and are more intense, clear and powerful".[21]

Herzog and de Meuron's works circa 1990 reflect to some degree Judd's stipulations, equating architecture with what they called "the autonomous reality of a painting or a sculpture".[22] The Minimalist connection, which is by now almost too tired to air, stands for more than a formal comparison. Indeed, Greenberg's

17 Ibid., p. 31.

18 Ibid., p. 32.

19 For example see Herzog and Vischer, 1997, pp. 213–215.

20 Donald Judd, quoted in Fried, 1968, p. 143.

21 Judd, 1992, p. 813.

22 Herzog and de Meuron, 1992, p. 144.

criticism of Minimalism as "too much a feat of ideation, and not enough anything else", can also be seen to apply.[23] One could consider in this context the "Swiss box" motif, symptomatic of the tension between aesthetic ambitions and the claims of inhabitation.

German-Swiss architects' relation to art in general and to Minimalism in particular is ambiguous. On the one hand they resist the charge of literal adoption and the vexed question of architecture in relation to art. On the other hand, they invoke art as a means to escape the burden of reality; art provides a model of self-regulation and conceptual coherence.

However, Swiss architecture's claims of integrity stem from its orientation not towards art but towards the common issues raised in relation to the city and Western urban society. It is this horizon of commonality that warrants access, as Meili has implied, to the constant values of human existence:

> We seek a kind of "authenticity of usage" […] we are no longer interested in the optimisation of the modes of usage in buildings but in the process of sedimentation of meanings into forms, such as results through the incessant repetition of everyday use. […] Our incursions into the world of the ordinary and the everyday constitute a search for collective meanings.[24]

This quest for a direct and intelligible architecture frames what Meili calls "authenticity" as the dilemma between pure form and the impositions of lived life. This differs from the meaning Kenneth Frampton has ascribed to "authenticity" as an inherent value of the architectural object.[25] The gravitas of empty, resonant spaces, the fascination with simple but tactile volumes has provided ample ground for essentialist readings. Yet Meili's proposal is more ambitious than an aesthetic of authenticity. Not only does he read common patterns directly in culture; he also identifies that these common patterns have less to do with architectural form than with a better understanding of architectural programme. To once again paraphrase Barthes, architecture should be seen as an unwritten pact between architect and society. The belief that form could encompass, in and by itself, cultural patterns transposes to architecture Greenberg's attempt to redefine an art form in crisis, by reiterating the boundaries and essence of its medium. The desired authenticity is not intrinsic to the simplified or reduced form, but something that emerges through architecture's dialogue with its wider context.

---

23 Greenberg, 1968, p. 183.

24 Meili, "Ein paar Bauten", 1991, p. 22. Translation from the German original.

25 See Frampton, "Minimal moralia", 2002.

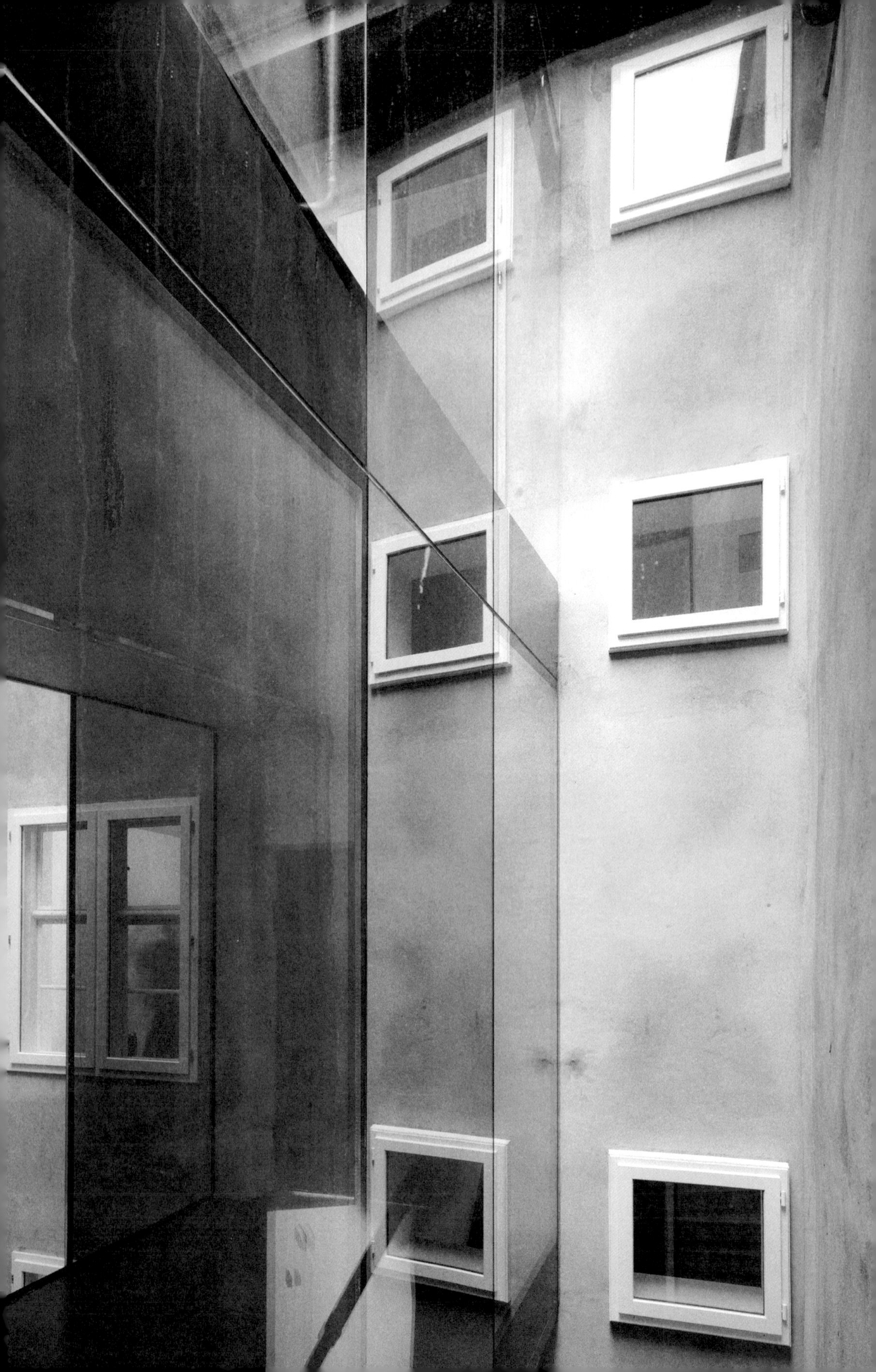

The Paradox of Realism

[1] Steinmann, 1998, p. 248.

[2] Adam and Wang, 2000, p. 8; Zaera, 1993, p. 16.

[3] Herzog and de Meuron, 2002, p. 8.

(Opposite) Herzog & de Meuron, Caricature and Cartoon Museum, Conversion and New Building, Basel, 1994–1996

Architecture is conditioned and is conditioning: architecture as a collective fact is inseparable from society, but "its principles are of a specific nature; they are derived from architecture itself," as Aldo Rossi writes.[1] **Martin Steinmann**

Architects and critics have repeatedly described Swiss projects in dialectic terms, like "normality and irritation", or "tradition and change".[2] In doing so, they indicate a dual preoccupation, firstly with the acknowledgement of norms and then with their transgression. Projects do not merely imitate existing type forms but subject them to degrees of distortion, initiating a friction with convention. This suggests the need for architecture to relate to a recognisable order of reality, yet remain capable of transcending it. In their early years, Herzog & de Meuron sought "an architecture with no distinguishing figuration, but with a hesitant non-imitating analogy".[3] This statement encapsulates the wider dilemma of communicability versus originality, or mimesis versus abstraction.

The ambition that buildings are, at once, integrated into their surroundings and distinct from them creates a tension between form and material on one side, and a more profound understanding of context on the other. The projects engender cultural associations almost despite themselves. Nevertheless the question of programme is seldom explicitly addressed; the artefact is expected to carry all such meanings implicitly in itself.

It is in the nature of practice that architects, through the external circumstances of each project, have found it hard to define their work philosophically with much precision. But the ethical claims implicit in Swiss production deserve a more explicit understanding. Its integrity lies in the attempt to mediate between typical, local and contemporary, global conditions. The potential problems stem from the devaluation of any "myths" by which Switzerland might identify common values other than global capitalism. The decreasing availability of meaningful references has meant buildings themselves are viewed as a means to re-establish integrity. Architecture represents either a turn to the physical aspects of each building or, alternatively, to the production of images for the style-market.

The painstaking coordination of theory and form comes from the effort to find a solid footing in the general cultural instability. The accent placed on the clarity of arguments and appearance, on construction that distinctly emphasises matter over technique, comes out of this need. And yet, the adoption of form and theory as vehicles of experimentation for the artist-architect leaves little scope for developing a deeper relationship with context. By themselves they fail to represent and resolve the multiple tensions a project needs to address.

One alternative has already been provided by Swiss architecture's involvement with actual structures of activity, in other words its role within human praxis. Potentially, the matrix of political and constructional practices that sustains the production could be seen as a different marker of architectural integrity. The integrity may be found not in the autonomy of artefacts, but in the acknowledgement of real conditions.

The reality of architecture

The organisational principle of autonomy, taken from international modernist theory, signals a breach between inner architectural coherence and wider societal issues. From the outset, Swiss architects have recognised that "external social factors are not an opposing alternative to architecture's internal specificity; they are different and mediate each other".[4] However, the nature of these factors seems to have been insufficiently addressed. Just as elsewhere Peter Eisenman turned autonomy to his own abstracting ends, the Swiss gravitated towards a self-consistent formal and material argument.[5]

Discussions about architectural reality cannot reach a consensus regarding what this reality consists of. In 1988, Herzog & de Meuron wrote about architectural reality as being primarily intellectual:

> Architecture creates its own reality outside of the state of [the] built or [the] unbuilt and is comparable to the autonomous reality of a painting or a sculpture. The reality [is] not the real building, the tactile, the material. Certainly we love this tangibility, but only in a relationship within the whole of the (architectural) work. We love its spiritual quality, its immaterial value.[6]

In contrast to that, Zumthor has seen "reality" precisely as tangibility:

> It is not the reality of theories detached from things, it is the reality of the concrete building assignment relating to the act or state of dwelling that interests me […]. The reality

4 Reichlin and Steinmann, 1977, p. 72. Translation from the French original.

5 See Hays, 2001.

6 Herzog and de Meuron, 1992, p. 144.

of architecture is the concrete body in which forms, volumes, and spaces come into being. There are no ideas except in things.[7]

[7] Zumthor, "The Hard Core", 2006, p. 37.

On the basis of these statements, Herzog & de Meuron prioritise the intellectual internal coherence of projects, whereas Zumthor focuses on the concrete relationships between material and detailing, place and form. These two opposing views converge on one point: the autonomous reality of the architectural object. A third view belongs to Marcel Meili, who connects architecture, through readings of local culture, with the deeper dimensions of existence. His argument transcends the object-oriented discourse and displays an explicit ethical ambition:

> The autonomy of architecture [...] is subjected here to a new interpretation. We could describe it as the hope that, in a city increasingly absorbed with management methods and marketing concerns, an architecture will survive whose efficacy emerges from a self-evident and precise architectural interpretation of the current modes of life.[8]

[8] Meili, 1996, p. 25.

In fact, in positing a connection with outer reality, this statement all but obliterates autonomy; architecture is being considered in the context of human activities. The relationship to the city offers a particular understanding of context. Firstly, it provides a critique of current market culture as having a destructive effect on urban order. Secondly, it refers to a more general reality, readable in society and culture rather than in architecture itself.

"Realism" has been one of the more enduring leitmotifs of the Swiss discourse from the 1970s onwards. ETH seminars, architectural journals and design studios all found an influential basis for design in the "reality" of peripheries, ordinary and vernacular architecture. Mike Guyer's statement exemplifies this understanding of the "real" as a necessity for design:

> We architects must learn better to view and to map that which is real today without prejudice. [...] Without an essentially open attitude to that which exists it seems impossible to find answers to the questions it raises.[9]

[9] Mike Guyer interviewed in Bräm, 1995, p. 53.

This open attitude accepts the distinct possibility that the "real" becomes an aesthetic category, as for example in the Analogue interpretations of Miroslav Šik's *altneu*. In other cases, the appeal to the "real" has become an essential component of architecture. For Diener & Diener in particular, the demands arising in practice are not a challenge to design but its fundamental point of reference:

> The question of Realism [...] is a prerequisite for our work. [...] The conditions of our production

do not appear to us to be a limitation but instead are the margins of play within which we design.[10]

[10] Diener and Righetti, 1991, p. 71.

This stance relates to a different aspect of Realism, the "reality of the building site" as the professional and cultural inheritance of *Neues Bauen*. The "conditions of production" are understood here as the codes and economic parameters determining urban development in the industrial age. The search for "archetypes with a more general validity" is based on the interpretation of established conventions, whether morphological or constructional.[11] As with Rossi, the actual city is seen as a repository of forms with collective relevance.

[11] Diener, 1989, p. 39. Translation from the German original.

Herzog & de Meuron have been less tolerant towards actual conditions and the limitations they imply. The point of departure for their design strategy, in their early career at least, was to assess and re-appropriate reality as a collage of reconstituted fragments.

> What else can we do but carry within us all these images of the city, or pre-existing architecture and building forms and building materials, the smell of asphalt and car exhaust and rain and to use our pre-existing reality as a starting point and to build our architecture in pictorial analogies? The utilization of these pictorial images, their dissections and recomposition into an architectural reality is a central theme in our work.[12]

[12] Herzog and de Meuron, 1992, p. 143.

While Swiss architects' statements regarding the "real" vary considerably, the discourse seems to make no definite distinction between aesthetic and practical factors:

> With an openly subversive intention, the project representations embrace a kind of photographic Realism which includes material textures and the spatial atmosphere and goes on to involve the user himself, as actor in this scenic event, to distil as much as possible the everyday world to which the object relates.[13]

[13] Meili, "Ein paar Bauten", 1991, p. 23. Translation from the German original.

One must note here the recourse to a common modernist strategy, whereby art becomes a vehicle for individual empowerment. The focus is less on the project's intelligibility within the urban continuum, than on its "representation" as a dominant mode of communication. Consequently the buildings seem less concerned with their specific situation than with the abstract theoretical discourse to which they defer. The appeal to the city is not sufficient to dispel the autonomous dimensions of architecture.

Swiss theory entails a variety of interpretations of "current modes of life", ranging from art-like isolation and claims of conceptual coherence, to a willing involvement with the given conditions.[14] Yet the production maintains a critical stance regarding reality, as if any architecture worth its name must question inherited assumptions. The architecture's differentiation from its surroundings reflects a typically modernist departure from traditional creativity.

So far the issue of Realism has been addressed at a general level, as valid for Switzerland as for other industrialised countries. The work's specificity becomes more apparent when mediating between theoretical conditioning and the possibilities of practice. While theory relates to an ongoing global academic discourse, design is circumscribed by changes to the local praxis – the architects' professional status, the enabling mechanisms of commissions (subsidies, competitions etc.), the existence of an informed and committed clientele, and the state of the construction industry.

The study *Switzerland – An Urban Portrait* is a record of architects' attitudes towards the "real" at the close of the twentieth century. The research on Swiss urbanisation represents at some level an extension of the architects' interests in practice, and the research methods resemble the "realist" strategies employed in design: an assemblage of "all the facts, all the everyday experiences, and even the platitudes in such a way that they start to glow".[15] For example, Herzog & de Meuron's copper-clad Signal Boxes in Basel were conceived as prototypes for a possible federal network that could, in time, replace threatened national institutions, like Swissair or Swiss Post, as "recognisable symbols of home".[16]

The study was intended as a feeler towards federal policy-making, although the authors remain sceptical about the effective application of their findings.[17] Both their practical experience and their analysis indicate a seemingly impossible situation. The differentiations on which Switzerland has relied for the creation of its political and cultural identity have also kept the country from urbanising at the pace required by the global economy. Unchecked participation in the global economy can only come at the expense of communal participation, local specificity, self-government etc. This balancing act between global interests and local concerns lies at the heart of the Realist thematic, and is acutely felt at the level of architecture.

Local / global
In 1959, Hans Schmidt's brother Georg remarked that the German term *Sachlichkeit* denotes Realism in the sense of objectivity. Steinmann and Reichlin have used this to argue that Realism and the modernist avant-garde are grounded in rational order.[18] The Swiss *Neues Bauen* sought to strip down design processes to an unquestionable calculus, free from style. Hans Schmidt's search for rational formulae, his rejection of *Baukunst*

14 Meili, 1996, p. 25.

15 Diener et al., 2006, p.136.

16 Mack, 2000, p. 83.

17 See Herzog and Meili, 2006, pp. 135–160.

18 Reichlin and Steinmann, 1977, p. 73.

for *Bauen*, reflected a re-emerging concern with conceptual coherence and objectivity, with the rational legitimisation of gesture.

In the 1980s, Swiss practice began looking at *Neues Bauen* precedents with a renewed interest. The recourse to local avant-garde models signalled a welcome detachment from the "alien" forms of Italian neo-rationalism.[19] Moreover, the early modernist fascination with objectivity resonated within the new generations. Despite the recognition that form is, inevitably, subjectively determined, the impulse remained to support formal gestures with buttresses of conceptual reasoning.[20]

This continuing fascination with rationality may be culturally, or even psychologically, motivated. The French political writer André Siegfried described the psychological profile of the German-Swiss as

> stolid, practical, opportunist, and little inclined to doctrinal attitudes. Their psychology reproduces one of the most striking traits of the German proper. [...] The word *Sachlichkeit* would no doubt express the thing [...], but the significant point is that we must turn to German here to express the idea of objectivity. In that state of mind the individual devotes himself to his work, identifies himself with his activity, and almost becomes the thing he produces by virtue of a sort of categoric imperative. [...] He loves common sense, practical ability and technical capacity.[21]

It's worth noting here Siegfried's appeal to the German term *Sachlichkeit*. The connection between Realism and objectivity offers a psychological reading of Swiss cultural character, which is also manifest in architecture. According to Meili, the *Neues Bauen* heritage was used by Swiss practitioners in the 1980s and 1990s not only as a repository of recognisable formal elements (a proposition inherent to typology) but also as a kind of *modus operandi* related to the local cultural psyche:

> The empiricism of Haefeli Moser Steiger or the timber Modernism of the 1930s, [...] Salvisberg's critical tolerance with regard to Swiss mediocrity, Egender's anti-intellectualism or the cold discipline of Emil Roth are types of behaviour which allow us to link what we perceive of Switzerland in terms of images with our own tradition of the modern project. Beyond their stylistic propositions, these architects lend us a precise vision of the possibilities of experimentation in the given cultural conditions.[22]

---

19   Meili, 1996; Steinmann, "Neueren Architektur", 2003, p. 95.

20   Reichlin and Steinmann, 1977, p. 72.

21   Siegfried, 1950, p. 156.

22   Meili, "Ein paar Bauten", 1991, p. 24. Translation from the German original.

The significance of *Neues Bauen* for the latter-day Swiss is therefore not simply a matter of ideology or pragmatics, but of cultural meaning. The widespread acceptance of Modernism during the 1930s and 1940s, the complex tug-of-war between avant-garde rationalism and nationalist nostalgia, the diluted *Landi* aesthetic shaped post-war building throughout Switzerland.[23] The architecture of anonymous prefabricated estates and benign monuments, whose individuality resides in detail rather than ensemble, represented the "humanisation" of Modernism under moderating processes of production and cultural demand.[24]

The post-war generation grew up with the experience of this architecture and later placed it under close scrutiny in its own work. This shared experience is a common denominator in the discourse, and a guarantor of wider intelligibility:

> Our incursions into the world of the ordinary and the everyday constitute a search for collective meanings. Following the collapse of national mythologies and territorial arrangements, this research attempts to recover the traces of an identity in the affected mobility of our contemporary culture [...]. Such identity resides less in traditional building types than in the everyday activities of contemporary modes of life in Switzerland.[25]

Meili's words reveal an interesting ambiguity. The need to address in design the given conditions is never too far from the unease in dealing with "Swissness" – a potentially problematic proposition, which could be easily subsumed within a nationalist agenda. Demystification comprises both freedom and rootlessness; the adjustment to the everyday can be defined as an adjustment to an economic landscape placed outside tradition.

This ambivalence is applicable not only to architecture, but to the wider Swiss cultural model. Switzerland's unity is defined by the acceptance of differences, whether attached to territory, language or religion. The urbanisation granted through participation in the world market is counteracted by the provincial outlook of communes, insistent on individual preservation. In the way Studio Basel has described the situation, "what is missing is an urbanisation of the mind".[26] The ancestral direct democracy that still operates in remote communes is an extreme example of this dilemma.

Surely, the architects' concern with the continuity of a modernist rationalist tradition deflects the focus on Switzerland's modes of life from the difficult connotations of conservatism and nostalgia. The notion of Regionalism, which arises especially with regards to the Alpine and rural architecture, has generally found little favour here. In the context in which it would seem relevant to tensions between local and global themes, this lack of interest is telling.

---

23 *Landi* was the popular shorthand for the Swiss Exhibition (*Schweizerische Landesausstellung*) organised in Zurich in 1939. Overseen by architect Armin Meili, the *Landi* exhibition set the design standards of moderate Modernism which remained effective for decades. Gubler, 1988, pp. 225–235.

24 Steinmann, *Forme forte*, 2003, p. 83.

25 Meili, "Ein paar Bauten", 1991, p. 22. Translation from the German original.

26 Meili, in Diener et al., 2006, p. 149.

Alan Colquhoun's sceptical view of Regionalism was promoted in the Swiss professional press in the early 1990s.[27] Regionalism, Colquhoun has argued, conceals the conflict between universal reason and assertions of cultural differences, related to territory: "The doctrine of regionalism is based on an ideal social model [...] according to [which] all societies contain a core, or essence, that must be discovered and preserved".[28] This model has only been conceived during its irretrievable erosion, while Romantic notions of traditional social structures were replacing their actual existence. Regionalism is therefore only available conceptually, as a representation rather than a fact:

> The question as to whether such an "authentic thing" ever existed is an idle one, as long as our only access to it is by means of its later conceptualisation. [...] The use of local materials, sensitivity to context, scale, and so on would all be so many ways of representing "the idea" of an authentic, regional architecture. The search for absolute authenticity that the doctrine of regionalism implies is likely to create an oversimplified picture of a complex cultural situation.[29]

In other words, Regionalism attempts to recover cultural integrity in an abstract aesthetic fashion, which further dissolves that integrity. The contemporary conditions only allow a superficial representation of authenticity. The more architecture appears to adjust itself to primitive culture, the more it stands for a refined construct. The formal and material motifs of local vernacular are integrated within the architecture as signifiers of a cultural unity that no longer exists.[30]

Colquhoun's refutation of Regionalism is helpful in establishing the limits of local culture in the Swiss theoretical imagination. His reading of Herzog & de Meuron's Stone House as a negation of Regionalism is no mere coincidence. This project establishes "an endless text", a *concetto* whose vernacular connotations are established only to be later dismantled through complementary associations.[31] Indeed, the issue here is that the very concreteness of matter is raised to the conceptual level – the stone walls as much as the formal diagram of the concrete frame. This is possibly deliberate. The house is not imagined as a local dwelling, but as occasional relief from the client's working life elsewhere in Europe. The Stone House responds to an image of Italy, in circulation since the eighteenth-century Grand Tour, as a setting for cultural renewal through a mix of revitalizing landscapes, edifying ruins and good food.

In Switzerland, the communes' political autonomy and the resulting network of differences impact on design processes in concrete ways. Conversely, the theoretical discourse tends to transcend these differences. The projects' conceptual basis renders them exportable, packages capable of establishing

[27] See Colquhoun, 1993, pp. 45–52.

[28] Colquhoun, "Regionalism", 2009, p. 282.

[29] Ibid., p. 283.

[30] Ibid.

[31] Ibid., p. 284.

superficial relations with "context" while preserving their autonomy regardless of their actual situation. The Swiss project thus oscillates between theoretical and practical imagination, between the terms of the over-arching discourse and the specific circumstances of each practice or building. Herzog & de Meuron is an extreme case of this ambivalence, divided between an internationalist agenda and the claims of a home base in and around Basel – which they see as already contaminated by global motifs.[32]

32 See for example Zaera, 1993, pp. 13–14

Realism as an ethical proposition

Interpretations of reality constitute one of the most substantial claims of a common vein running throughout Swiss production. At the same time, we have seen that "the reality of architecture" means different things to different people, and the spectrum of interpretation is so vast as to undermine the thesis of unity.

A shared invocation of ordinariness in its Venturian sense doesn't by any means finalise the matter. Venturi and Scott Brown's appeal to popular culture as a measure of objectivity is itself ambivalent. A Realism modelled on the Vegas commercial strip entails an aesthetic of disconnected referents, available to be picked and chosen at will. One may infer here the possibility of finding something desirable and subversive, not in urban order, but precisely in its absence.

The Realism debate is grounded in the decline of confidence in the traditional European city. The unquestionable domination of the periphery in spatial terms has been extended to its identification with a new paradigm for settlement. The critiques of Georg Simmel and Walter Benjamin have shifted emphasis to urban economic activity and to new, more abstract frameworks of representation.

Early Modernism displaced questions of civic order to a dialogue between large-scale infrastructure and architectural fragments. Mass housing, as a pattern of repeated modules, was most representative of this exchange. The matrix of equally distributed modules was architecture's response to quantitative statistical thinking. Housing units, rather than dwellings, combined the technical details of *Existenzminimum* with an aesthetic discourse arising from art and art criticism. This dislocation reflects the tensions between the sciences and humanities in a secular society more focused on individual freedom than on the nature of collective existence.[33]

33 See Taylor, 1991.

If Postmodernism originated in the post-war reaction against the abstraction of late Modernism, in an effort to recover architectural meaning, by the end of its run the reverse was the case. Already in 1971, Denise Scott Brown relocated meaning away from space and into the structures of communication. "Space", she wrote, "is not the most important constituent of suburban form. Communication across space is more important, and it requires a symbolic and a time element in its descriptive systems".[34] These

34 See Scott Brown, 1998, p. 64.

communicative systems were seen to behave more or less in the manner of marketing demographics, as a field of referents without a clear gravitational centre. The association of new advertising techniques with the development of the periphery and the extension of infrastructure to outward commercial zones meant urban development became less dependent on traditional means, for example typological coherence. The "decorated sheds" illustrate a concern with architectural surface over and against traditional urban order.[35]

This is partly due to the secondary role played by aesthetics since Kant and Hegel, in relation to a more primary philosophy. This has allowed anything from personal psychology and intuition to formal systems to become legitimate bases for the perception of art. The early postmodern period voiced existentialist concerns regarding alienation. Soon it became dominated by structuralist motifs, notably semiotics, whereby concepts like "code", "reference" and "system" could be freely applied to culture, language, law and politics.

Structuralism directly correlated the prevalent theories of meaning with the behaviour of references in free-market capitalism. This behaviour oversaw all notions of order or reaction against order. It is under these conditions that the space of the museum and that of the shop have become virtually identical. The juxtaposition of art and commerce are equivalent to understanding meaning as a matter of individual consumption.

Consequently any question of the "real", in Switzerland as elsewhere, has been reduced to personal reactions expressed in individual works and in the array of concepts being offered by architects and critics alike. In the name of "reality", the periphery has attracted attention as a domain more faithfully corresponding to the new conditions of meaning. At the same time, any call for Realism is a reaction against these very conditions. It entails a call for authenticity, for something like firm ground, for, indeed, something like the traditional attributes of architectural ordering. Under these circumstances, the appeal to Realism involves a paradox – an attempt to embrace both the dispersal of meanings as well as an affirmation of profound meaning.

This paradox was already operating in Venturi's support for the new icons of commerce as manifestations of popular culture.[36] To regard what was effectively the product of the advertising industry as a manifestation of popular values is tantamount to understanding the basic exploitation of individual desires as a manifestation of something more profound, which should be oriented around the ethical concerns of the society.

Postmodernism has dealt with this paradox through irony, which is preserved in Rem Koolhaas' attitude of "anything goes". Its obvious effect has been to render ethics superfluous. While the Swiss production is characterised to a large extent precisely by its resistance to this predicament, its earnest appeals to objectivity

---

[35] See Hays, 2001, pp. 102–103.

[36] The semiotics of *Learning from Las Vegas* (1972) is grounded in the formal, structuralist basis demonstrated in Venturi's earlier *Complexity and Contradiction in Architecture* (1966).

in the attempt to re-animate the nature of Realism have proven to be equally provisional. On the one hand the adherence to a bourgeois topography, in opposition to the multiple claims of the town, develops into a reading of Switzerland as mega-urbanism. This has been encountered in the spectrum of research, from André Corboz to Studio Basel. On the other hand, there is also an element of primitivism, of redeeming the problematic periphery through the provision of magical objects.

An illustration of this, albeit atypical, is the case of Herzog & de Meuron. Their description of Basel in terms of "abrupt" urban breaks implies an interest in disjointed urban conditions, all the better for individual buildings to carry architectural meaning in themselves.[37] Basel is presented less as a coherent topography of powerful institutions, which it manifestly is, than as a heterogeneous collection of varying urban characters. In opposition to the preserved city centre, the more permissive peripheral topographies are interpreted as fields of suburban sheds, industrial storage, railway tracks, roads and highways, into which more aesthetically astute objects can still be inserted.

To a certain extent, this vision describes the concrete possibilities of architecture with respect to historical centres frozen under the pressure of conservation and restoration. Thus Realism implies a moment of irony, even regret. The admission that contingent peripheries are the main urban topographies in which architecture is allowed to operate is equivalent to making the best of a bad situation. Nevertheless, one should understand the city as more than the expanding conurbations that increasingly make up the territory. Just as language doesn't only transmit messages but guarantees understanding, just as identity is not intrinsic to individuals but dependent upon their participation in a cultural context, so a city is fundamentally not a formal, but an ethical proposition.

[37] Zaera, 1993, pp. 13–14.

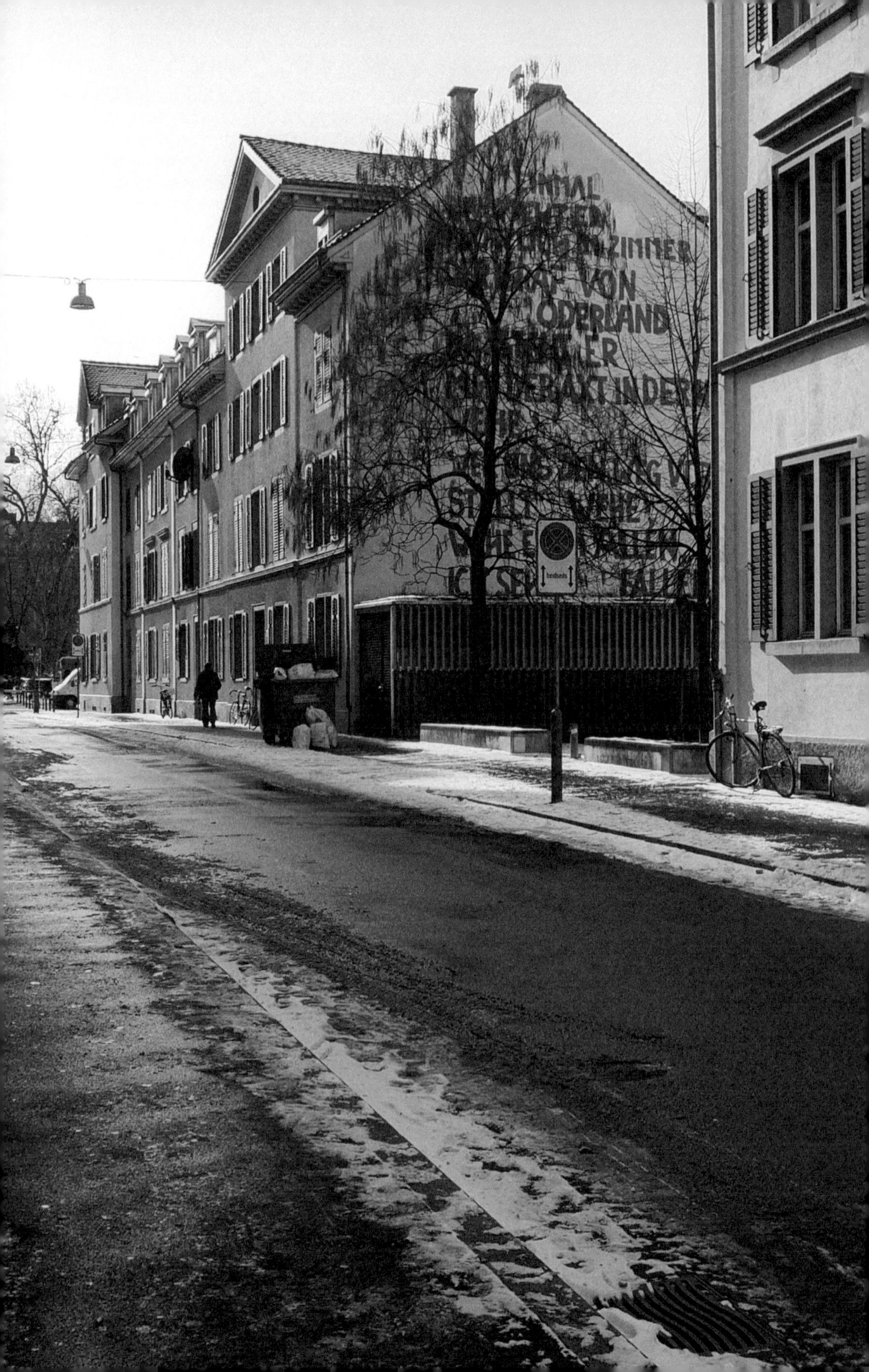
ZIMMER
VON
ODERLAND
beidseits

A Landscape of Signs

[1] Lucan, 2001, pp. 128–129.

Throughout this book, the effort towards conceptual coherence has emerged as a pervasive motif of Swiss architecture. Various aspects of design are integrated into the unity of the single object, or into the relational unity of "constellations".[1] The more the tension between parts and whole is subsumed under the overall logic, the stronger the design is perceived to be. What Herzog & de Meuron wrote about their early work illustrates – or perhaps has itself generated – a more general ambition:

> In our projects we have always tried to establish as many links as possible between the different systems at work. Our best projects are the ones in which the visibility of such links has been reduced to zero, in which the links have become so numerous you don't "see" them anymore. Everything then becomes almost self-evident.[2]

[2] Zaera, 1993, p. 21.

At the same time, it is in the nature of this magical "self-evidence" that despite its conceptual basis architecture is to be perceived directly, that is, non-conceptually:

> Such architecture approaches the […] ability to first affect people physically and emotionally before they are intellectually aware of what is going on.[3]

[3] Ibid.

This ambition to make intellectual constructs available in a pre-intellectual manner expresses a tension between the theoretical and practical frameworks for architecture. This polarisation corresponds to a wider conception of practice as the application of science. Since the Enlightenment, instrumental thinking has separated theory from praxis. This schism is central to the impasse of modern creativity, and Swiss architecture's concern with authentic meaning is an eloquent illustration of this dilemma.

The production has been defined by a sense of loss or of absence, whether this void has been lamented or embraced. Herzog & de Meuron's renunciation of the "Utopia of tradition", Meili's aim to preserve "the last vestiges of a collective sensibility" or Diener's attempt to "prevent a single meaning where it cannot exist" are various strategies for coping creatively in a world understood as perpetually contingent.[4]

The understanding of architectural integrity as a matter of conceptual consistency is rooted in this unstable ground. The focus on typological objects conceived according to a theoretical framework overlooks the proposition that architecture draws meaning from its participation in human praxis. It contradicts the more profound, often unexpressed, ethical orientation of the work.

Without irony

In this context, praxis is understood as a shared framework that enables communication. In Greek thought, *praxis* arose from "a need for enlightened choice, just deliberation, and right subordination under common ends".[5] *Theoria* provided the model for a shared reality which, unlike material goods, actually gains from being shared. If theory and practice have been largely separated in post-Enlightenment thought, in the classical sense they are integrated within the sphere of informed actions, deliberations and interactions through which we negotiate our position in the world.[6]

Based on the classical notion of *praxis*, Hans-Georg Gadamer built an understanding of practice as a manner of commitment.[7] The act of deliberation through which decisions are reached mediates between individual and society, between law and its application. The collective significance acquired through deliberation provides a ground of wider intelligibility, a link between the few and the many. "Practice is conducting oneself and acting in solidarity. Solidarity however is the decisive condition and basis of all social reason".[8] As the deliberate action of free citizens, *praxis* is rooted in the order of the *polis*. This was the basis of Aristotle's practical philosophy which, whilst reflective, was concerned with active contributions to political life.

Inescapably, the practice of architecture also mediates between concrete and theoretical circumstances, possibilities and limitations, ambitions and ideas. It is affected by interactions between architect and client, community and statutory bodies, contractors, craftsmen and critics. Each building's primary purpose is not the propagation of a theoretical discourse, but the creation of a framework for further action. The acknowledgement of architectural creativity as a collective act, with a collective purpose, brings into question the theoretical model of architectural autonomy.

We have seen earlier that the mediation between contingent peripheries and values of permanence involves a paradox of realism. The loss of meaning is embraced in order to generate new meanings. In this context, the formal restraint of Swiss architecture should be understood not as an aesthetic proposition but, at its best, as a means to grasp a universal dimension of human existence through the "generality" of situations.

4 Herzog and de Meuron, 1992, p. 143; Meili, 1996, p. 24; Steinmann, 1995, p. 18.

5 Gadamer, 1981, p. 76.

6 See Vesely, 2004, pp. 373–374.

7 Gadamer, 1981, p. 81.

8 Ibid., p. 87.

This ethical aim is nevertheless subverted by the reliance on form to convey meaning. The focus on autonomous objects hinders architecture's orientation towards the city as a manifestation of collective existence. The Swiss understanding of reality seems to pertain to a dispersed territory of theme parks connected by highway strips. Refurbished medieval town centres, prettily framed villages and Alpine landscapes are all viewed as the products of a more general process of conceptualisation. They are fictions sustained by the less scenic reality of sprawling suburbs, rail- and motorways, commercial and industrial infrastructure. In this territory, architectural interventions take the form of disconnected objects, which can only extend their internal order to the immediate context.

This view is permeated with disenchantment. Switzerland is acknowledged as a privileged place for architectural practice, but this admission is often undercut by allusions to its threatened status. Its most particular situations, such as local construction customs, are seen as anachronistic. The architectural impasse points beyond a theoretical quandary to wider uncertainties regarding the country's cultural, political and economic conditions. This sense of insecurity is reflected in the rhetorical questions asked by Studio Basel: "Is Switzerland a hole? Is Switzerland an island?"[9]

9   Diener et al., 2006, pp. 56–59.

The oscillation between internationalism and nationalism that Jacques Gubler had perceived in early Swiss Modernism is reconstructed today in cultural economic terms, as the tension between the preservation of political freedom on the one hand, and participation in the world economy and market culture on the other. In these conditions, architecture's call to Realism involves the slight sense of subversion that can be detected in the production of the 1980s and 1990s.

The artefact's autonomy and its refusal to comply unquestioningly with convention represents not only an avant-garde position but also a challenge to bourgeois established order. This manifests itself particularly in the ossified structures of the historical city, protected by statute and conservationist lobbies, virtually closed to new development. The architects' attitude towards this centre has been ambivalent – on the one hand they seem resentful of its privileged status, on the other they value the sense of continuity and permanence it represents. Outside the frozen centre, the earnest engagement with reality calls for the insertion of cultural objects in the dispersed landscape.

Postmodernist architecture appealed to irony as a manner of coping in this situation. If Venturi used irony up front, this attitude survived more implicitly in the works of Koolhaas, Gehry, Hadid and the array of international architects planting extraordinary object-buildings wherever in the world the need arises for a brand. In the late 1980s, Swiss projects established a province of "resistance" to the commodification of architecture, an architecture without irony. This opened their work to the criticism of being too sincere, even pious. In return, more recent works have taken a U-turn and aligned themselves with the status quo, the production of objects. In the twenty-first century, reflecting the encroaching global economic conditions, Swiss production has manifested an increasing tendency towards market architecture. So, could one ascribe to this work a similar impulse to that of the Postmodernism it opposed earlier?

The answer lies firstly in the production's profound ambiguity. In spite of its intention to preserve a collective relevance, Swiss architecture falls back on the structuralist understanding of reality. Structuralism understands meaning to reside in structures inherent in the artwork itself, rather than its relation to the outside world. "We understand architecture to be autonomous": Meinrad Morger's words speak for generations of practitioners.[10] Under the sign of autonomy, architecture reaches an impasse similar to that experienced by Minimal Art. The withdrawal into form, the "degree zero" of intelligibility, becomes commodified and understood itself as a product. Meanwhile, the concern with preserving dimensions of collective relevance meets accusations of self-righteousness. As architects attempt to define their own positions at the expense of a potential commonality, the situation leads back to the restorative potential of irony.

An example of latent, latter-day irony is found in the architecture of Valerio Olgiati, whose carefully rationalised bases are contrasted with "irrational" moves. Nevertheless, the nature of his wit is not in the vein of Koolhaas's carefree cynicism, but appears as a self-conscious and deliberate endeavour. This is perhaps most apparent in his Yellow House project in Flims, where the "broken pillar" on the top floor discloses the structure's misalignment with the centre of the pyramidal roof. The immediate effect is similar to that of Mannerist simulations of imminent collapse. However, its juxtaposition with a calming palette of over-all whitewash turns the drama of the broken pillar into a kind of anti-academic satire. Olgiati has acknowledged that, at design stage, the pillar's eccentric position was undecided for a long time. This seemingly Dada gesture against academic conventions, carried off with panache, is in fact the result of long and careful consideration.

Between the "actual" and the "real"

As Swiss architecture becomes identified with a definite brand and demand pours in for exports, its roots in native conditions are abstracted or distorted to suit other cultures. The most radical example is that of Herzog & de Meuron, oscillating between the Basel power base and the declared internationalist ambition to insert magical objects in a world of signs.

On the one hand, this architecture seeks to participate in the production of meaning through the focus on objects, as advocated by structuralism in alignment to the market. In this respect, one could call it "actual". The "actual" may be seen as a matrix of disconnected referents, like the urban periphery that can be improved through the addition of remarkable objects.

[10] Morger, 2007, p. 17.

(Page 252) Zurich streetscape, 2011

Valerio Olgiati. The Yellow House, Flims, 1998–2000. The "broken pillar" on the top floor

On the other hand, the architecture attempts to say something about universality, about what is common to all human beings. In this respect, it could be seen as "real". The "real" implies the depth of human existence, the reconciliation of human condition with the world. However, little is said about the latter aspiration, presumably to avoid accusations of piety or nostalgia. The more one operates in the belief that all cities, or indeed metropolitan Switzerland, tend towards versions of megalopolis, the more one's thoughts are dominated by actual dispersal.

With its interest in backgrounds, Diener & Diener's work can be seen as a kind of polar opposite to Herzog & de Meuron's. Yet the notion of everyday that Diener exploits is subjected to a similar lack of distinction between what is actual and what is real. It is hard to say if the melancholy photographs of speculative offices and housing blocks pertain to typology as a question of demographics, or to the provision of typical backgrounds for everyday situations. The staged emptiness of uninhabited rooms allows little insight into how housing and office buildings engage with urban or private life.[11] The order of plans oscillates between the undetermined space of commercial buildings for rent and undemonstrative, yet controlled residential inhabitation patterns.

Elsewhere, Zumthor's domestic interiors appear as carefully framed still-lives in which art, nature and household objects are composed to evoke particular atmospheres. In public settings, the elements of the composition are reduced to light, shadow and material texture. The external expression of the buildings is generally that of extraordinary objects, simple prisms defined by evocative or elaborate surfaces. While Zumthor's architecture seems to readily engage with the connotations of the "real", this contention is undermined by an unambiguous retreat into private aesthetics.

Swiss production can be seen to reflect a tension between individual freedom (autonomy) and collective responsibility (solidarity). This topic recalls Charles Taylor's essay *The ethics of authenticity* (1991), in which individualism is presented as a contemporary malaise. Modern freedom, with all its unquestionable advantages, has come at the expense of belonging in a traditional cosmic order, in which each person, thing, activity had its assigned place and role. The terms of this loss demand reconsideration. Following Alexis de Tocqueville, Taylor raises questions regarding the participative freedom that the individual is still allowed in the present context. He maintains that an authentic life is not achieved through inwardness, but through recognizing the "dialogical character" of human life, formed in the light of the commitment to the anonymous whole – in other words, in the all-encompassing context of praxis.[12]

Taylor challenges the primacy of the "rationality we draw on when we calculate the most economical application of means to a given end".[13] Much of modern disempowerment and the retreat into private endeavour is rooted in the perceived hegemony of

---

11 See Carrard, Diener, and Dubuis, 1998.

12 Taylor, 1991, p. 33.

13 Ibid., p. 5.

economic mechanisms, that which Max Weber called "the iron cage" of capital. Taylor rejects the idea that economy is beyond human control. The perception of economy as a distribution of desires or self-interests, as an anonymous aggregate of individual initiatives rather than a collective ethos, is damaging. "We can't abolish the market, but nor can we organise ourselves exclusively through markets".[14]

14 Ibid., p. 111.

This argument should also apply to architecture. Rossi's melancholy concern with "small things, having seen that the possibility of great ones was historically precluded" expresses a characteristic late modern impasse.[15] Just as the inward focus of individualism "flattens and narrows the meaning out of life", the claim of architectural freedom produces autonomous objects in a flattened city.[16]

15 Rossi, 1981, p. 23.

16 Taylor, 1991, p. 3.

Rossi's architecture does not renounce the idea of town as much as some Swiss proposals do. The formal similarities between the Gallaratese housing and Modena cemetery are not simple reiterations of geometric forms with universal validity, but invoke a more profound complementarity between city and necropolis.[17] Rossi's attempts to revive the reciprocity of house and tomb in the Roman world betray a concern with cultural continuity. The translation into matters of form constitutes an adaptation to the twentieth century, to a world where collective values are more implicit and originality is increasingly a goal in itself.

17 Nesbitt, 1996, p. 346.

The Swiss took autonomy to a different level through their adherence to Venturi's "affirmative" Modernism. Consequently, they concentrated on the peripheries as a new paradigm for dwelling. The acceptance of this model for loose configurations of dispersed objects comes at a cost. The more each individual is free, and each building an autonomous magical object, the more the collective dimensions of urban order are lost.

Seen through a theoretical filter, suburbia conjures the aesthetic appeal of the everyday as recorded, for example, by Swiss artists Peter Fischli and David Weiss. Von Ballmoos and Krucker embraced this aesthetic in their research for the Stöckenacker estate. What the project yielded under examination was the ambiguous aspiration to create urbanity through the coherence of form, material and construction. And yet the estate would be a mere reflection, a mirage of urbanity, were it not caught in actual urban growth. This case is illustrative of a more general fascination with the disaggregated topography of suburbia, which allows architectural claims to accumulate in individual objects.

The Stöckenacker project is exemplary in its consideration of urban, rather than suburban, models for dwelling, in the rejection of stylistic models grounded in theoretical imagination (such as "the Swiss box") and in the collaborative nature of its decision-making process. All these indicate the presence of societal and cultural claims on architecture. Decisions are accounted for in the tension between inherited theoretical knowledge and the possibilities arising from practice.

Stöckenacker's emphatic materiality articulates another distinction between Swiss architecture and its neo-rationalist roots. If, for Rossi, architecture operated dominantly as image, with little thought to its embodiment as long as the right associations were raised, in Swiss architecture the material matters a great deal. This is due less to a theoretical incentive than to a condition arising in practice. The representational content of construction does exist, and varies from project to project. It is, by and large, less an end in itself than a means to an end. An excessive focus on construction is considered either too pious or too dry, and one will find in metropolitan architecture an impatience with the time-celebrated values of handicraft invoked in the more remote, hands-on Alpine culture. This suggests that the perfectionism of construction arises from the local culture and economy, rather than from a common theoretical background.

Ethics, praxis, town

The theoretical content of Swiss architecture is not as unassailable as the buildings, through their conceptual and formal clarity, suggest. The interpretations of theory are understood as tokens of originality, or of individual freedom. Theory is, however, applied to a discourse focused on buildings, in a context more generally understood as a distribution of objects with potential meanings. What is, in practice, a negotiation of programme and the means at hand is measured against an increasingly stringent set of standards. A building is not just shelter, the background for the unfolding of human activities; it becomes necessarily a statement, a claim to artistic and professional status. This duality is summarised in architecture's hesitation between practice and theory.

In this respect, Swiss architecture expresses a much wider cultural dilemma. It poses questions at a global level regarding architecture's domination by positivism. Even where a culturally motivated sobriety remains, the sense of integrity is projected straight onto artefacts, which are denied participation in a larger continuity. Unsurprisingly, in the new century the issue of architecture's deeper cultural relevance has been deemed as overly idealistic, and temporarily silenced.

This problem could be summarised as a mistrust of the city. The architects' frustration with unassailable urban centres has allocated excessive meaning to the growing periphery, where spaces are still open for intervention. While part of a general conception of the ever-advancing metropolis, this is a particularly charged issue in a dense habitat. *Switzerland – An Urban Portrait*, with its superimposition of infrastructural statistics on the territory, renounces urban coherence in the very effort to preserve it. It feels as if, despite its sense of commitment, Swiss architecture cannot fully commit to the deep structure of continuities established within the urban domain.

This indicates not an architectural but a cultural problematic. What Studio Basel showed is, after all, the degree to which the federal construct has struggled to sustain the network of local autonomies. The insistence on communal autonomy has led to an insufficient overlap of interests. Continuity has become a matter of adjacencies rather than interactions, resulting in the "genuinely antiurban character" of territory.[18] Once the urban dimension has been relinquished, all that remains is a landscape of signs, a scattered collection of possible referents.

18   Meili in Diener et al., 2006, p. 142.

The alternative is an architecture rooted in conventions and customs as communicative structures, representing values that are still held in common. These collective structures are still present, even though they tend to receive less attention than the conditions of emancipation. The city is richer than an aggregate of infrastructures crystallised in types, collective dwelling is more than the anonymous background for individual performance. The orientation towards the urban enables the development of structures for discourse and negotiation.

It is therefore praxis, not formal restraint, which constitutes a basis for common intelligibility. In relation to praxis, the perceived permanence of objects is itself contingent. Architecture needs to relinquish its preoccupation with artefacts and turn instead towards an assessment of programme in which the building becomes a real framework for praxis. In this way, architecture can mediate between the universal conditions of human existence and the particular situations it addresses. Architecture is a form of practice committed to the creation of urban structures, mediating between individuals and the anonymous collective. As a network of such structures, the city remains open to interpretation. A sustainable architecture, in an ethical sense, pertains to the collective sphere, and to the preservation of the urban realm in contemporary conditions.

Bibliography

Adam, Hubertus, and Wilfried Wang, "A Conversation with Annette Gigon and Mike Guyer", in: *El Croquis* 102 (2000), *Annette Gigon / Mike Guyer 1989 – 2000, The Variegated Minimal*, 6–23

Allen, Graham, *Roland Barthes*, London 2003

Allenspach, Christoph, *Architecture in Switzerland. Building in the 19th and 20th Centuries*, Zurich 1999

"Alpine Fallow Lands, Alpine Resorts", in: Diener, Roger, et al., *Switzerland – An Urban Portrait*, Basel/Boston/Berlin 2006, 876–885

Argan, Giulio Carlo, "On the Typology of Architecture", in: *Theorizing a New Agenda for Architecture: An Anthology of Architectural Theory 1965–1995*, Kate Nesbitt (ed.), New York 1996, 242–246

Bachmann, Jul, and Stanislaus von Moos, *New Directions in Swiss Architecture*, New York 1969

von Ballmoos, Thomas, and Bruno Krucker, interview with the author, Zurich, 15 November 2006

Barber, Benjamin R., *The Death of Communal Liberty. A History of Freedom in a Swiss Mountain Canton*, Princeton 1974

Barbey, Gilles, and Roger Diener (eds.), *Fenêtres habitées. Die Wohnung im Fenster*, Basel 1989

Barthes, Roland, *Writing Degree Zero*, London 1984

Bergier, Jean-François, et al., *Switzerland, National Socialism and the Second World War. Final Report of the Independent Commission of Experts Switzerland – Second World War,* Zurich 2002

Berman, Marshall, *All That Is Solid Melts Into Air: The Experience of Modernity*, London/New York 1983

Bernet, Zita, and Rafael Sommerhalder (dir.), *Schwere Vorfabrikation. Die Entsehung der Wohnsiedlung Stöckenacker in Zürich-Affoltern*, 2002 [on DVD] in: *Dialog der Konstrukteure*, Zurich 2006

Bichsel, Peter, *Des Schweizers Schweiz*, Zurich 1969

Bowie, Andrew, *Aesthetics and Subjectivity: From Kant to Nietzsche*, Manchester/New York 1990

Bräm, Matthias, Annette Gigon, Mike Guyer, "The Grammar of Materials", in: *Daidalos* 56 (August 1995), *Magic of Materials II*, 48–55

Breitschmid, Markus (ed.), *The Significance of the Idea in the Architecture of Valerio Olgiati*, Sulgen/Zurich 2008

Burckhardt, Jacob, *Reflections on History (Weltgeschichtliche Betrachtungen, 1868–1871)*, London 1943

Burckhardt, Jakob, Adolf Max Vogt, and Paul Hofer, *Reden und Vortrag zur Eröffnung*, Basel/Stuttgart 1968

Burckhardt, Lucius, "Gli anni Trenta e gli anni Settanta: Oggi vediamo le cose in modo diverso", in: *Werkbund: Germania, Austria, Svizzera*, Venice 1977, 94–101

Burckhardt, Lucius, Max Frisch, and Markus Kutter, *achtung: die Schweiz. Ein Gespräch über unsere Lage und ein Vorschlag zur Tat*, Basel/Zurich 1955

Bürgi, Bernhard Mendes (ed.), *Ernst Ludwig Kirchner – Mountain Life. The Early Years in Davos, 1917–1926*, Kunstmuseum Basel, Stuttgart 2003

Bürkle, J. Christoph, "Befreiung des Raumes. Valerio Olgiati: Schulhausweiterung Paspels 1996–98", in: *archithese* 3 (1998), 62–68

Caragonne, Alexander, *The Texas Rangers: Notes from an Architectural Underground*, Cambridge/London 1995

Carrard, Philippe, Roger Diener, and Laurène Dubuis (eds.), *Stadtansichten – Diener & Diener*, Zurich 1998

Cohen, Jean-Louis, "The Italophiles at Work", in: *Architecture Theory Since 1968*, K. Michael Hays (ed.), Cambridge/London 1998, 508–520

Colquhoun, Alan, *Modernity and the Classical Tradition. Architectural Essays 1980–1987*, Cambridge/London 1989

Colquhoun, Alan, "Kritik am Regionalismus", in: *werk, bauen+wohnen* 3 (March 1993), 45–52

Colquhoun, Alan, *Modern Architecture*, Oxford 2002

Colquhoun, Alan, "Changing Museum", in: *Collected Essays in Architectural Criticism*, London 2009, 335–345

Colquhoun, Alan, "Regionalism 1", in: *Collected Essays in Architectural Criticism*, London 2009, 280–286

Conzett, Jürg, interview with the author, Chur, Graubünden, 31 August 2006

Corboz, André, "Grossstadt Schweiz? Stadt der Planer – Stadt der Architekten", in: *archithese* 6 (1998), 14–20

Corboz, André, and Sebastien Marot, *Le Territoire comme palimpseste et autres essais*, Besançon/Paris 2001

Davidovici, Irina, "The Dilemma of Authenticity in Recent German Swiss Architecture" (paper presented at the "The Complexity of the Ordinary. Context as key to architectural strategies" conference, The Royal Danish Academy of Fine Arts, Copenhagen, 5 October 2006).

Decasper, Gebhard, "[Paspels School] Structural aspects. The engineer's report", in: *Constructing Architecture: Materials, Processes, Structures,* Andrea Deplazes ed., Basel/Boston/Berlin 2005, 334

Dell'Antonio, Alberto, "Schoolhouse in a Wheat Field", in: *Paspels,* Valerio Olgiati and Dino Simonett eds., Zurich 1998

Deplazes, Andrea (ed.), *Constructing Architecture: Materials, Processes, Structures. A Handbook*, Basel/Boston/Berlin 2005

Diamond, Rosamund, and Wilfried Wang (eds.), *From City to Detail. Selected Buildings and Projects by Diener & Diener*, London 1992

Diener, Marcus, and Roger Diener, "The Tradition of the Modern in the Present: Four Projects Composed from Fragments", in: *Assemblage* 3 (July 1987), 76–107

Diener, Roger, "Zum Entwurfsprozess und zu verwendeten Mitteln", in: *Fenêtres habitées. Die Wohnung im Fenster, Architekturmuseum Basel*, Ulrike Jehle-Schulte Strathaus (ed.), Basel 1989, 32–40

Diener, Roger, "The Seduction of the Architect", in: *Luigi Snozzi. Costruzioni e progetti – Buildings and Projects 1958–1993*, Peter Disch (ed.), Lugano 1994, 25–31

Diener, Roger, interview with the author, Basel, 27 October 2005

Diener, Roger, et al., *Switzerland – An Urban Portrait*, Basel/Boston/Berlin 2006

Diener, Roger, and Dieter Righetti, "The Few Things That Are Necessary", in: *Diener & Diener. Projects 1978–1990*, Ulrike Jehle-Schulte Strathaus and Martin Steinmann (eds.), New York 1991, 71–78

Diener, Roger, and Martin Steinmann, *Das Haus und die Stadt. The House and the City*, Lucerne/Basel 1995

Disch, Peter (ed.), *Architektur in der Deutschen Schweiz*, Lugano 1991

Dürrenmatt, Friedrich, "A Monster Lecture on Justice and Law, Together with a Helvetian Interlude (A Brief Discussion on the Dramaturgy of Politics)", in: *Plays and Essays*, Volkmar Sander (ed.), New York 1982, 263–312

ETH Executive Board, "Mission Statement of the Swiss Federal Institute of Technology Zurich", http://www.ethz.ch/about/missionstatement/index_EN, date accessed: 12 November 2007

Flaig, Egon, "Jacob Burckhardt, Greek Culture, and Modernity", in: *Out of Arcadia: Classics and Politics in Germany in the Age of Burckhardt, Nietzsche and Wilamowitz*, Ingo Gildenhard and Martin Ruehl (eds.), London 2003, 7–39

Forster, Kurt W., "Architektur in der Schweiz = Schweizer Architektur?", in: *archithese* 2 (1997), 4–7

Forty, Adrian, *Words and Buildings: A Vocabulary of Modern Architecture*, London 2000

Frampton, Kenneth, "In (De)nature of Materials: A Note on the State of Things", in: *Daidalos* 56 (August 1995), *Magic of Materials II*, 11–19

Frampton, Kenneth, "Apropos Ulm: Curriculum and Critical Theory", in: *Labour, Work and Architecture. Collected Essays in Architecture and Design*, London/New York 2002, 45–63

Frampton, Kenneth, "Minimal moralia: Reflections On Recent Swiss German Production", in: *Labour, Work and Architecture. Collected Essays in Architecture and Design*, London/New York 2002, 324–331

Frei, Hans, "Museum für sauber gelöste Details – Zur neuen Deutschschweizer Architektur", in: *archithese* 2 (1994), 68–71

Frei, Hans, "Birth of the Cool. In memoriam for "Swiss-German architecture"", in: *SD* 401 (February 1998), 68–70

Fried, Michael, "Art and Objecthood", in: *Minimal Art. A Critical Anthology*, Gregory Battcock (ed.), Berkeley/London 1968, 116–147

Frisch, Max, "Cum grano salis – eine kleine Glosse zur schweizerischen Architektur", in: *Werk* 10 (1953), 325–329

Frisch, Max, *I'm Not Stiller*, London 1982

Frisch, Max, "Foreignization I", in: *Novels, Plays, Essays*, Rolf Kieser (ed.), New York 1989, 336–339

Frisch, Max, "Switzerland as 'Heimat'", in: *Novels, Plays, Essays*, Rolf Kieser (ed.), New York 1989, 340–347

Gadamer, Hans-Georg, *Reason in the Age of Science*, Cambridge/London 1981

Gigon, Annette, and Mike Guyer, *Gigon / Guyer. The 2000 Charles & Ray Eames Lecture*, Michigan 2000

Gilbert, Mark, and Kevin Alter (eds.), *Construction Intention Detail. Five Projects from Five Swiss architects*, Zurich/London 1994

Gossman, Lionel, "Basel", in: *Geneva, Zurich, Basel: History, Culture, and National Identity*, Lionel Gossman (ed.), Princeton 1994

Gossman, Lionel, *Basel in the Age of Burckhardt: A Study in Unseasonable Ideas*, Chicago/London 2000

Gossman, Lionel, "A Comment on Egon Flaig's Essay", in: *Out of Arcadia: Classics and Politics in Germany in the Age of Burckhardt, Nietzsche and Wilamowitz*, Ingo Gildenhard and Martin Ruehl (eds.), London 2003, 41–45

Gossman, Lionel, "Per me si va nella città dolente: Burckhardt and the Polis", in: *Out of Arcadia: Classics and Politics in Germany in the Age of Burckhardt, Nietzsche and Wilamowitz*, Ingo Gildenhard and Martin Ruehl (eds.), London 2003, 47–59

Greenberg, Clement, "Recentness of Sculpture", in: *Minimal Art. A Critical Anthology*, Gregory Battcock (ed.), Berkeley/London 1968, 180–186

Greenberg, Clement, "Modernist Painting", in: *Art in Theory 1900–1990*, Charles Harrison and Paul Wood, Oxford 1992, 754–760

Grisebach, Lucius, "Living Among the Peasants of Frauenkirch...", in: *Ernst Ludwig Kirchner – Mountain Life. The Early Years in Davos, 1917–1926*, Bernhard Mendes Bürgi (ed.), Stuttgart 2003, 91–98

Gubler, Jacques, *Nationalisme et internationalisme dans l'architecture moderne de la Suisse*, Geneva 1975

Harries, Karsten, "Light Without Love", in: *The Broken Frame: Three Lectures*, Washington 1989, 1–32

Hays, K. Michael, *Modernism and the Posthumanist Subject: the Architecture of Hannes Meyer and Ludwig Hilberseimer*, Cambridge/London 1992

Hays, K. Michael (ed.), *Architecture Theory Since 1968*, Cambridge/London 1998

Hays, K. Michael, "Prolegomenon for a Study Linking the Advanced Architecture of the Present to That of the 1970s through Ideologies of Media, the Experience of Cities in Transition, and the Ongoing Effects of Reification", in: *Perspecta 32* (2001), *Resurfacing Modernism*, 100–107

Heidegger, Martin, "The Age of the World Picture", in: *The Question Concerning Technology and other Essays*, New York/London 1977, 115–154

Henze, Wolfgang (ed.), *Kirchner Museum Davos – Katalog der Sammlung*, Davos 1994

Herzog, Jacques, and Pierre de Meuron, "The Hidden Geometry of Nature (1988)", in: *Herzog & de Meuron*, Wilfried Wang (ed.), Zurich/Munich/London 1992, 142–146

Herzog, Jacques, and Pierre de Meuron, "The Pritzker Architecture Prize 2001", in: *a+u Architecture and Urbanism* 2 (February 2002), *Special Issue Herzog & de Meuron 1978–2002*, 6–10

Herzog, Jacques, and Marcel Meili, "Conversation", in: *Diener, Roger, et al., Switzerland – An Urban Portrait*, Basel/Boston/Berlin 2006, 135–162

Herzog, Jacques, and Theodora Vischer, "Conversation, May 1988", in: *Herzog & de Meuron 1978–1988*, Gerhard Mack (ed.), Basel/Boston/Berlin 1997, 212–217

Hoesli, Bernhard, "Addendum (1982)", in: *Colin Rowe and Robert Slutzky, Transparency*, Basel/Boston/Berlin 1997

Jansen, Jürg (ed.), *Architektur lehren: Bernard Hoesli an der Architekturabteilung der ETH Zürich / Teaching Architecture: Bernhard Hoesli at the Department of Architecture at the ETH Zurich*, Zurich 1989

Jenzer Bieri, Martina, "Die Umnutzung des Warteck-Areals in Basel", http://www.sgti.ch/uploads/media/In-Ku-49_01.pdf, date accessed: 10 February 2008

Jud, Markus G., "geschichte-schweiz.ch.", http://history-switzerland.geschichte-schweiz.ch/spiritual-defense-world-war-ii.html, date accessed: 15 December 2005

Judd, Donald, "Specific Objects", in: *Art in Theory 1900–1990*, Charles Harrison and Paul Wood (eds.), Oxford 1992, 809–813

Kipnis, Jeffrey, "A Conversation with Jacques Herzog", in: *El Croquis* 84 (1997), *Herzog & de Meuron 1993–1997*, 6–21

Krucker, Bruno, Gian-Marco Jenatsch, and Daniel Cavelti, *Wechselwirkungen. Interactions in Teaching, Research and Practice*, Zurich 2005

Lefebvre, Henri, *The Production of Space*, Oxford 1991

Lefebvre, Henri, *The Urban Revolution*, Minneapolis/London 2003

Loos, Adolf, "Vernacular Art", in: *The Architecture of Adolf Loos: an Arts Council exhibition*, Yehuda Safran, Wilfried Wang (eds.), London 1985, 110–113

Lucan, Jacques (ed.), *Matière d'art. Architecture contemporaine en Suisse / A Matter of Art. Contemporary Architecture in Switzerland*, Paris/Basel 2001

Lucan, Jacques, and Martin Steinmann, "Obsessions", in: *Matière d'art. Architecture contemporaine en Suisse / A Matter of Art. Contemporary Architecture in Switzerland*, Jacques Lucan (ed.), Paris/Basel 2001, 8–25

Mack, Gerhard (ed.), *Herzog & de Meuron 1978–1988: Complete Works, Vol. 1*, Basel/Boston/Berlin 1997

Mack, Gerhard (ed.), *Herzog & de Meuron 1992–1996: Complete Works, Vol. 3*, Basel/Boston/Berlin 2000

Mallgrave, Harry F., *Gottfried Semper. Architect of the Nineteenth Century*, New Haven/London 1996

Maspoli, Flavio, and Jürg Spreyermann, "Aldo Rossi an der ETH Zürich. Quelle der neuren Deutsch-Schweizer Architektur", Thesis Zurich, 1993

Maurer, Bruno, "Von der Aussenstation zum Campus Hönggerberg", in: *Hochschulstadt Zürich. Bauten für die ETH 1855–2005*, Werner Oechslin (ed.), Zurich 2005, 106–133

Meili, Marcel, "Ein paar Bauten, viele Pläne", in: *Architektur in der Deutschen Schweiz*, Peter Disch (ed.), Lugano 1991, 22–25

Meili, Marcel, "The Luzernerring Housing Project", in: *Diener & Diener. Projects 1978–1990*, Ulrike Jehle-Schulte Strathaus and Martin Steinmann (eds.), New York 1991, 39–46

Meili, Marcel, "A Few Remarks Concerning German Swiss Architecture", in: *a+u Architecture and Urbanism* 309 (June 1996), 24–25

Meili, Marcel, interview with the author, Cambridge, 18 June 2004

Meili, Marcel, interview with the author, Zurich, 14 November 2006

Meili, Marcel, "Is the Matterhorn City?", in: Diener, Roger, et al., *Switzerland – An Urban Portrait*, Basel/Boston/Berlin 2006, 919–926

Meseure, Anna, Martin Tschanz, and Wilfried Wang (eds.), *Schweiz: Architektur im 20. Jahrhundert*, Munich 1998

von Moos, Stanislaus, "Zum Stand der Dinge", in: *Die Architekturabteilung der ETH 1957–1968*, Zurich 1971, 15–17

von Moos, Stanislaus, "Editorial zu Realismus in der Architektur", in: *archithese* 19 (1976)

Moravánszky, Ákos, "Swissboxes etcetera", in: *a+u Architecture and Urbanism* 410 (November 2004), 12–17

Moravánszky, Ákos, "Constructs", in: *Bearth & Deplazes. Konstrukte/Constructs*, Heinz Wirz (ed.), Lucerne 2005, 19–35

Moravánszky, Ákos, "Concrete Constructs. The Limits of Rationalism in Swiss Architecture", in: *Architectural Design* 77 (September/October 2007), 30–35

Moravánszky, Ákos, and Judith Hopfengärtner (eds.), *Aldo Rossi und die Schweiz*. Architektonische Wechselwirkungen, Zurich 2011

Morger, Meinrad, "The Course of Things", in: *Three Architects in Switzerland*, Markus Breitschmid (ed.), Lucerne 2007

Nesbitt, Kate (ed.), *Theorizing a New Agenda for Architecture: An Anthology of Architectural Theory 1965–1995*, New York 1996

Oechslin, Werner, "Zur 'Befindlichkeit' der Schweizer Architektur", in: *archithese* 1 (1992), 8–16

Oechslin, Werner, "Introduction" in Colin Rowe and Robert Slutzky, *Transparency. With a Commentary by Bernhard Hoesli and Introduction by Werner Oechslin*, Basel 1997, pp. 9–20

Oechslin, Werner, "Helvetia Docet", in: *Schweiz: Architektur im 20. Jahrhundert*, Anna Meseure, Martin Tschanz and Wifried Wang (eds.), Munich 1998, 55–60

Oechslin, Werner (ed.), *Hochschulstadt Zürich. Bauten für die ETH 1855–2005*, Zurich 2005

Olgiati, Valerio, "Iconographic Autobiography" in: *El Croquis* 156 (2006), *Valerio Olgiati 1996–2011*

Olgiati, Valerio, interview with the author, Chur, Graubünden, 31 August 2006

Olgiati, Valerio, "School, Paspels", in: *2G* 37 (2006), *Valerio Olgiati*, 42–55

Olgiati, Valerio, "Conversation with Valerio Olgiati", in: *The Significance of the Idea in the Architecture of Valerio Olgiati*, Markus Breitschmid (ed.), Zurich 2008

Paquot, Thierry, "Paroles sur la ville: Lucius Burckhardt, avril 1998" in: *Urbanisme* 8 (August 1998), http://urbanisme.univ-paris12.fr/1134766281383/0/fiche___article/&RH=URBA_1Paroles, date accessed: 10 April 2007

Pearlman, Jill, "Book Review: A. Caragonne, The Texas Rangers", in: *Journal of Architectural Education* 50 (November 1996), no. 2, 127–128

Pender, Malcolm, *Max Frisch: His Work and Its Swiss Background*, Stuttgart 1979

Poeschel, Erwin, "Das flache Dach in Davos", in: *Werk* 15 (1928), 102–109

"Porträt Kanton Graubünden," Economy and Tourism Office Graubünden, http://www.awt.gr.ch/bibliothek/de/statistik/zusammenfasungen/INET_Portraet%20GR.pdf, date accessed: 27 February 2007

Quatremère de Quincy, Antoine-Chrysostome, "Le dictionaire historique d'architecture", in: *The True, the Fictive, and the Real: the Historical Dictionary of Architecture of Quatremère de Quincy*, Samir Younés (ed.), London 1999

Reichlin, Bruno, "When Modern Architects Build in the Mountains", in: *2G* 14 (2002), *Building In The Mountains,* 132–134

Reichlin, Bruno, "This is not Das Gelbe Haus", in: *Valerio Olgiati*, Laurent Stalder and Dino Simonett (eds.), Köln 2008

Reichlin, Bruno, and Martin Steinmann, "Zum Problem der innerarchitektonischen Wirklichkeit", in: *archithese* 19 (1976), 3–11

Reichlin, Bruno, and Martin Steinmann, "À propos de la réalité immanente", in: *L'architecture d'aujourd'hui* 190 (1977), 72–73

Rosenblatt, Helena, *Rousseau and Geneva, From the First Discourse to the Social Contract, 1749–1762*, Cambridge 1997

Rossi, Aldo, *Texte zur Architektur,* Vol. 4: Aldo Rossi – *Vorlesungen, Aufsätze, Entwürfe*, Zurich 1974

Rossi, Aldo, *Aldo Rossi in America: 1976 to 1979*, Cambridge 1979

Rossi, Aldo, *A Scientific Autobiography*, Cambridge/London 1981

Rossi, Aldo, *The Architecture of the City*, Cambridge/London 1982

Rossi, Aldo, "Fragments", in: *Aldo Rossi Architect,* Milan 1987, 12–13

Rossi, Aldo, "An Analogical architecture", in: *Theorizing a New Agenda for Architecture: An Anthology of Architectural Theory 1965–1995*, Kate Nesbitt (ed.), New York 1996, 348–352

Rousseau, Jean-Jacques, "Lettres écrits de la montagne", in: *Œuvres complètes de Jean-Jacques Rousseau*, Bernard Gagnebin and Marcel Raymond (eds.), Paris 1964

Rousseau, Jean-Jacques, "A Discourse on Inequality", New York 1984

Rowe, Colin, and Robert Slutzky, *Transparency*, Basel/Boston/Berlin 1997

Rüegg, Arthur, "Architectural Education at the ETH and Swiss German Architecture", in: *SD* 401 (February 1998), 89–90

Rüegg, Arthur, and Bruno Krucker, *Konstruktive Konzepte der Moderne*, Zurich 2001

Safran, Yehuda, and Wilfried Wang (eds.), *The Architecture of Adolf Loos*, London 1987

Schaub, Christoph, "The Vrin Project", in: *2G* 14 (2002), *Building In The Mountains*, 136–143

Schmid, Christian, "Theory", in: Diener, Roger, et al., *Switzerland – An Urban Portrait*, Basel/Boston/Berlin 2006, 163–192

Schmidt, Hans, 'The Swiss Modern Movement 1920–1930', in *Architectural Association Quarterly*, volume 4, 2, 1972, pp. 32–41

Schwartz, Frederic J., *The Werkbund: Design Theory and Mass Culture before the First World War*, New Haven/London 1996

Scolari, Massimo, "The New Architecture and the Avant-Garde", in: *Architecture Theory Since 1968*, K. Michael Hays (ed.), Cambridge/London 1998, 126–145

Scott Brown, Denise, "Learning from Pop", in: *Architecture Theory Since 1968*, K. Michael Hays (ed.), Cambridge/London 1998, 60–66

Scotti, Roland ed., *Ernst Ludwig Kirchner und Die Brücke*, Davos 2005

Seligmann, Werner, "The Texas Years and the Beginning at the ETH Zurich 1956–61", in: *Architektur lehren*, Jürg Jansen ed., Zurich 1989

Siegfried, André, *Switzerland: A Democratic Way of Life*, London 1950

Šik, Miroslav, "Analogous Architecture", in: *Quaderns* 175 (October/December 1987), 60–64

Šik, Miroslav, *Altneu / Old-New*, Lucerne 2000

Šik, Miroslav, A*ltneue Gedanken. Texte und Gespräche 1987–2001*, Lucerne 2002

Solt, Judit, "Neues am Stadtrand", in: *archithese* 1 (2003), 38–42

Somol, Robert E., "Operation Architecture", in *Inchoate: An Experiment in Architectural Education*, Zurich 2003, p. 11.

Sorell, Walter, *The Swiss. A Cultural Panorama of Switzerland*, London 1972

Spier, Stephen (ed.), S*wiss Made. New Architecture from Switzerland*, London 2003

Spier, Stephen, "There's Just Something About Switzerland. The Swissness of Swiss Architecture", in: *AA Files* 59 (2009), 51–55

Stauffer, Marie-Theres, "Writing About Writing About Architecture", in: *SD* 401 (February 1998), 93–94

Steinmann, Martin, "Le sens du banal. Bâle, immeuble de bureaux à la Hochstrasse", in: *Faces* 13 (1989), 6–11

Steinmann, Martin, "The Most General Form. On the Development of Diener and Diener's Work", in: *Diener & Diener. Projects 1978–1990*, Ulrike Jehle-Schulte Strathaus and Martin Steinmann (eds.), New York 1991, 25–31

Steinmann, Martin, "The Presence of Things. Comments on Recent Architecture in Northern Switzerland", in: *Construction Intention Detail*, Zurich/Munich/London 1994, 8–25

Steinmann, Martin, "Notes on the Architecture of Diener & Diener", in: *Diener, Roger, and Martin Steinmann, Das Haus und die Stadt / The House and the City*, Lucerne/Basel 1995

Steinmann, Martin, "Reality As History: Notes for a Discussion of Realism in Architecture", in: *Architecture Theory Since 1968*, K. Michael Hays (ed.), Cambridge/London 1998, 248–253

Steinmann, Martin, "La forme forte. Vers une architecture en deçà des signes", in: *Forme forte. Écrits / Schriften 1972–2002*, Jacques Lucan and Bruno Marchand (eds.), Basel/Boston/Berlin 2003, 189–208

Steinmann, Martin, "Neuere Architektur in der Deutschen Schweiz", in: *Forme forte. Écrits / Schriften 1972–2002*, Jacques Lucan and Bruno Marchand (eds.), Basel/Boston/Berlin 2003, 93–109

Steinmann, Martin, interview with the author, Lausanne, 12 March 2004

Steinmann, Martin, Michael Alder, Jacques Herzog, Pierre de Meuron, and Peter Zumthor, "Bauen mit Holz / Propos sur le bois", in: *archithese* 5 (1985), 6–15

Steinmann, Martin, and Thomas Boga, *Tendenzen. Neuere Architektur im Tessin*, Zurich 1975

Tafuri, Manfredo, *Theories and History of Architecture*, London 1980

Tafuri, Manfredo, and Francesco Dal Co, *Modern Architecture*, London/Milan 1976

Taylor, Charles, *The Ethics of Authenticity*, Cambridge/London 1991

Tessenow, Heinrich, "Die äussere Farbe der Häuser", in: Heinrich Tessenow, *Geschriebenes*, Braunschweig 1982, 45–51

Tewsen, Isabell, "Ein Dorf leistet sich Architektur", in: *Neue Zürcher Zeitung* 175, 31 July 1999

Tschanz, Martin, "Tendenzen und Konstruktionen von 1968 bis heute", in: *Schweiz: Architektur im 20. Jahrhundert*, Anna Meseure, Martin Tschanz and Wifried Wang (eds.), Munich 1998, 45–52

Tschanz, Martin, "Essentially Realism", in: *Swiss Made. New Architecture from Switzerland*, Stephen Spier (ed.), London 2003, 236–243

Tschanz, Martin, "Of Heavy Mass and Apparent Heaviness", in: *Constructing Architecture: Materials Processes Structures. A Handbook*, Andrea Deplazes (ed.), Basel/Boston/Berlin 2005, 255–257

Ursprung, Philip ed., *Herzog & de Meuron: Natural History*, Montréal/Baden 2002

Vesely, Dalibor, *Architecture and Continuity. Diploma Unit 1 Projects 1978–81*, London 1982

Vesely, Dalibor, *Architecture in the Age of Divided Representation*, Cambridge 2004

Vidler, Anthony, "The Third Typology", in: *Oppositions* 7 (1977), 1–4

"Viele Mythen, ein Maestro. Kommentare zur Zürcher Lehrtätigkeit von Aldo Rossi, Teil I", in: werk, *bauen + wohnen* 12 (1997), 37–44

"Viele Mythen, ein Maestro. Kommentare zur Zürcher Lehrtätigkeit von Aldo Rossi, Teil II", in: werk, *bauen + wohnen* 1/2 (1998), 37–44

Vogt, Adolf Max, "Das Institut, seine Aufgabe, seine Verpflichtung", in: *Reden und Vortrag zur Eröffnung*, Basel/Stuttgart 1968, 13–19

Wang, Wilfried, (ed.), *Herzog & de Meuron*, Zurich/Munich/London 1992

Weber, Max, *The Protestant Ethic and the Spirit of Capitalism*, London/New York 2001

Wirz, Heinz ed., B*earth & Deplazes. Konstrukte/Constructs*, Lucerne 2005

"Wohnüberbauung Stöckenacker, Zurich. Werk-Material: Mehrfamilienhäuser, 01.02 / 419", in: werk, *bauen + wohnen* 7/8 (2003)

Zaera, Alejandro, "Continuities: Interview with Herzog & de Meuron", in: *El Croquis* 60 (1993), *Herzog & de Meuron,* 6–23

Zimmermann, Michael F., "Art and Crisis: Kirchner Paints Kirchner", in: *Ernst Ludwig Kirchner - Mountain Life. The Early Years in Davos, 1917–1926*, Bernhard Mendes Bürgi (ed.), Stuttgart 2003, 59–70

Zumthor, Peter, "Stone and Water", in: *Thermal Bath at Vals*, Mohsen Mostafavi ed., London 1996

Zumthor, Peter, in: *a+u Architecture and Urbanism* 2 (February 1998), Extra Edition: Peter Zumthor

Zumthor, Peter, *Atmospheres*, Basel/Boston/Berlin 2006

Zumthor, Peter, "The Hard Core of Beauty", in: *Thinking Architecture*, Basel/Boston/Berlin 2006, 32–37

Zumthor, Peter, interview with the author, Haldenstein, Graubünden, 31 August 2006

Zumthor, Peter, *Thinking Architecture*, Basel/Boston/Berlin 2006

Zumthor, Peter, "A Way of Looking At Things", in: *Thinking Architecture*, Basel/Boston/Berlin 2006, 7–27

"The Zurich Metropolitan Region", in: Diener, Roger, et al., *Switzerland – An Urban Portrait*, Basel/Boston/Berlin 2006, 605–646

Index

Names

Alder, Michael 97, 98
Alig, Simon 203
Antonioni, Michelangelo 60
Argan, Giulio Carlo 55
Aristotle 254
Asplund, Gunnar 65

von Ballmoos Krucker 171–186, 207, 259
von Ballmoos, Thomas 171–186, 259
Barber, Benjamin R. 198
Barthes, Roland 234–237, 239
Bearth & Deplazes 195, 214
Bearth, Valentin 7, 15, 195, 203
Benjamin, Walter 234, 249
Berman, Marshall 237, 238.
Bichsel, Peter 30, 31
Bill, Max 48, 78
Boga, Thomas 58
Botta, Mario 33
Bowie, Andrew 13
Burckhardt, Jacob 23–26, 30–32, 156
Burckhardt, Lucius 50, 51
Burkhalter + Sumi 97
Burkhalter, Marianne 7

Calatrava, Santiago 64
Caminada, Gion A. 7, 199, 203, 204
Campi, Mario 53, 57
Cohen, Jean-Louis 72
Colquhoun, Alan 68, 70, 84, 120, 248.
Consolascio, Eraldo 53, 57
Constant, Benjamin 24
Conzett, Jürg 15, 198, 203
Corboz, André 34, 35, 251

Deplazes, Andrea 7, 64, 155, 195, 207
Diener & Diener 33, 97, 133–152, 166, 171, 176, 200, 207, 214, 224, 228, 229, 238, 243, 258
Diener, Marcus 135
Diener, Roger 7, 15, 35, 51, 70, 135, 231, 253
Diggelmann, Peter 203
Durand, Jean-Nicolas-Louis 13, 45
Dürrenmatt, Friedrich 30, 156

Egender, Karl 246
Eisenman, Peter 13, 242
Eyck, Aldo van 45

Fellini, Federico 60
Fischli / Weiss 172, 184
Fischli, Peter 172, 259
Fisker, Kay 65

Forster, Kurt W. 206
Frampton, Kenneth 7, 110, 239
Frei, Hans 110
Fried, Michael 70, 237
Frisch, Max 26, 28, 30–33, 191, 230
Fustel de Coulanges, Numa Denis 24

Gaberel, Rudolf 97, 117, 118
Gadamer, Hans-Georg 254
Gartmann, Patrick 203
Gehry, Frank Owen 255
Giedion, Sigfried 44, 45
Gigon / Guyer 115–130, 207, 213, 220
Gigon, Annette 7, 15
Godard, Jean-Luc 184
Gossman, Lionel 134
Greenberg, Clement 237–239
Gubler, Jacques 257
Gutmann, Rolf 50
Guyer, Mike 7, 15, 243

Hadid, Zaha 255
Haefeli Moser Steiger 246
Hagmann, Andreas 97, 203
Harries, Karsten 70, 93, 224
Hays, K. Michael 62, 71
Hegel, Georg Wilhelm Friedrich 250
Heidegger, Martin 38
Herzog & de Meuron 9, 33, 51, 64, 77, 81–94, 97, 108, 110, 115, 128, 164, 171, 200, 207, 208, 213–216, 220–224, 227, 228, 236, 238, 241–245, 248, 249, 251, 253, 256, 258
Herzog, Jacques 7, 35, 38, 51, 98, 108
Hoesli, Bernhard 21, 44–46, 48, 50, 51, 53, 55, 62, 73, 135
Hofer, Paul 51, 53, 62

Judd, Donald 88, 94, 123, 238
Jung, Carl Gustav 11, 60
Jüngling Hagmann 203
Jüngling, Dieter 203

Kant, Immanuel 93, 250
Keller, Gottfried 156
Kerez, Christian 155, 218
Kirchner, Ernst Ludwig 115–131
Koolhaas, Rem 115, 250, 255, 256
Krucker, Bruno 171–186, 259
Künzel, August 140
Kutter, Markus 32

Le Corbusier (Charles-Édouard Jeanneret-Gris) 45, 46, 110, 230
Lefebvre, Henri 35
Loos, Adolf 110
Lynch, David 172

Maldonado, Tomás 49, 50
Maranta, Paola 7, 64
Märkli, Peter 7, 15, 128, 208, 209, 216, 218
Meier, Richard 128
Meili & Peter 97
Meili, Armin 34
Meili, Marcel 7, 9, 14, 15, 34, 35, 38, 48, 50, 57, 62, 66, 68, 70, 77, 126, 194, 196, 202, 203, 228, 229, 239, 243, 246, 247, 253
Metron 51
Meuron, Pierre de 7, 35, 51, 81–94, 98
Meyer, Hannes 50, 148, 191
Mies van der Rohe, Ludwig 46
Milizia, Francesco 13, 55
Miller, Quintus 7, 64, 155
Moos, Stanislaus von 15, 51, 52
Moravánszky, Ákos 64
Morger, Meinrad 256
Moser, Karl 44, 73

Oechslin, Werner 33
Office for Metropolitan Architecture (OMA) 115
Olgiati, Rudolf 155
Olgiati, Valerio 7, 15, 64, 155–169, 203, 204, 207, 208, 216, 218, 222, 256
Ortelli, Luca 64

Pestalozzi, Johann Heinrich 156
Peter, Markus 97
Poeschel, Erwin 118

Quatremère de Quincy, Antoine Chrysostôme 10, 54
Rabinowitch, David 178, 184
Reichlin, Bruno 52, 53, 56, 62, 166, 196, 236, 245
Reinhart, Fabio 53, 64
Riedi, Erwin 158
Rittel, Horst 50
Rogers, Ernesto Nathan 53
Rolland, Romain 1 33, 134
Rossi, Aldo 9, 11, 13, 52–57, 60, 62, 64, 66, 71, 73, 81, 90, 135, 140, 162, 171, 214, 224, 236, 237, 241, 244, 259, 260
Roth, Alfred 44, 73
Roth, Emil 97, 246
Rousseau, Jean-Jacques 22–25, 30, 31, 34, 156
Rowe, Colin 45, 56

Salvisberg, Otto Rudolf 44, 73, 246
Saussure, Ferdinand de 235
Schmid, Christian 35
Schmidt, Georg 245
Schmidt, Hans 191, 245
Schnebli, Dolf 52, 53
Scolari, Massimo 54, 60
Scott Brown, Denise 9, 60, 64, 238, 249
Semper, Gottfried 44, 73
Siegfried, André 246
Šik, Miroslav 53, 62, 64, 65, 70, 243
Simmel, Georg 249
Slutzky, Robert 56
Snozzi, Luigi 53, 57, 135

Steinmann, Martin 13–15, 48, 52, 58, 62,66, 70, 98, 108, 115, 122, 138, 140, 202, 216, 233, 234, 236, 241, 245
Stirling, James 128
Sumi, Christian 7
Suter+Suter 136

Tafuri, Manfredo 52, 71, 72, 236
Taylor, Charles 258, 259
Tessenow, Heinrich 144
Tocqueville, Alexis de 24, 258
Tschanz, Martin 15, 77, 78, 162

Venturi, Robert 9, 60, 64, 71, 166, 238, 249, 250, 255, 259
Vesely, Dalibor 10
Vogt, Adolf Max 51

Wang, Wilfried 213
Weber, Max 13, 25, 134, 259
Weiss, David 172, 259
Wright, Frank Lloyd 46

Zaugg, Rémy 128
Zinn, Hermann 51, 135
Zumthor, Peter 7, 9, 15, 33, 64, 97–112, 115, 128, 148, 172, 202–204, 206,207, 213–216, 218, 220, 222, 224, 227, 234, 242, 243 258

Places and buildings
Basel 23, 66, 115, 133, 134, 136, 144, 152, 200, 214, 249, 256
    Administration Building Picassoplatz 138
    Apartment Building with Bank Branch Office Burgfelderplatz 138, 238
    Hammerstrasse Housing 138, 238
    St. Alban-Tal Housing 97, 138
    Kunsthalle 120
    Kohlenberg Office Building 166
    Signal Boxes 216, 222, 245
    Warteck Brewery Housing and Office Buildings 133–152, 176, 216, 220
Berlin 116
Berne 36
Biel
    School for Wood Technology 97
Bottmingen
    Plywood House 81, 97
Bregenz
    Kunsthaus 115

Chur 100
    Condominium 222
    Protective Housing for Roman Archaeological Excavations 97–112, 195, 214, 216, 218, 222
    Rhaetian History Museum 100, 102

Davos 115–118, 123, 126, 130, 207
    Kirchner Museum 115–130, 171, 192, 195, 213–216, 218, 220
    Skating Rink Building 97
    Town Hall, Davos Platz 116–118
    Zürcher Heilstätte Clinic 118

Fällanden
    Youth hostel 97
Flims 155
    Yellow House (Das Gelbe Haus) 216, 222, 256
Frauenkirch 116
Freiburg im Breisgau 36

Geneva 22, 23, 36
Giornico
    La Congiunta 216, 218

Haldenstein
    Zumthor Studio 100, 104, 214

Itingen
    Hagmann House 97

Laufen
    Ricola Warehouse 81
Levittown 240
Lucerne
    University 222

Marfa 88
Milan 54
    Gallaratese 57, 62, 259
Modena
    San Cataldo Cemetery 57, 62, 259
Mulhouse 36
Munich
    Goetz Gallery 115

Oberwil
    Blue House 214, 238

Paspels 156–159, 222
    School 155–168, 192, 195, 198, 199, 204, 207, 208, 216, 218, 220

San Gimignano 84
Sevgein
    Willimann-Lötscher House 214

Tavole
    Stone House 81–94, 108, 164, 208, 216, 218, 220, 248
Trieste
    Palazzo della Ragione 57
Turbenthal
    Forest Works Depot 97

Vals
    Thermal Baths 106, 204, 216, 218, 222
Vella
    School 214
Vrin 199, 200, 204

Weil am Rhein
    Photographic Studio Frei 81, 97, 238

Zurich 32, 33, 36, 64, 66, 172, 182, 200, 208
    Apartment Building on
Forsterstrasse 218
        Kunsthaus 57
        Stöckenacker Housing, Affoltern 171–186, 216, 259, 260
        University 57

Higher education courses and institutions
Accademia di Architettura, Mendrisio 8
Analoge Architektur 53, 64–66, 155, 171

Basel School of Design (Schule für Gestaltung Basel) 100, 206
Bauhaus 45, 46, 48, 65, 184, 186, 206
Beaux-Arts 42, 45, 164

Cornell University, Ithaca 45
The Cooper Union, New York 45

École Polytechnique Fédérale de Lausanne (EPFL) 8, 51
ETH Studio Basel 35–39, 172, 196, 247, 251, 255, 261

Fachhochschulen, 206, 207

Grundkurs 45, 48, 51, 135

Institute for the History and Theory of Architecture (gta) 51, 52, 71, 77, 236

Pratt Institute, New York 100

Swiss Federal Institute of Technology (Eidgenössische Technische Hochschule, ETH) Zurich, former Polytechnikum 8, 9, 11, 12, 15, 26, 41–73, 78, 81, 98, 100, 135, 155, 158, 171, 184, 199, 203, 206, 207, 214, 236, 243

Ulm School of Design (Hochschule für Gestaltung Ulm) 48, 50
The University of Texas at Austin 45

Acknowledgements

The timescale of this book has been equivalent to that of a building and, like a building, it exists thanks to the collective efforts of many. My first debt of gratitude goes to Peter Carl, for his long-term guidance during my doctoral study, for his intellectual restlessness and great generosity. The research benefited from the kind advice of Ákos Moravánszky, Adrian Forty, Jacques Herzog, Annette Gigon, Valentin Bearth, Tony Fretton, Stephan Mäder, Micha Bandini, Matthew Barac, David Etherton, Matei Manaila, Jean-Paul Jaccaud and Diana Periton. Dalibor Vesely, Marion Houston and Wendy Pullan at the University of Cambridge gave their support to the early stages of research. I remain deeply grateful to Robert Maxwell and Iain Boyd Whyte for their far-reaching comments at the end of my doctorate. During the preparation for publication I received extraordinary help from Alan Colquhoun, whose immense knowledge, patience and precise use of the English language are truly a great inspiration.

The most valuable primary material was gathered through discussions. I'd like to thank my Swiss interviewees, some of them many times over, for their time and benevolence: Marcel Meili, Martin Steinmann, Roger Diener, Valerio Olgiati, Peter Zumthor, Harry Gugger, Mike Guyer, Peter Märkli, Bruno Krucker, Thomas von Ballmoos, Jürg Conzett, Arthur Rüegg, Miroslav Šik, Martin Tschanz, Stanislaus von Moos, Emanuel Christ, Andrea Deplazes, Philip Ursprung and Adolf Max Vogt.

I remain greatly indebted to those who generously provided rare material, in particular Marianne Burkhalter and Christian Sumi, Isabel Halene, Fortunat Dettli, Hanspeter Müller, Markus Breitschmid, Oya Atalay Franck, Jürg Rageth at the Graubünden Office for Cultural Affairs, Hans-Ulrich Minnig of the Graubünden Building Office, Arno Caluori of the Rhaetian Museum Chur, Moises Puente at *2G*, Hannes Mayer at *archithese*, Christian Mueller Inderbitzin and Isabelle Abele at ETH Studio Basel, Alienor de Chambrier at Herzog & de Meuron, Jennifer Hauger and Veronika Weisner at Gigon / Guyer, Christa Schmid and Barbara Soldner at Atelier Peter Zumthor. Hélène Binet, Georg Aerni, Danielle Brauchbar, Bernhard Strauss, Christian Vogt, Henry Pierre Schultz, Heinrich Helfenstein, Sarah Maunder and Walter Mair generously donated their beautiful photography. I am grateful to Sprüth Magers Gallery for the kind permission to reproduce work by Peter Fischli and David Weiss.

I remain indebted to Britta Callsen, Timo Keller, Max Sternberg, Claudia Schrag and Anne Hultzsch for their help with translating original texts from German.

Special thanks are due to Bruno Maurer and Daniel Weiss for their friendly and remarkably efficient support at the gta Archive. The research and implementation were greatly facilitated by the unfailing efforts of staff at the British Library, Cambridge University Library, the RIBA Library, the Department of Architecture and History of Art library in Cambridge, the City of Zurich Architectural History Archive, Swiss National Museum Archive and Kirchner Museum Archive.

This book would not have happened without the sharp eye, enthusiasm, organizational and fundraising skills of my publishers at gta, Veronika Darius and Ursula Bein. My warm gratitude to Marina Aldrovandi, for the many months she spent editing the manuscript and securing image rights. Thanks are due to Ian Cartlidge and staff at Cartlidge Levene for their time, generosity and exquisite graphic sensibility. I am deeply indebted to Sergison Bates Architects, London for their friendship and long-term sharing of resources. I'd like to thank my colleagues at the School of Architecture and Landscape, in particular the Head of School Daniel Rosbottom, and Fran Lloyd and Jane Nobbs from the Visual and Material Culture Research Centre at Kingston University, for their support in completing this project. The publication was greatly endorsed by the RIBA's Award for Outstanding Research, PhD category, 2009.

This book and the research behind it were made possible through the financial help of the Visual and Material Culture Research Centre at Kingston University, the Swiss Arts Council Pro Helvetia, the British Arts and Humanities Research Council, and Kettle's Yard Travel Fund. I gratefully acknowledge the kind sponsorship of Dixon Jones and Sergison Bates Architects.

Finally, paper thanks do not begin to repay a long-standing debt to my family. This work was supported along the entire way by Jonathan's loving patience, encouragement and expertise. I am grateful to my mother for her reliable presence during and after maternity leave and to Maia, for teaching me to balance architecture with playtime.

My interest in German-Swiss architecture is linked to the sparseness and visual order I first encountered on my father's army airfield. This book is dedicated to his memory.

Credits and copyrights

pp. 20, 27, 29, 205: Swiss National Museum Archive

p. 37: courtesy of ETH Studio Basel

p. 43 (top): Zurich City Archives

pp. 47, 49: gta Archive, ETH Zurich, B. Hoesli collection

pp. 59, 61 (top): Eredi Aldo Rossi / Fondazione Aldo Rossi

pp. 61 (bottom), 99 (top left): gta Archive, ETH Zurich

p. 63: courtesy of archithese / Niggli Publishers Sulgen

pp. 67, 69: courtesy of Miroslav Šik Archive, ETH Zurich

pp. 80, 83, 85-87, 215 (top left), 217 (top right), 225 (photos), 240: Margherita Spiluttini

pp. 89, 91, 221 (top left): courtesy of Herzog & de Meuron Basel, © 2012

pp. 96, 101, 105, 107, 109 (top right), 113, 217 (top left), 219 (bottom): courtesy of Hélène Binet

pp. 99 (middle left), 139 (plans, photos middle left, bottom right), 141, 143, 146: courtesy of Diener & Diener Architects

p. 99 (top right) Michael Alder Archive, courtesy of Hanspeter Müller

p. 99 (middle right) Heinrich Helfenstein, courtesy of Burkhalter + Sumi

pp. 99 (bottom right), 170, 174 (top), 175 (bottom right), 179: courtesy of Georg Aerni

pp. 103, 225 (top): courtesy of Atelier Peter Zumthor & Partner, Haldenstein

pp. 109 (bottom), 111: courtesy of Peter Zumthor

pp. 114, 121 (top), 127, 129 (top left), 157 (top), 160 (bottom), 163, 219 (top left): courtesy of Heinrich Helfenstein

pp. 119 (top and middle), 121 (bottom): Kirchner Museum Davos

pp. 119 (bottom), 124, 129, 225 (top right): courtesy of Gigon / Guyer

pp. 132, 137 (top): Christian Vogt

p. 137 (middle and bottom right): Paolo Rosselli

pp. 139 (middle right), 147, 149, 151, 226: courtesy of Bernhard Strauss

pp. 154, 169: courtesy of Danielle Brauchbar

pp. 157, 160 (top), 161, 163, 165 (top and bottom), 221 (middle), 257: courtesy of Archive Valerio Olgiati

p. 165 (photo): Sophia Zelov, courtesy of Markus Breitschmid

pp. 174 (top), 177, 181: courtesy of von Ballmoos Krucker

p. 174 (middle): courtesy of Sprüth Magers Gallery

p. 175 (top right): courtesy of Morger + Dettli

p. 193 (bottom left): courtesy of Henry Pierre Schultz

pp. 193 (bottom right), 197 (top): courtesy of Bearth + Deplazes

p. 197 (bottom): courtesy of 2G

p. 215 (bottom): Ralph Feiner

p. 219 (top right): courtesy of Walter Mair

p. 251: courtesy of Sarah Maunder

All otherwise uncredited photographs are by Irina Davidovici.

Swiss Federal Institute of Technology Zurich
ETH Zurich

DARCH **gta**

Department of Architecture
Institute for the History and Theory of Architecture

Copy editing
Marina Aldrovandi, London

Proof reading
Ulla Bein, Michael Robertson

Graphic design
Cartlidge Levene, London

Printing and binding
The Colourhouse, London

Paper
Olin High White Regular 300gsm and 120gsm

Fonts
Helvetica Neue 65 Medium, 55 Roman and 56 Italic

© Texts by the author
© Illustrations by the photographers, artists, and their legal successors

Every reasonable attempt has been made by the author and the publisher to identify owners of copyrights. With appropriate notifications errors or omissions will be settled within the usual limits.

© 2012 gta Verlag, ETH Zurich, 8093 Zurich, Switzerland
www.verlag.gta.arch.ethz.ch

ISBN 978-3-85676-307-7

Bibliographic information published by the Deutsche Nationalbibliothek

The Deutsche Nationalbibliothek lists this publication in the Deutsche Nationalbibliografie; detailed bibliographic data are available in the Internet at http://dnb.dnb.de

Kindly supported by

Kingston University
Pro Helvetia
Ricola AG